WK

The En...
of the Terr...

The End
of the Terraces

The Transformation
of English Football
in the 1990s

Revised edition

Anthony King

Leicester University Press
London and New York

Leicester University Press
A Continuum imprint
The Tower Building, 11 York Road, London, SE1 7NX
370 Lexington Avenue, New York, NY 10017–6550

First published in 1998
This revised paperback edition published in 2002

British Library Cataloguing-in-Publication Data
A catalogue record for this book is available from the British Library.

ISBN   0–7185–0127–6 (hardback)
        0–7185–0259–0 (paperback)

Library of Congress Cataloging-in-Publication Data
King, Anthony, 1967–
    The end of the terraces: the transformation of English football
in the 1990s/Anthony King.
        p.   cm.
    Includes bibliographical references (p. 219) and index.
    ISBN 0–7185–0127–6 (hardcover) — ISBN 0–7185–0259–0 (paperback)
    1. Soccer—Social aspects—Great Britain.   2. Popular culture—
Great Britain.   3. Soccer fans—Great Britain—Social conditions.
I. Title.
GV943.9.S64K56   1997
796.334'0941–dc21   97–19569
                                                              CIP

Typeset by BookEns Ltd, Royston, Herts.
Printed and bound in Great Britain by Bookcraft (Bath) Ltd, Midsomer Norton

Contents

Contents

Preface

The research for this book was mainly carried out between 1993 and 1995 as part of a doctoral dissertation when it was clear that a profound transformation was occurring in English football reflecting wider historical developments. However, although something important was plainly happening to English football in the early 1990s, the extent of the subsequent changes have gone far beyond anything which could have been envisaged at that time. Above all, the European context has changed dramatically since my original research, fundamentally altering the situation in which clubs have to operate and, in turn, demanding new forms of solidarity and strategies from the fans. This European dimension is briefly highlighted at the end of the book but it is not systematically analysed since its form was still only a blurred outline at the time of writing. Growing from these first thoughts and in the light of the transformations which occurred in European football in the second half of the 1990s, I have undertaken a research project called 'Football and Post-national Identity in the New Europe' which has been funded by the Economic and Social Research Council and from which I hope eventually to produce a book which will be called *The European Ritual*. These wider changes to European football in the 1990s which have created a genuinely transnational context for the clubs necessitate a correspondingly transnational analytical perspective and I hope that my current work will succeed at that level. Nevertheless, while in the new millennium a transnational perspective is now essential, this does not invalidate *The End of the Terraces*; rather it merely alters the book's relevance. In the light of this rapid European transformation, *The End of the Terraces* becomes a historical document which analyses the transformation of English football at a level of consciousness which typified the period with which it was concerned; namely, a national one, albeit with a brief recognition of the relevance of more international forces. *The End of the Terraces*' primarily national orientation is not wrong therefore but, writing in 2000, it is certainly a limited vision. However, given this limitation, it is hoped that the book will be a useful resource for those interested in the transnational dynamics which are now in operation in European football, especially since this new transnational context emerged out of a period whose basis of organization was primarily national.

Though I believe that the general orientation of the book remains valid, I am aware of shortcomings in Chapter 1. While I stand by that chapter's general purpose of emphasizing the wider sociological relevance of the study of football and encouraging more rigorous work in the field, it is over-critical of other writers' work and has even been seen as dismissive of the fans, which was plainly not my intention. Since I now recognize that some of the arguments which I make in Chapter 1 are overstated, I have altered certain of the most provocative phrases but the polemical character necessarily persists; only a total revision, which has not been possible, could change it fundamentally.

Were I to re-write the book now, there are several other alterations that I would make. I stand by the general categories which I employed to differentiate fans, but I would position certain individuals differently in these categories, as well as emphasizing the fluidity of these groups more. Above all, the most important individuals in the fans' movement would probably be classified not as members of the 'New Football Writing' group but in the 'Lads' group, although they are more politically committed and active than most of the other masculine fans. Nevertheless, for the most part, with only a few minor amendments for the larger audience which the paperback edition of this book is likely to receive, I have left the text as it is, reflecting the conditions in which it was written in the mid-1990s.

Anthony King
Exeter
January 2002

Acknowledgements

I am extremely grateful to all those who helped in various ways over the years in the writing of this book. To the following, I am especially indebted: Crisca Bierwert, Peter Boyle, Graham Byrne, Grant Cass, Steven Doyle, John Early, Eric Dunning, Mick Gibson, David Gildea, Hugh Gildea, Tim Holloway, Brian Longhurst, David Mitchell, Andy Mitten, Anthony Southgate, Robert Sutton, Ian Taylor, Stephen Wagg, Andy Walsh, all the individuals who allowed me to interview them and finally, but not least, my wife Cathy.

One of the most pleasing aspects of this book is that it has been the medium through which I have come back into contact with an old teacher of mine, Keith Hart. I have benefited enormously from our renewed exchanges. I am also grateful to my colleagues in the Sociology Department at Exeter University for their assistance over the past three years.

For my mother and father

PART I

THEORETICAL AND HISTORICAL FRAMEWORKS

1

For the Sociology of Football

The Premier League and the New Consumption of Football

Over the last twenty-five years, academic analysis of football has focused overwhelmingly on the issue of hooliganism. This has been neither surprising nor unjustified in the light of the extensive public debates which it has engendered, the seriousness of some of these violent confrontations and the self-evident sociological interest of the ritualistic activities of these young males. However, it may be the case that legitimate concerns about hooliganism have unreasonably biased research into football, so that issues such as the administration of the game and its political economy have been wrongly relegated to a secondary position. Duke (1991) and Moorhouse (1991b) have argued along these lines, suggesting that sociological research into football should give hooliganism its proper position as only one of a number of important issues surrounding football. In particular, Duke has suggested the need to highlight the question of modernization in any future research (1991, p. 637).

The call to widen the sociological focus into issues of modernization and political economy could never be more apposite than in the 1990s, when English football has undergone an apparently unprecedented sea-change. After the disasters at Bradford, when 55 people died as the main stand burnt down, and Heysel, when Liverpool fans accidentally caused the deaths of 39 Juventus fans, it was widely felt that football was in permanent decline – unless it could radically transform itself. Despite the unlikelihood of such a transformation in a nation which has persistently rejected dynamic reform in favour of the tried and tested tradition of muddling through, many of the bigger clubs in English professional football have undergone rapid change in the 1990s. On the one hand, the political economy of the league has been completely restructured through the creation of the Premier League in order to assist the top clubs in their pursuit of increased television and admission revenues. On the other hand, partly as a result of the Premier League's new wealth, the grounds have been reconstructed into all-seater stadia in order both to attract wider audiences and to reduce potentially lethal crowd violence, with its deleterious effects on attendances and the image of the game.

The Inadequacy of the Contemporary Sociological Study of Football

The primary task which this book sets itself is to analyse the 'new consumption of football' in the 1990s. In doing so, a more general methodological point is being made, one which is unlikely to be welcome among the academic circles that have worked in the sociology of sport, and of football more particularly, in recent years. Over the last twenty-five years, research into hooliganism has been, despite the various short-comings of the different accounts, sociological in intent. The analysis of hooliganism by Taylor (1971), Marsh *et al.* (1978) and Dunning *et al.* (1988) – to name only the main figures in the field – is informed by what C. Wright Mills would have called a 'sociological imagination' (Wright Mills, 1959). Explanations for the violent actions of certain football fans are critically sought in the transformation of those fans' social circumstances and in their (potentially blundering) attempts to make sense of them.

We can criticize Taylor's argument that hooligans were attempting to regain their share in formerly democratic football clubs through violent confrontation for its lack of empirical evidence. We can point up the shortcomings of the sociobiological conclusions of Marsh *et al.* or we might suggest that Dunning's Eliasian approach tends, in its less self-critical moments, towards teleology. Nevertheless, despite the inevitable shortcomings in the sociological study of hooliganism, the examination has been informed by an awareness of sociological theory and procedure.

Therein lies the problem of the contemporary sociology of football in Britain. At the very time when the dramatic transformation of the game is occurring, almost all of the work concerning aspects of this transformation of football has been inadequately theorized or, indeed, not theorized at all. Much of the work is insufficiently theorized and does not engage closely enough with the empirical detail of the subject matter under analysis. Consequently, while these texts almost always include very interesting passages and information, they often unfortunately fail to link specific empirical observations with wider historical contexts or to employ sociological theory to raise those interesting descriptions to the level of genuine and sustained sociological analysis. These texts remain informative in the journalistic sense, even though they occasionally employ sociological terms.

Redhead established himself as a leading commentator on new styles of fandom towards the end of the 1980s and into the 1990s. Although one of his articles (Redhead, 1991a) is an informative account of some of the changes in (mainly) masculine terrace culture in the light of the Hillsborough disaster and the development of new musical styles, subsequent work has been both undertheorized and lacking in empirical evidence. Although Redhead does not cite Baudrillard, it is evident that he has been influenced by the style and tone of Baudrillard's increasingly assertive, obscure and problematic later writing.[1] Leaving aside the problematic Baudrillardian form which Redhead's writing has taken, the main flaw is that its central point is not fully sustained or developed. Redhead's fundamental argument is that (masculine) football fan culture is heavily informed by popular music culture and vice versa (Redhead, 1991b). Such an observation is certainly valid. The specific ways in which young men and women re-negotiate the culture in which they live through this constant re-articulation of their sporting and musical interests is a potentially rich field of study which could throw useful light on the transformation of youth culture in Britain, thereby contributing to the sociological analysis of subcultures. In that way, Redhead would update the important work of the Birmingham Centre for Contemporary Cultural Studies in the 1970s. In his uncritical imitation of Baudrillard's style, however, Redhead has passed over the opportunity to make some genuinely novel contributions to sociology.

Haynes' recent work on football fanzine culture (Haynes, 1995) has demonstrated some similar weaknesses. Although Haynes does not vitiate his work through the adoption of an unhelpful intellectual style, he does, in fact, go too far the other way. His prose is too straightforward, reflecting a perhaps insufficiently critical approach to his subject matter. The development of fanzines – fan magazines produced by and for fans at low cost, increasingly on home-publishing equipment – has been an important aspect of the transformation of fandom in the late 1980s and 1990s, as fans have debated the transformation of English football through these publications. Yet, like Redhead, Haynes has not fully exploited the opportunity to make an important contribution to the field by merely reporting some of the developments of certain fanzines over the last decade.[2] There are practically no references to the sociological canon in the work and there is certainly no overarching sociological theory which informs the work throughout. The acknowledgement of other writers would not be so important if Haynes had adopted a critical and analytical position of his own. Yet this he singularly fails to do, a failure which is demonstrated with clarity at two particular points in the texts. First, discussing the argument in 1991 between *When Saturday Comes*, a national fanzine, and *Red Issue*, a Manchester United fanzine, over *Red Issue's* publication of cartoons and articles which scurrilously portrayed Liverpudlians as predisposed to larceny. As a result, *When Saturday Comes* refused to include *Red Issue* on its monthly list of fanzines. (As we shall see in Chapters 12 and 13, this argument between the two fanzines marked a quite decisive cultural and social rift between the producers and consumers *of When Saturday Comes* and those of *Red Issue*, a rift which is of importance in comprehending the new consumption of football in the 1990s.) Haynes has missed the very different social origins of these publications, including them both in an unfortunately flaccid category – 'the fanzine community'. He concludes his account of this above dispute with the statement: '*When Saturday Comes* is socially and culturally representative of its readership, despite the occasional run in with dissenting voices from within the fanzine community itself' (Haynes, 1995, p. 78). The potential shortage of critical awareness emerges at its starkest in almost the last line of the book. Having listed many of the fanzines available in Britain, Haynes adds the proviso 'Many of the fanzines listed above no longer exist, many have changed their name, and many have new editors and writers. This is the nature of football fanzine culture' (Haynes, 1995, p. 156). Yet while his discussions are interesting, Haynes has not explained to the reader why the evanescence of these publications is 'the nature of football fanzine culture'. Furthermore, the disappearance of certain titles implies that the continued production of fanzines after the initial surge in new titles is a complex process which cannot be captured by the uncritical notion of the 'rise of fanzine culture', which is both the subtitle of this book and the overarching framework of his analysis.

The neglect of sociological theory and the descent into uncritical journalism is perhaps revealed with greatest clarity in the ethnographic accounts of Armstrong (1994) and Armstrong and Harris (1991) of the activities of violent fans at Sheffield United. There is no questioning Armstrong's admirable submersion into the group which he studies and that deep ethnographic acquaintance has produced some very interesting (and amusing) accounts. However, Armstrong has failed to situate that ethnography within a critical sociological or anthropological framework – perhaps because he was too close to those he ostensibly studied to maintain a critical distance from them. Thus, in the first piece, he attempts to employ his rich ethnography against an overly simplified account of Hall's theory of labelling and moral panics, while assaulting the claim of Dunning *et al.* that football hooligans generally come from the 'rough' working class (Armstrong and Harris, 1991, pp. 428–9). In trying to undermine these theorists, at which they are less successful than they might be, Armstrong and Harris actually obscure the potential of their own data from themselves.

Throughout this account of the activities of the 'Blades', Sheffield United's hooligan crew, the most significant feature which emerges is the discrepancy between the violent fans' own descriptions of themselves and their opposition to others (principally Sheffield Wednesday fans – 'the Owls') and the realities of these social interactions. The confrontations between these groups is heavily informed by notions of masculinity and honour, but Armstrong and Harris never get down to a detailed examination of how the fans' (often fanciful) construction of their violent rivalries become incorporated into those relationships and those fans' understandings of themselves. There is a comic example of this discrepancy between the fans' construction of their absolute opposition to 'the Owls' and the actual complexity of their relationship with the latter (Armstrong and Harris, 1991, pp. 441–3). After a match, the Blades decided to go to a pub which Wednesday fans were known to frequent. There was much excitement at the prospect of 'mashing' some Owls, and the group prepared for battle. On their arrival at the pub, the Blades vastly outnumbered the Owls, some of whom were known by and, indeed, were almost friends of some of the Blades. Furthermore, since the Blades were gathered at the entrance to the pub, there was no method of escape for the Owls.[3] The whole escapade descended into farce as some of the hardened (Owl-hating) Blades refused to attack these individuals whom they knew well (and who would receive a very severe beating, since there was no possibility of escape). In the end, the only punch thrown was between Blades, one of whom still wanted to 'mash' the Owls and the other who had no inclination to set about a friend.

The richness of this ethnography demands a detailed analysis of the construction of fan identities and the way in which those constructions inform and are informed by the reality of social interaction. Armstrong and Harris unfortunately do not exploit the rich data they have uncovered and descend into an indefensible refutation of the point of theoretical critique *tout court*. After all this ethnography, Armstrong and Harris have only this to say about the activities of the Blades: 'The worst that can be said was that most of these fans were willing on occasions to get into relatively minor physical conflict with rivals' (Armstrong and Harris, 1991, p. 455). Both Dunning *et al.* (1991, p. 465) and Moorhouse (1991b, pp. 490–4) rightly highlight the disappointment of this retreat from sociology, which undermines the manifest importance of Armstrong's ethnography.

Giulianotti's recent contributions to the analysis of hooliganism constitute a very special case of this trend of uncritical, undertheorized writing because, on the surface, Giulianotti's sentences are replete with philosophical terminology, and they are obscurely constructed in a manner which suggests theoretical sophistication and erudition. In two articles, in which he analyses violent Aberdonian (Giulianotti, 1993) and Hibernian fans (Giulianotti, 1994b), Giulianotti employs two of Habermas's writings, *Knowledge and Human Interests* (Habermas, 1972), and 'What is universal pragmatic?' (Habermas, 1979) as the putative theoretical frameworks for his analyses of the cultural practices of these fans. I will direct my comments only to the second piece (Giulianotti, 1994b), both because it is more recent and, therefore, likely to be a maturer statement of Giulianotti's position and because it involves less of the committed obfuscation of the first piece and, therefore, requires less exposition. It is easier to get to the point.

In this second piece, Giulianotti sets himself the interesting task of examining the way in which Hibernian fans construct the world for themselves. The term 'ontology' in the title refers to the constitution of the Hibernian fans' social world – what exists for these fans. Into this analysis of the construction of a social world, Giulianotti inserts Habermas' famous 'universal pragmatic'. For Habermas, social domination is the result of distorted communication, when individuals are mystified into accepting improper and inegalitarian social norms. The universal pragmatic was Habermas' attempt to propose a theoretical situation in which such distorted communication and, therefore, domination might be obviated. The universal pragmatic was arrived at by means of an Ideal Speech Situation, which was a theoretical and, frankly, utopian moment of total discursive transparency, when all social power was put to one side and individuals in society faced each other to agree upon the rules which would best govern the society. In the transparency of the Ideal Speech Situation, power would be supposedly annulled and only the unforced 'force of a better argument' (Giddens, 1985, p. 95) would triumph. Reason and not power would be the deciding force in society.

Giulianotti attempts to apply this abstract formulation of political philosophy to the conduct of violent hooligans. Since this chapter is mainly concerned with demonstrating the theoretical inadequacy of much recent work in the sociology of football, it may seem potentially contradictory to criticize Giulianotti for employing high-level theory. This contradiction is only apparent, for Giulianotti employs Habermasian concepts out of their own philosophical context and he fails to integrate these concepts into his arguments; thus his empirical data stand apart from his theory and are not critically informed by it. Thus Giulianotti argues that the battle for honorific supremacy between football hooligans, violently and stylistically, constitutes an Ideal Speech Situation in which one group attempts to gain the upper hand over the other:

> The very endeavour to achieve this competitive pre-eminence indicates that any casual formation is appealing to a common set of standards, a subcultural standard of truth, against which this claim of superiority may be judged. Habermas defines this underlying objective as the Ideal Speech Situation. (Giulianotti, 1994b, p. 332)

Besides the fact that Habermas rules violence out from the start in the Ideal Speech Situation – it is rational arguments which triumph – the purpose of the Ideal Speech Situation is not for groups to gain superiority, as is the case for football hooligans, but, on the contrary, for a set of (democratic and fair) rules which will govern social interaction to be agreed upon in egalitarian fashion. A particular argument wins in the Ideal Speech Situation and the whole community benefits. Certainly, Giulianotti is right to argue that hooligans operate within the same cultural framework which gives their actions meaning; they know the stylistic and combative rules and, therefore, who has won, but how the Habermas universal pragmatic aids our understanding of this process is unclear. Rather than employing the highly philosophical and utopian idea of the Ideal Speech Situation, Giulianotti would have been better advised to look to less philosophical and more sociological theories of intergroup rivalries, cultural norms and honour, on which there is an extensive literature, to provide a critically informed and textured account of how the hooligans' construction of social reality contributes to the possibility of and the particular nature of violent confrontations.

The fact that Habermas' universal pragmatic cannot directly inform Giulianotti's analysis or encourage him to deepen his empirical analysis means that, in the end, despite the appearance of heavily theorization, the article is actually an interesting but straightforward description of the main categories which Hibernian fans use to describe others. No historical dimension is given, and nor, more importantly, is the way in which these categories inform social practice discussed. The appeal to the Habermasian universal pragmatic is then, in the end, unnecessary ornamentation which does not improve the initial description.

Giulianotti's failure to utilize Habermas in any serious way is no crime in itself. Giulianotti's use of Habermas distracts him from the proper issue, but it is a common academic problem that theories sometimes float unhelpfully above the data, without really assisting in their interpretation. However, the manner in which Giulianotti draws upon Habermas and the style which he uses throughout his writings suggest a more reprehensible academic strategy at work. The integration between theory, on the one hand, and empirical material, on the other, fails in the writings of Giulianotti because the theoretical framework is employed for the most part as a decoration. It merely dresses the material in more impressive clothing than is warranted and, unfortunately, distracts Giulianotti from deepening his potentially insightful analysis of the fans themselves. This stylistic obfuscation is easily highlighted if we examine what Giulianotti actually means by the use of certain grandiloquent terms. When talking of the hooligan rivalries and their struggle for supremacy, Giulianotti writes 'The neutralisation [of the Other] is, in a transcendental sense, a simulation of 'the Ideal Speech Situation' (Giulianotti, 1994b, p. 337). We have noted that Giulianotti is simply mistaken in his belief that the competition for honour between hooligans constitutes an Ideal Speech Situation. Besides the theoretical short-comings of this sentence, its significance lies in the use of the term, 'in a transcendental sense', for this term reveals Giulianotti's deliberate strategy of obscurity.

It is difficult to comprehend what a transcendental neutralization of the Other might be. For Kant, the term 'transcendental' refers to those synthetic *a priori* categories of the human mind which make experience possible (Kant, 1996, pp. 298–9, 318–19, 432, 483; Körner, 1955, pp. 35, 44–5; Ewing, 1974, pp. 25–6; Habermas, 1979, p. 21). Habermas employs the word in *Knowledge and Human Interests* (Habermas, 1972) to mean the same thing, although he has very different transcendental categories in mind than Kant. If Giulianotti means transcendental in this sense (as he should when referring to a philosopher who is very consciously in line with the rich Germanic heritage), the sentence means nothing. A neutralization could never have the cognitive capacity of making an experience possible in the Kantian sense; it simply does not refer to mental faculties or experience. The meaning of this sentence, although this is by no means certain, appears, I think, if we recognize that Giulianotti has confused transcendental with the other important Kantian word 'transcendent', which means beyond the limits of possible human experience (God, immortality and freedom) (Kant, 1996, pp. 298–9, 318–9; Ewing, 1974, pp. 25–6). Again, if we take the Kantian sense literally, the sentence means nothing. If neutralization is beyond human experience, then we cannot talk of it and it seems hard to describe the activities of violent men as transcendent in any of the essentially theological or cosmological ways that Kant intended. However, if Giulianotti confuses transcendental with transcendent and then by the latter means 'in theory' in the loosest sense – i.e. above and beyond everyday action – then the sentence begins to have some meaning, which belies its use of difficult Kantian terminology. In the end, the sentence means that if we idealize the battles of hooligans into theoretical models detached from the actual practices of those males, then they begin to look like (simulate) the Ideal Speech Situation. The problem with this is that, as I have argued above, it is actually not correct and this 'transcendental' theorizing does not cast any useful light on this social practice; in fact, it diverts us from the properly sociological task of examining the way in which meanings inform everyday actions and the interactions between individuals.

Giulianotti's writings display the same faults that I have documented in other sociological studies of football, in that they are undertheorized at exactly the point where critical analysis would be most useful. It would be illuminating to hear how the Hibernian fans' social ontology informs their relations with others or how these fans construct an imagined social reality which belies actuality in the way which Armstrong and Harris unknowingly revealed for the Blades fans (Armstrong and Harris, 1991). Giulianotti compounds critical inadequacy, which he shares with much recent writing on football, with stylistic obscurity, so that his texts are doubly flawed. They are under-theorized with insufficiently detailed empirical analysis and are, in places, practically impenetrable, concealing their potential interest behind unnecessary stylistic complexities and theoretical superfluities.

The False Populism of the Contemporary Sociology of Football

Although it is not universally the case, particularly for Giulianotti's mystifying prose, the critical and theoretical inadequacies of much of the contemporary sociology of football can be traced to a conscious political orientation which is found among the writers mentioned above. The majority of contemporary British writing on football is written from a populist position. Emerging sociologists have quickly taken the position of the 'fans' in any contemporary debates and, with little attention to the historical, social or gender specificities of those arguments, endorsed them in sociological accounts.

Sociologists of football are, in this country, overwhelmingly white and male, and they have adopted the position of a large majority of white, male fans who also attend football matches. This assumption of the political position of a particular group in a process under study is nothing new in sociology – Marx, of course, is a paradigmatic example. Yet the particular problem which emerges in many of the writings of British football sociologists is that they uncritically adopt the views of a certain group of fans and interpret this socially specific and gender-specific political position as an example of universal populism. The reaction of white, male fans to the new consumption of football in the 1990s – which is viewed more or less negatively – is regarded as evidence of a genuine and universal populist uprising, which the sociologists of football – as white, male football fans – support. In effect, sociologists of football conveniently legitimate their own position by pointing to its populist origins. Political engagement is admirable and doubtless important but the mantel of academic research insists that any political aspirations are raised beyond the level of naiveté.

There are numerous examples of this exaggeration of the views of the white male fan into a broad populism which is uncritically endorsed in the literature. For instance, in the Preface to his work on fanzines, Haynes properly notes his fandom of the game:

> Entry into the football fan subculture as an ethnographer was premised upon my previous knowledge and experience of football – reflecting the symbolic relation I and many other mates of my generation (I was born in the 60s and grew up to love the game in the 70s) have with the previous generations and cultural traditions of football in British society. (Haynes, 1995, p. viii)

Here, Haynes demonstrates his close relationship to a particular kind of fandom. He writes that he intends to be 'self-reflective' about this fandom, but at the same time he notes 'my love of football would often conflict with my intellectual scrutiny of the sport' (Haynes, 1995, p. x). I would suggest that this is indeed the case and that Haynes has been unable to detach himself from his own fandom in order to mount an effective critical appraisal of the fanzine movement, which he romanticizes in line with his own construction of the game as a fan.

It is not just Haynes who slips into this uncritical populism, though, and this assumption of the rectitude and universality of the white male's beliefs across all of football fandom is to be found in much of the contemporary sociology of football. In their introduction to their collected volume, Giulianotti and Williams (1994b) draw upon some of the same uncritical and unacknowledged populist premises to mount a criticism of some of the aspects of the 1994 World Cup in the USA. They are especially critical of new methods of broadcasting football: 'In the globalised future of televisual sports, the collage of traditional methods and the importance of the cultural rootedness of place and established localisms seems to count for increasingly little in the desperate pursuit of commercial success' (Giulianotti and Williams, 1994b, p. 13). The implication of this sentence is that the televisual coverage of football disrupts the natural and proper connection between the football club and the local community. Consequently, televised football is a debased currency, the inauthentic representation of an authentic original. Giulianotti and Williams argue that the origin of football fandom lay in the connection between the football club and its local community, and make an immediate and unsustained jump from that premise to the conclusion that this original relationship with the club is authentic and any development which threatens the original attachment is necessarily inauthentic and impoverished.

This leap simply cannot be sustained, for, as fandom in the age of the car reveals, it is perfectly possible for fans to be the supporters of a club even when they live many miles away from that club. It is merely reactionary to deny the reality of the attachment which these fans have to their club, and this denial blinds the academic to a very interesting area of research about the way in which fans construct their relationship with the club in the light of this loss of immediate geographical attachment. The television is central to these new forms of attachment, and is completely transforming football fandom, but, in the eyes of reactionary authenticity, this new fandom can only be regarded as inauthentic.

Both the consumption of football at the ground, by a local community, and the consumption of football on television require the interpretation of the spectator. Neither is more immediate or authentic than the other, but rather both involve active individual interpretation. It is simply that the interpretations are different in each case. Giulianotti and Williams assume that the historically prior form of spectatorship must be theoretically prior and existentially superior because (as white, male football fans) they unwittingly exaggerate this relationship with the game to the level of an archetype against which any developments are to be judged. Although their populist assumptions are less forthright than those of Haynes, in the end Giulianotti and Williams make the same mistake of exaggerating their own preferences and personal experiences into an authentic populism and, therefore, the appropriate critical standard by which to judge the contemporary transformation of the game.[4]

Much of the contemporary sociological commentary on aspects of the transformation of football is inadequate. It is poorly theorized and uncritical. In particular, the contemporary sociology of football fails because it unselfconsciously assumes the views of generally white, male, 'working-class' fans to be both representative of the football crowd as a whole and politically populist in sentiment. Recent writings have failed to situate the views of these white, male fans in a wider social, historical and gender context and have tended to romanticize the attitudes of these individuals because they reflect the sociologist's own imagined relations with football. The critical standard which these sociologists have then been able to apply to the contemporary transformation of football is overly influenced by the potentially exclusive views which individuals who are part of this large but limited group of fans sometimes adopt.

Criticism must start at home. If sociologists of football are to extract themselves from the marginal position in which they find themselves in the academic world and if their work is to be employed to inform wider sociological debate, then improving the theoretical rigour of contemporary work and its critical content is absolutely essential. Indeed, such an improvement is incumbent upon those writing about football, since football is patently an important cultural phenomenon. The marginalization of the study of football in sociology because the academic work on it is inadequate finally weakens the discipline as a whole. Sociological accounts of contemporary transformations, falsely diminish the role of football in contemporary social transformations, because the sociology of football fails to highlight its relevance to sociological theorists more generally. There is no single remedy to these problems, and to suggest one would be both arrogant and imperialistic. However, Adorno's arguments for a negative dialectics provides some useful insights which those academics working in football might well take to heart: 'Dialectics is the consistent sense of nonidentity. It does not begin by taking a standpoint. My thought is driven to it by its own inevitable insufficiency, by my guilt of what I am thinking' (Adorno, 1990, p. 5). The process of thinking is not a static one in which we elaborate upon and clarify what we already know; we should not take a standpoint. Rather, thinking proceeds by examining the inadequacy of what one thinks. That is, the first question any thinker must ask themselves is why they think what they think. This self-conscious reflection will begin to highlight the curious biases and partialities of our thought, and these naive biases will thereby begin to be removed. Of course, we inevitably speak from some standpoint and our views are inevitably inadequate – as Adorno knew – but at least by subjecting ourselves to the dialectical critique which Adorno outlines we will avoid the most obtuse errors of unselfconsciousness. Contemporary sociological accounts of football need to submit themselves to such a dialectical critique to highlight their own inadequacies and, in particular, to avoid the uncritical adoption and reification of the views of a narrow range of football fans. Such self-conscious critique provides a potential avenue for the sociological analysis of football which grounds itself in and contributes to current theorizing about contemporary social change.

Conclusion

To begin a work by mounting a critique of recent contributions is a strategically questionable endeavour, since it invites equal criticism in response. This is unavoidable, since the criticisms mounted above needed making and the hostility of the response may, I hope, serve to drive the analysis of football onwards and upwards. It is hoped that this book will demonstrate some of the features whose absence I have noted in contemporary sociological writings, namely, being theoretically informed and critical. Yet writers are invariably among the worst judges of their own work, and this account may fall below the very standards that it has set for others. If it does fail by its own standards, that in no way negates the arguments which I have proposed here, and at least the work will have failed in an attempt to be critical rather than merely never having left the complacent starting place of unacknowledged populism.

Finally, the extensive critiques which I have made in this chapter might imply a certain hubris about the following analysis: namely, that since I have criticized other approaches to the study of football, the following analysis should be the model for all future research. Nothing could be further from the truth. I have approached the question of the transformation of football in a way which seemed appropriate to me. Others must approach their own research questions with their own theoretical frameworks. Indeed, the development of competing styles of analysis would seem to be utterly essential if the sociology of football is to establish itself as a serious pursuit in the academic world. The central problem in contemporary writings is that they are all concerned with a romanticized populism which represents the standards of certain white, male fans as the standard of academic critique. We require analyses of football which are informed by theories of gender and which are carried out by women. We need interpretations which situate themselves in current sociological theories on race, which are carried out by individuals from ethnic minorities, and we need studies which examine fans other than white males, who have stereotypically filled the imagination of sociologists. If nothing else, it is hoped that the following analysis of the transformation of football in the 1990s will inspire future research into a field which is potentially replete with sociological interest and significance.

Notes

1 For a critique of Baudrillard's later writings see King (1998b).
2 The fandom which has developed around *When Saturday Comes* is discussed in Chapter 13.
3 For a discussion of the construction of hooligan confrontations and the creation of boundaries of acceptable violence see King (1997c).
4 Rogan Taylor's *Football and its Fans* (Taylor, 1992) falls into both of the traps described in this chapter, since it is undertheorized and is premised on a romantic notion of football fans. The recent collection by Giulianotti *et al.* (1994) on football hooliganism is another example of an undertheorized work, which amounts in the end to little more than journalism.

2

Football, Ritual and Historical Change

The Ritual of Football

Irving Scholar, the chairman of Tottenham Hotspur Football Club from 1982 to 1991, regarded the place which this football club held in public consciousness as being extraordinary, considering that Tottenham Hotspur was effectively only a small north London business (Scholar, 1992, p. 296; Horrie, 1992, p. vi). The overwhelming importance which is attached to professional football clubs, in spite of their financial modesty (in comparison with the vast multinationals of the post-Fordist world), lends the football club what Barthes might call a 'mythic quality' (Barthes, 1972, p. 19). The significance of football lies primarily not in its financial value but rather in the fact that many individuals – particularly males – in English society have regarded it as critical to their lives. Football is a regularized activity which provides an arena for the expression of meanings and identities for a particular section of the class and gender order of English[1] society. Football is, then, a ritual, and, consequently, this examination of its transformation in the 1990s can usefully draw on the anthropological analysis of ritual as a source of methodological and theoretical insights.

To this end, Geertz's seminal analysis of Balinese cock-fighting (Geertz, 1973) provides a theoretical approach to the study of ritual which might be usefully applied to the case of English football. Geertz's account of Balinese cock-fighting is both a piece of anthropological analysis and a statement of method. For Geertz, a society is not a mechanistic instrument of function and structure, but rather comprises a set of cultural values and meanings which inform everyday practice. The task of the anthropologist is to infiltrate the self-understandings of other cultures to demonstrate the ways in which individuals in a specific culture interpret their situation in order to negotiate their relations with other members of that culture. Geertz suggests that these self-understandings are inscribed in a culture's texts, by which he means various social practices. This view of culture implies an anthropological method which differs quite radically from that of Geertz's functionalist and structuralist predecessors: 'The culture of a people is an ensemble of texts, themselves ensembles, which the anthropologist strains to read over the shoulders of those to whom they properly belong' (Geertz, 1973, p. 452)

For Geertz, the task of the anthropologist is not simply to outline the structure of kinship or the structure of the 'savage mind' which the natives invariably reproduce in their social practice. Rather, the anthropologist has to attempt to discern the way in which natives actively interpret the meanings and values which their culture provides in their creation of identity. From this hermeneutic position, which highlights the meanings that individuals give to their lives and actions, Geertz argues against the functionalist view of the ritual. Whereas functionalist accounts of ritual propose a mechanistic view, wherein the ritual simply inculcates values into the natives, ensuring their compliance to the social hierarchy, Geertz suggests that through the ritual of the cock-fight, Balinese men express their own self-understandings to themselves: 'Its function, if you want to call it that, is interpretive; it is a Balinese reading of Balinese experience, a story they tell themselves about themselves' (Geertz, 1973, p. 448). For Geertz, not only is the active participation of the Balinese necessary in creating themselves as Balinese, but the story, which they tell themselves, involves both the expression of the strict hierarchy in Balinese society and a commentary upon it: 'it [the cock fight] provides a metasocial commentary upon the whole matter of assorting human beings into fixed hierarchical ranks and then organizing the major part of collective existence around that assortment' (Geertz, 1973, p. 448). Geertz argues that the cock-fight does not create status distinctions in a simplistic functionalist way but that, through the expression of self-understandings, status is brought under consideration for debate and re-negotiation.

However, in his assault on deterministic functionalist explanations, Geertz understates the issues of power and domination which are at work in the ritual. Although Geertz is right to highlight the agency of individuals and their negotiation of social meanings, this does not preclude the fact that relations of power are established in and through the ritual. These relations of power are not created functionally but only through the active interpretation of social agents. Individuals are effectively forced into conceding the political superiority of the rich in the Balinese cock-fight, even though there is some opportunity to pass comment on this inequality. For instance, the rich in Balinese society are able to express their status through cock-fighting because they are involved in the 'deep play' of the large bets which they stake, rather than the small side-bets of the poor. Through this 'deep play', the rich demonstrate their status, but that demonstration, as Geertz points out, is not automatic; the poor have to interpret the demonstration, and in their interpretation will question and negotiate the status of the rich. Geertz's notion that the ritual provides an opportunity merely for commentary about the social hierarchy is too weak. Through the ritual, the dominant groups in society attempt to establish their hegemony over the society. That is, these groups attempt to establish a particular set of meanings which legitimate their domination as the universal commonsense across the whole society (Gramsci, 1971, pp. 419–23; Hall *et al.*, 1978, p. 156). The ritual is not only an opportunity for social commentary, but is an arena of intense political struggle and contestation.

Once we have added this intensely political dimension to Geertz's analysis of the Balinese cock-fight, Geertz's hermeneutic method becomes very useful as a framework for the analysis of the transformation of English football in the 1990s. In the ritual of football, individuals express their notion of themselves and of their culture through their consumption of the game. Through that consumption, social relations and the understanding which inform them are expressed and contested. Thus, football becomes 'central to how we see ourselves as a nation' (Tomlinson and Whannel, 1986, p. 120; Bromberger, 1993, pp. 90–1; Critcher, 1991, p. 83). The point is that 'how we see ourselves' is anything but automatic. Rather, it is the result of continuous political struggle over the meanings which are expressed in rituals like football. The transformation of football in the 1990s can be usefully viewed and analysed in terms of this struggle over social meanings, wherein dominant and subordinate groups have contested the values which are expressed through football.

There are two further additions which are necessary in the context of the analysis of the new consumption of football in England in the 1990s. First, Geertz's analysis almost wholly excludes the excitement which is engendered by the ritual. This is particularly serious in so far as this study is concerned, as this communal excitement is a central element of the experience of football (Elias and Dunning, 1986; Dunning, 1996). However, the centrality of the experience of excitement to football does not invalidate Geetz's hermeneutic method, but suggests that such a method should be taken even more seriously. In the heightened emotional states which football fans experience, their identities and social relations with others are not subsumed in some primordial return to a natural state of adrenalin-induced hysteria but, on the contrary, are realized at a particularly visceral level. Social identities and relations emerge from the abstract dilution of the everyday to be forcefully actualized in the swaying body of the crowd. Durkheim (1964) famously analysed this ritualistic realization of the social in his study of aboriginal religion in Australia. There the clans would spend most of the year engaged in the profane and dispersed activity of hunter-gathering across the outback, but when the time for ritual came, the whole clan would gather and, through the ecstatic celebration of their totem, would physically experience the presence of their society, in the form of the bodies of other tribespeople around them and in the sensations of ecstasy which the celebrations induced. The point is that the excitement which is induced by football intensifies the political debates – or the metasocial commentary, as Geertz would call it – which go on around the game, intensifying negotiations about power and domination.

In addition, Geertz's hermeneutic theory needs to be more critical. If we only read the social texts over the shoulders of the actors, then we merely present a description of those texts to the reader. This may be enough in the ethnography of other societies, when the cultural differences are so wide that any critical judgement may sound imperialistic. However, as emphasized throughout Chapter 1, it is imperative that the contemporary analysis of football should be critical. We must do more than merely read the texts over the shoulders of actors. We have to interpret the debates around football critically, for the very reason that they are political. The metasocial commentary which informs the transformation of football is inevitably and explicitly political, reflecting the understandings and interests of particular groups.

Geertz's passive reading can be transformed into a critical hermeneutics by reference to Gadamer's own work on hermeneutics. Gadamer (1979) argued that hermeneutics primarily involves the circular process of moving between the whole of a text and its parts; it is through our comprehension of the whole that the parts become meaningful. However, since a text is only composed of its parts, the meaning of the whole is constantly transformed through the reinterpretation of the parts. The hermeneutic process operates around an upward spiral of constantly changing understanding through the incessant interplay of the parts and the whole. In the context of the analysis of football in the 1990s, this hermeneutic circle can be employed to interpret the arguments of various individuals and groups involved in the transformation of the game by situating their arguments within a wider social and historical whole. That is, we have to situate the particular actions and demands of fans, government, the media and entrepreneurs within the wider context of contemporary Britain. By interpreting particular interventions within this wider context, the political disposition and social relevance of these interventions is revealed and, in this realization of the particularity of each intervention, we arrive at a standpoint which is superior to and critical of the social transformation which we study. In this way we achieve a properly sociological perspective on what we are studying.[2]

A slightly reformulated hermeneutic method, which is self-consciously critical and which takes into account the ecstatic aspects of ritual celebration, comprises one of the major theoretical frameworks which informs this study throughout. However, the object of study here is social change. I am concerned with how the Premier League was established and how the new consumption of football – all-seater stadia, new televisual coverage, increased ticket prices – came into existence. Consequently, the hermeneutic theory which I have proposed above is not in and of itself sufficient to the task in hand. To that end, Gramsci's Hegelian reading of Marx,[3] which emphasizes historical transformation rather than its structuralist elements, provides the most useful resource for the construction of a theory of social change and which will inform this analysis of the transformation of English football in the 1990s.

Historical Change

Gramsci regarded Marx's Preface to *A Contribution to the Critique of Political Economy* (*Zur Kritik*) (1971) as a fundamental resource for the development of his 'philosophy of praxis' – the term which he used to describe his theory of revolutionary practice. The importance of 'The Preface' to Gramsci's thought is revealed by his regular reference to it in *The Prison Notebooks* (Gramsci, 1971, pp. 106, 177, 409, 432) and is highlighted in Gramsci's critique of the Italian Communist Party's *Popular Manual*.

> It is worth noting that the *Popular Manual* does not quote the passage from the Preface to *Zur Kritik* nor even refer to it. This is pretty strange, given that this is the most important authentic source for a reconstruction of the philosophy of praxis. (Gramsci, 1971, p. 460)

Since Gramsci endows the specified passage from *Zur Kritik* with such importance, it is worth quoting the passage in full:

> No social order is ever destroyed before all the productive forces for which it is sufficient have been developed, and new superior relations of production never replace older ones before the material conditions for their existence have matured within the framework of old society. Mankind thus inevitably sets itself only tasks as it is able to solve, since closer examination will always show that the problem itself arises only when the material conditions for its solution are already present. (Marx, 1971, p. 21)

In *The Prison Notebooks*, Gramsci argues that it is possible to develop a whole set of historical methods from this passage, and one of the crucial methodological divides which the passage suggests to Gramsci is the separation between the 'organic' and the 'conjunctural' (Gramsci, 1971, p. 177; Joll, 1977, p. 85). For Marx, the emergence of a new social formation cannot be attributed to immediate and conjunctural factors, because it is necessary to consider what gave rise to these immediacies and what rendered them significant in the first place. Any particular historical transformation has to be predicated on vast (organic) economic changes which problematize the existing form of social relations. Society resolves these crises in accordance with the economic conditions which produced that crisis in the first place. The economic development of a society prescribes the possible horizon of future social forms.

Although Gramsci cites the passage from *Zur Kritik*, his own historicist arguments take a somewhat different turn from those presented by Marx, for whereas Marx is, in this passage, very economistic, pointing to a direct relationship between a society's economic development and its subsequent historical transformation, Gramsci gives the economy a less decisive determining influence. He asks the rhetorical question of whether fundamental historical changes can be caused directly by economic crises (Gramsci, 1971, p. 178) and replies:

It may be ruled out that immediate economic crises of themselves produce historic events: they can simply make the terrain more favourable to the dissemination of certain modes of thought and ways of posing and resolving questions involving the entire subsequent development of natural life. (Gramsci, 1971, p. 178)

In contradistinction to the Marx of *Zur Kritik*, therefore, Gramsci does not regard the economy as the primary force of historical change. Rather, the economic development of a society is itself embedded within the wider ideological framework of that society.

For Gramsci, the material realities of a society are dependent upon the wider cultural framework which makes those material conditions and their transformation possible. Gramsci makes his position quite explicit at various points in *The Prison Notebooks* (e.g. 1971, pp. 161–7, 178, 337, 407–8). For instance, Gramsci writes:

The analysis of these propositions tends, I think, to reinforce the conception of the historical bloc in which precisely the material forces are the content and ideologies are the form, though this distinction between form and content has purely didactic value, since material forces would be inconceivable historically without form and ideologies would be individual fancies without material forces. (Gramsci, 1971, p. 377)

The material conditions of any society, then, do not stand separately from the cultural formation of that society. Nor do the former determine the latter in a relation of base to superstructure but rather a society's ideology provides a framework for the kind of mode of production which is possible. Ideas and values are implicit in social and economic transformation from the very outset.

Gramsci argued that historical change occurs through the organic development of the economy which consists of myriad everyday exchanges which are informed by the framing ideas. At certain points, this economic development will come into conflict with the framing ideas of society which originally informed that economy and there will arise a contradiction in the social formation wherein the formally recognized values and meanings are in opposition to emergent economic conditions. At this conjunctural moment, new framing ideas are developed which highlight the trajectory of organic development and formally recognize these developments.

For Gramsci, then, historical change must be explained by reference to organic, economic developments which give rise to certain conditions in which change is necessitated, and to conjunctural, ideological moments when the specific nature of these changes is debated and realized. However, as we have seen, emergent economic conditions do not stand prior to cultural and ideological frameworks but are informed by them. Furthermore, as the concept of hegemony, by which Gramsci meant this dominant ideological framework, implies, neither the ideas which get established as dominant in conjunctural moments nor the historical trajectory of a society are determined equally by all members of a society. On the contrary, dominant groups, which are favoured by organic developments, have a privileged say over the values and principles which frame a society's historic development. This dual historical method, utilizing the concepts of the organic and the conjunctural (and emphasizing issues of power), provides a useful framework with which to analyse the development of the Premier League and the new consumption of football. This method necessitates the consideration of the long-term developments which gave rise to the Premier League and the new consumption of football. However, those organic economic developments of the *longue durée* did not automatically determine the subsequent establishment of the Premier League or the new consumption of football. Those specificities have to be analysed as particular results of the conjunctural moment. Yet, since the organic developments have substantially stimulated the need for reform, the organic also privileges certain arguments and the classes which express them. In other words, although historical change cannot be read off from organic development directly, there is, nevertheless, a certain logic to historical development whereby the historical trajectory of a culture limits the kinds of transformation which can take place.

Conclusion

The analysis of the transformation of football must be inserted into this theory of historical change. Following Geertz, I have argued that in the ritual, the self-understandings which inform individual action and are constitutive of a culture are expressed. It follows, then, that the ritual will express (in admittedly complex and resisted ways) the dominant framework of any society – the hegemony, as Gramsci would have called it. However, as organic developments render that hegemony obsolete, the meanings which the ritual itself expresses will become obsolete and transformation of that ritual will be insisted upon by the progressive and emergent dominant classes. In addition, the ritual itself is not a static social form. It, too, is a sphere of social interaction, involving economic exchanges, and it also therefore undergoes organic transformation. Significantly, because the ritual is informed by ideas similar to the wider social formation (and therefore involves similar economic exchanges), its course of development reflects the organic developments of the wider society. Thus, at a particular moment in history, as a result of its organic development, the ritual will supersede the hegemonic framework of understanding which was originally adequate to it. At that conjunctural moment, when a new ritual form has 'matured within the framework of the old' ritual, arguments are proposed at various important social sites by emergent social groups which demand the reformation of the ritual (in line with the reformation of wider society). For English professional football, the conjunctural moment at which the ritual was out of step with wider social changes and with its own development was the mid-1980s to the early 1990s and, in particular, from 11 May 1985, the day of the incineration of Bradford's main stand,[4] until solutions to the Hillsborough disaster began to be implemented after the publication of the Taylor report in 1990.

Since both the organic (political economic) development of football and its conjunctural moment of crisis in the mid-1980s can only be explained through an understanding of the wider social transformations in which these organic and conjunctural moments occurred, it is necessary to provide at least a brief outline of the major social developments which have occurred in post-war Britain. In particular, it is important that we recognize the significance of the collapse of the Keynesian post-war consensus, the rise of Thatcherism and the development of Britain's peculiar version of post-Fordism.

Notes

1   Some clarification of the use of the terms English and British is required. This book examines the transformation of the top flight of English professional football. However, in order to explain that transformation, wider social and economic changes which have occurred across the whole of Britain more generally have to be acknowledged. In particular, it is necessary to recognize the importance of transformations of government policy under Thatcherism, which have affected the whole of Britain, though in regionally different ways. In this book, although I point to the government policies which have been applied to the nation as a whole, my claims about the transformation of football are limited only to England.

2   The argument for a critical hermeneutics is a good deal more controversial than I have claimed here, as is witnessed by the extensive debates between Habermas and Gadamer (see McCarthy (1978) and How (1995) for summaries of these debates). It is impossible to go into these debates here, and the proof that hermeneutics can be critical must be found in the eating; if my analysis of the various arguments about the transformation of football in the 1990s is convincing, it will demonstrate practically the possibility of a critical hermeneutics.

3   Boggs (1976) and Joll (1977) have both argued that Gramsci was committed to a Hegelian perspective, which emphasized historical development and the importance of ideas to that development.

4   The main stand at Bradford City's Valley Parade burnt down during the last day of that season, killing 55 people (see Chapter 7). The Hillsborough disaster occurred on 15 April 1989 and resulted in the eventual deaths of 96 Liverpool fans (see Chapters 8 and 9).

3

The Post-war Consensus and the Emergence of British Post-Fordism

The Post-war Settlement

Although not universally acknowledged in the academic literature (e.g. Pimlott, 1988), the existence of a post-war settlement or consensus between the end of World War II and the 1970s, which was characterized by the broad agreement between the government, the opposition and the public on the central principles of national economic and social policy, is widely accepted (e.g. Marquand, 1988; Kavanagh and Morris, 1989; Brooke, 1992; Hall *et al.*, 1978; Gamble, 1988; Holmes and Horsewood, 1988; Hutton, 1996). This post-war consensus and, more particularly, its collapse and replacement by an emergent, Thatcherite, post-Fordist consensus forms the essential historical context for this study.

The most important and celebrated element of the post-war consensus was the Keynesian economic settlement which lay at its heart. Keynesian economic theory had been developed in response to the Depression of the late 1920s and 1930s, the chief cause of which, Keynes famously maintained, was underconsumption, which had provoked a vicious circle of unemployment (as workers were laid off because the goods they produced could no longer be sold) and further underconsumption; once unemployed, workers were even less likely to make purchases. Keynes insisted that the state must intervene in the economy to prevent any future repetitions of this underconsumption and, in particular, that the state had to ensure full employment through public spending. A fully and securely employed population would feel free to spend its earnings, thereby preventing underconsumption (Marquand, 1988, pp. 18–21; Kavanagh and Morris, 1989, pp. 36–7). In addition, the post-war governments sought to overcome the antagonism which had character-ized British industrial relations through the creation of a corporatist settlement between state, capital and labour. The state would intervene to mediate in disputes between capital and labour in order to maximize productive efficiency by reducing the levels of trades union actions.

Whatever the details of Keynesian economic theory, the central economic commonsense of the post-war consensus, which was derived from Keynes, was the priority of full employment, and this was related to a deeper notion of universality, whereby the citizens of the entire nation would be protected by the state (Marquand, 1988, p. 34).

The social aspect of the post-war consensus involved the welfare and educational developments which were proposed during the World War II and implemented by post-war governments. The most important element of the social settlement was Beveridge's creation of a welfare state which was designed to act as a safety net 'from cradle until grave' (Marquand, 1988, p. 23; Addison, 1982, pp. 14, 17, 211; Sked and Cook, 1979, p. 20). In particular, the institution of national insurance and the national health service were fundamental to the security of the population. Again, these welfare institutions were themselves predicated on a deeper social-democratic belief in the universality of the provision of state benefits; the need to ensure a decent standard of living for everyone (Marquand, 1988, p. 28; Sked and Cook, 1979, p. 20; Brooke, 1992, pp. 239, 248, 272–3).

In addition to these governmental policies, there were marked social transformations from the 1950s, the most striking of which was the emergence of 'affluence'. Partly as a result of Keynesian economic and Beveridgean social policies but, more particularly, because of the long post-war boom which was substantially based on the success of American Fordist systems of mass production, there was something of a revolution in affluence from the late 1950s. This affluence initiated a quite radical transformation of class relations and of working-class culture, as the extensive 'embourgeoisement' debate in sociology in the late 1950s and 1960s[1] has testified. These profound social transformations have been important to the possible form which British post-Fordism has been able to take. When the Keynesian post-war consensus eventually collapsed in the 1970s, any social reformation had to take into account the new affluence of the 1960s, as well as, of course, Britain's historic economic bias towards the City and to external financial investment. In other words, the new balance of class relations which developed under Keynesianism was crucial to subsequent historical transformations.

The success of the post-war settlement overwhelmingly lay in the fact that it coincided with a long economic boom which ensured the full employment and the improved living standards which were at the heart of the settlement. However, the settlement came under strain in the 1960s as rates of profit began to fall, and by the early 1970s there was a full crisis of the consensus. The importance of the collapse of the post-war settlement to this book lies in what replaced it: Britain's idiosyncratic and, according to Hutton (1996), 'unredeemable' post-Fordist settlement. This post-Fordism and the Thatcherite ideas which informed its creation constituted the framework for the transformation of football in the 1990s.

British Post-Fordist Society

The Economy

Despite its claim of being the 'first industrial nation', Britain was, ironically, never fully industrialized, relying more on the relatively easy wealth which its Empire provided and which the 'habitus' of its ruling class (a curious blend of aristocracy and bourgeoisie) regarded as an appropriate method of accumulation (see Weiner, 1985; Landes, 1989). Thus Britain's manufacturing base was always somewhat patchy and *ad hoc*, and Britain's industries were never organized as rigorously as those in the US or Germany. From the late eighteenth century, Britain's economy was oriented towards the City with its bias towards immediate financial reward through foreign investment in the Empire rather than long-term investment in indigenous British industry (Nairn, 1981, p. 23; Gamble, 1985, pp. 3, 23, 60, 85, 112; Landes, 1989, p. 326–58 Hutton, 1996, pp. 111–31).

In the light of Britain's amateurish industrialization, it is not surprising that, in the face of the new global economy of the 1970s, the easiest response for the British economy was to promote the financial markets of the City, benefiting from the sizeable invisible income which those markets brought (to the south), and to focus not on the production of post-Fordist goods but on their sale in an increasingly service-oriented society. In short, the easiest strategy for Britain to adopt in the light of intense competition in the new post-Fordist global economy was to retrench along its traditional lines of strength. In effect, this involved implementing policies which favoured the City at the expense of the manufacturing sector, which would require much greater and more imaginative investment if it were to be made competitive in the global markets. Consequently, post-Fordist economic developments in Britain have been characterized not so much by the development of flexible specialization systems of production (Piore and Sabel, 1984) as by the quite radical decline in manufacturing employment. For instance, whereas 8 million people were employed in manufacturing in 1971, only 5.5 million were still employed in the same sector in 1984 (Lash and Urry, 1987, p. 99), while the number of individuals employed in the service sector increased from 11.3 million in 1971 to 13.3 million in 1984 (Lash and Urry, 1987, p. 99).

In their later work, Lash and Urry (1994) have argued that a central element of post-Fordism is the development of a new type of commodity which has 'sign value'. The post-Fordist commodity is concerned with the creation of identity, endowing its consumer with meaning, rather than providing that consumer with a tool which has a function (Lash and Urry, 1994, p. 4). In relation to this argument for the creation of commodities with sign value, Lash and Urry dubiously assert that individuals in contemporary culture are somehow more 'reflexive' than before and are therefore more concerned with the issue of their identity than in the past (Lash and Urry, 1994, pp. 3, 5, 55–8). Although Lash and Urry's arguments for reflexivity and sign value are overstated,[2] they are useful in so far as the new consumption of football is concerned, because they highlight the new use to which football has been put by certain entrepreneurs in the 1980s and 1990s. Football has, in the 1990s, become a very important sign value in the economies of signs and space of which Lash and Urry speak, and certain entrepreneurs have effectively attempted to commodify the identity which the football club offers. The football club has become, then, a typically British post-Fordist enterprise; it is a service industry which sells symbolic values.

The New Class Structure

The shift away from manufacturing has radically altered the class formations and relations in Britain. In particular, the class structure of British society has been reformulated by the division of the workforce into a core and periphery, which was noted as a typical process in the global phenomenon of post-Fordism (Murray, 1990a, p. 58). The division of the post-Fordist workforce into a core and a periphery has elsewhere been described as the development of a 'two-thirds, one-third' society (Therborn, 1990; Hall and Jacques, 1990, p. 34; Hall, 1990, p. 118) or the development of a thirty, thirty, forty society (Hutton, 1996, pp. 14, 106–10). The core comprises a well-paid, secure and skilled workforce, which is supported by an increasingly private welfare system, based on insurance, while the periphery consists of a casualized, low-paid workforce, dependent on an inadequate public welfare system, which has been problematically termed the 'underclass' (Murray, C., 1990; Murray, R., 1990, p. 58; Lister, 1996; Marris, 1996). In Britain, this developing 'underclass' is generally situated in those areas which were formerly economically dependent on heavy industry, such as the north of England, South Wales and Clydeside. Working-class individuals living in those areas have been consigned to practically permanent unemployment, poverty and crime. They comprise the periphery of British society (Lash and Urry, 1987, p. 99).

However, although the decisive rift in post-Fordist society lies between the core and the periphery, the core is itself divided, so that it has been argued that post-Fordist Britain has become a trichotomous society (Therborn, 1990, pp. 111–12; Burrows, 1991, p. 8; McDowell *et al.*, 1989, pp. 1–3; Hutton, 1996, pp. 14, 105–10). The actual constitution of this core is complex and has led to differing accounts of its constituency. For instance, Hutton is more pessimistic than Therborn about the less affluent section of the core, describing its members as the 'marginalized' and 'insecure' (Hutton, 1996, p. 106), but despite these discrepancies, I will attempt to draw a tenable picture of the current state of the social formation.

The two essential groups within the core, which comprise the relatively affluent two-thirds, according to this argument, are the lower-grade white-collar workers, who perform menial (and boring) functions in the bureaucracies of large service corporations, and the professional middle classes employed in more secure, more skilled and generally better-paid employment at the highest bureaucratic levels. Sociological discussion of the white-collar workforce has been principally concerned with whether this group constitutes a proletariat (see Crompton and Jones, 1989). The significant point about these arguments so far as this account is concerned is that the 'traditional' divide between the working- and middle-class employment has been blurred. The middle-class bureaucrats have been deskilled by the development of computer technology, and service corporations have looked to employ more women at the lower levels, as they are usually more deferential and can be paid less.[3] The need for low-grade white-collar employees in the bureaucracies of the service industries has meant that many working-class individuals have attained jobs which would never have been open to their parents. Consequently, there has been a convergence between the lower-middle-class white-collar workers and certain upwardly mobile sections of the working class.

The professional middle class has become increasingly divided as a result of certain post-Fordist developments. Various commentators have noted the increasing concentration of capital in the post-Fordist economy with the development of very large multinational corporations (Amin and Malmberg, 1994, pp. 234–6; Lash and Urry, 1987, p. 90) which have become increasingly politically and economically dominant. This growing dominance of multinationals has had the important effect of promoting those members of the middle classes employed by these private multinationals above those professionals employed in the public sector. This increasingly dominant private sector of the professional middle class has been called the 'service class'; it operates in the highest ranks of the service bureaucracies, performing functions of control for capital (Abercrombie and Urry, 1983, p. 122), and has become the object of sociological scrutiny (Goldthorpe, 1980; Abercrombie and Urry, 1983; Lash and Urry, 1987; Savage *et al.*, 1992).

The sociological concentration on divisions in the middle classes and the development of the service class, in particular, has obscured the existence of the capitalist class. It is certainly true that the growth of very large multinationals, which are owned by institutional shareholders and administered by boards, has reduced the importance of entrepreneurial capitalists who have sole or majority ownership of their companies. Nevertheless, these entrepreneurial individuals do exist, especially, as we shall see in Chapter 11, in the interstices between the markets of the multinationals, although there are notable exceptions to the new pattern of institutional shareholding. Rupert Murdoch, who still owns and controls his vast News Corporation, is the most prominent example of this persistence of the entrepreneurial capitalist at the highest economic levels, and he, as we shall see, is important to the discussion of the transformation of football.

Consequently, we are left with a system of social classification which categorizes post-Fordist Britain into four groups: the 'underclass', the new affluent manual and white-collar workers, the professional middle class (divided into private sector service class and public sector) and the entrepreneurial capitalists. These groups are not monolithic; they are internally differentiated in their styles of consumption and self-under-standings and, perhaps most importantly, by their differential engagement with and dependence on the private and public sectors.[4]

The Ideology and Politics of Post-Fordist Britain: Thatcherism

Thatcherism is central to the examination of the transformation of football, because this ideological and political project established a new set of meanings as hegemonic over British society which informed the reform of the game. Gamble has argued that there were three potential strategies for renewal in the face of the crisis of the post-war settlement: de-industrialization or two forms of industrial regeneration pro-grammes, which Gamble terms industrial regeneration I and II (Gamble, 1983, pp. 123–4). 'Industrial regeneration I' involved restructuring the industrial base by destroying the trade unions and reaffirming the power of management, while 'industrial regeneration II' referred to a re-structuring which would involve the state and would be carried out with the collaboration of all classes (Gamble, 1983, p. 124; Overbeek, 1990, p. 154).

Although there were three potential solutions to the crisis of the 1970s, the free-market strategy was adopted. The adoption of the free market is explicable by reference to some of the arguments made above. The free-market strategy was adopted because it was the easiest way of defending emerging class interests in the face of intense economic competition. In particular, the free-market strategy promised to defend as much of the affluence which had been gained under Keynesianism as possible. Furthermore, and more importantly, the free market arguments which Thatcherism espoused supported Britain's historic orientation to financial capitalism and to the City, in particular. Free-market methods of reform, therefore, promised to maximize Britain's economic competitiveness in the new global order at the least cost of restructuring (Jessop *et al.*, 1988, p. 18; Gamble, 1985, pp. 195, 204, 226). Thatcherism envisaged economic retrenchment along the lines of Britain's traditional financial strengths.

The free market and the strong state

Gamble has argued that in 1979 the Conservative Party under Thatcher set itself five tasks.[5] Those tasks were to restore the health of the economy and social life, to restore incentive, to uphold Parliament and the rule of law, to support family life and to strengthen Britain's defences (Gamble, 1988, p. 121). The first two projects were concerned with creating and extending the free market, while the last three would be achieved through the application of a strong state (Gamble, 1988, p. 121).

Thatcherism's espousal of the free market and the strong state appear contradictory. However, a closer examination of these ideological elements will reveal their compatibility. One of the main causes of the collapse of the post-war consensus had been the raging world inflation of the 1970s. That inflation made capital investment very insecure and had a deleterious effect on economic development. Consequently, it was regarded by Thatcher as the central target for her economic policies. This concern was derived from monetarist theories such as that of Hayek, who (wrongly) argued that inflation was due solely to public spending and that the reduction of public spending was the only solution to the problem of inflation. Consequently, Thatcher attempted to apply monetarist measures which would reduce public spending and thereby restrict inflation. In addition, Thatcher promoted the free market as a method of re-invigorating capitalist enterprise in Britain, and thus she reduced both corporate and high-income taxation as an 'incentive' to entrepreneurs. Finally, the free-market ideology justified the government's withdrawal from the corporatist relationship with the unions and capital which had been attempted but which had spectacularly failed during the 1970s. The government had no duty to intervene in industrial disputes, although, in fact, this free-market *laissez-faire* attitude actually legitimated the state's active support of business in these disputes. The free-market ideology of Thatcherism dismissed the concept of 'One-Nation' Toryism which had informed the Conservative Party's political strategies in the post-war years.

Once it is understood that the demand for a strong state was similarly related to class interests and understandings and to a strategy of economic retrenchment along lines which historically favoured the City, the apparent contradiction between the appeals for a strong state *and* a free market disappears. Dispensing with the 'One-Nation' strategy of the post-war settlement and introducing economic policies which would cause unemployment meant that Thatcher would require a strong state to control the civil disorder that these measures would engender, in the form of demonstrations, riots and crime. In particular, although Thatcher's free-market ideas dispensed with the notion that the state had a negotiating role to play in the disputes between business and labour, the idea of the strong state legitimated the active suppression of union dissent. The development of a strong state was essential for the continued security and prosperity both of large businesses which benefited from free-market policies, and of those individuals who worked in those businesses, from the service class down to the affluent working class. The development of the strong state was designed to allay these classes' anxieties for their persons and property. In Gamble's analysis of Thatcherism, therefore, the authoritarian populist strand, to which Hall (1983) gives pride of place, actually constitutes only one element in an ideological complex. In addition to the strong state's repressive defence of property, such a state is essential to the smooth running of the free market, through its system of laws and its control over currency.

Gamble is not merely concerned, however, with ideology in the abstract. He also discusses the way in which this ideology was implemented into policy. To this end, Gamble divides Thatcher's premiership into two periods, which parallel the schema of Jessop *et al.* Gamble terms the first period from 1979 to 1982 'the slump', when Thatcher attempted to impose monetarist policies (Gamble, 1988, p. 98) but was actually forced to increase government spending due to the recession (Gamble, 1988, p. 105). Gamble's second period runs from 1982 to 1987, and he calls this 'the recovery'. Gamble argues that by 1987 monetarism was quite unimportant as a guide to what the government was doing.

Despite his long discussion of the ideological principles of Thatcherism, Gamble finally argues that Thatcherism is much better explained as statecraft than as ideology (Gamble, 1988, p. 141). Despite the admirableness of concentrating on the specifics of Tory policy, the claims that Thatcherism was only a form of statecraft do not fit in well with the rest of Gamble's work. Nor are they finally theoretically defensible. If the ideological element of Thatcherism was a mere side-issue to the real point of Thatcher's premiership – the pragmatic implementation of policy – then it is difficult for Gamble to justify the extent to which he goes to analyse the ideological formulations of the free market and strong state. Furthermore, if Thatcher was no more than a pragmatist, then her extensive efforts to broadcast her project by means of speeches and the publication of policy documents by (heavily funded) right-wing think-tanks, such as the Institute for Economic Affairs, seems incomprehensible. Most importantly, the very suggestion of the possibility of an entirely pragmatic and un-ideological statecraft is itself unsustainable. The very decision to be practical (and it is not at all clear that Thatcher was inspired by mere practicality in policy-making) requires a judgement based on standards (of what is practical) to be made. These standards are necessarily ideological, as they are actively derived from interpretations.

Gamble makes the error of concluding that, just because the Thatcher government was unable to implement monetarism, the ideological commitment to the free market was, therefore, irrelevant. Such a dismissal is unwarranted. It ignores the important work which the ideology has done in spite of its failure to become policy. For instance, the monetarist strand of Thatcherite ideology has not been ineffective in the reforms which the Tory governments of the 1980s were able to institute. Pure monetarist policy may well have been impossible to impose on the British economy but the central doctrine of monetarism, the value of the free market, has informed reforms in private and public sectors. The notion of the free market has legitimated the government in giving business a freer hand in its own affairs in the private sector, while (ironically) the application of the free market in the public sector has been the means by which ever-greater governmental controls over spending have been brought about. The technicalities of Hayek's thought may be irrelevant to understanding Britain's response to the post-war crisis, but his mediated influence on reforming policy in the 1980s in the guise of a commitment to the free market is difficult to deny.

Despite the eventual retreat to mere pragmatism of Gamble's analysis of Thatcherism, Gamble's account nevertheless provides a good account of Thatcher's project, incorporating both ideological strands and linking them (admittedly not entirely satisfactorily) to the actuality of her policy. It is the definition of Thatcherism which will, consequently, be used to interpret the debates around the reformation of football from the mid-1980s to the late 1980s (in Part III) and in which Thatcher, herself, played an important role.

Notes

1   The embourgeoisement debate concerned itself with the issue of whether the working class were becoming more middle class or not. The following texts were important in the debates: Abrams (1960), Goldthorpe *et al.* (1968a,b, 1969), Young and Wilmott (1986), Roberts (1983), Dennis *et al.* (1956), Jackson (1968), Klein (1970), Anderson *et al.* (1966), Frankenburg (1970), Hoggart (1957) and Zweig (1962).

2   I am unconvinced by the arguments of Lash and Urry that post-Fordism has involved the introduction of new symbolic commodities in place of functional ones with use value, or that contemporary culture is any more 'reflexive' than other cultures. Did not Hegel have some notion of the centrality of self-consciousness to human existence nearly two hundred years ago, and have not anthropologists demonstrated that objects in all cultures, in all places and at all times are symbolic? Furthermore, the recent commonplace in sociology that we have suddenly become 'self-reflexive'

seems to fly in the face of biological evidence, for this new reflexivity must be predicated on the development of new functions in the human brain. Contemporary human conduct would not suggest such an epochal evolutionary development in the cerebral faculties of *Homo sapiens*.

3　The spate of 'Essex girl' jokes in the City in the 1990s have been concerned with reasserting distinctions by the traditional white-collar workforce and the service class concerning the influx of female workers of working-class origin into formerly middle-class employment.

4　See Edgell and Duke (1991) for an interesting, though problematic, discussion of the effects of the division between private and public sectors on class formation.

5　I focus my discussion of Thatcherism on Gamble's analysis; there are, however, other important contributions (e.g., Hall and Jacques, 1983; Jessop *et al.*, 1988) which I have not been able to discuss for reasons of brevity.

PART II

THE ORGANIC ORIGINS OF THE NEW CONSUMPTION OF FOOTBALL

4

The Decline of Attendance and the Abolition of the Maximum Wage

Declining Attendances at Football League Grounds

In this chapter, drawing on the theoretical and historical frameworks sketched in Part I, I will examine the organic origins of the new consumption of football through the examination of two developments in English professional football. I want to show how the differential decline of match attendances of League football, on the one hand, and the transformation of labour regulations between professional footballers and their clubs, on the other, set professional English football on an organic historical trajectory, whereby the big city clubs became increasingly financially autonomous of the clubs of the lower divisions from the 1960s onwards. I will go on to argue that this financial autonomy created the possibility of a Premier League and, therefore, the possibility of the new consumption of football.

In describing the organic origins of the new consumption of football, I want to connect the regulation of football in the post-war period with the wider Keynesian consensus to argue that the administration of football in the middle decades of the twentieth century, and perhaps earlier, echoed the corporatist and universalist ethic of that Keynesian common sense. Crucially, from the 1960s, the decline in attendances at Football League grounds and the increased wage bills after the abolition of the maximum wage rendered this corporatist regulation of football increasingly inadequate to the reality of League football, just as the Keynesian consensus became inadequate to wider economic realities. Thus, the organic development of football echoed the wider historical development of British society and the solutions which would be hit upon to come to terms with these developments in the 1980s would also echo those in wider society. In order to demonstrate the connection between the corporatist administration of the League and the wider Keynesian consensus, and to show that the abolition of the maximum wage constituted the emergence of a set of free-market principles which were at odds with that consensus, it is necessary to examine the conjunctural moment of the abolition of the maximum wage in some depth. The apparently academic debates for and against the maximum wage, which are discussed below, are, consequently, of great prescience to the transformation of English football in the 1990s.

The 1948–1949 season constituted the high-water mark in attendance at Football League games – there were 41.3 million match attendances that season – but from then until 1986, excepting a slight bulge after 1966–1967, when England won the World Cup, attendances fell steadily, so that in the 1985–1986 season attendances were only 16.5 million (Football Trust, 1991, p. 9). This decline in attendance, as might be expected, was not uniform across the League. Rather, Third and Fourth Division clubs bore the brunt of this decline in patronage. From 1960 to 1974, there was a decline of 11 per cent in attendance at First Division games, but in the Second Division the decline was 27 per cent, in the Third Division 42 per cent and in the Fourth Division 49 per cent (Commission on Industrial Relations, 1974, p. 7). Thus by 1974, the average attendance in the First Division (28,290) was seven times that of the Fourth Division (3918). Other statistics tell a similar story. During the 1960s, attendances for the top two divisions rose by 15 per cent and 7.8 per cent respectively, whereas the Third and Fourth Divisions showed declines, respectively, of 11.7 and 24.5 per cent (Chester, 1983, p. 14).

The decline of attendances within the League, and particularly within the Fourth Division, was offset by the increase in admission prices, but this compensatory device was inevitably less effective in the lower divisions, as they had smaller attendances from which to extract raised admission prices (Chester, 1983, p. 14). For example, the Chester report of 1983 analysed the gross receipts from League games of 10 First Division clubs, and found they had risen by a factor of 11 between 1958–1959 and 1981–1982, whereas the receipts of the 10 Fourth Division clubs which the report also analysed had risen by less than three and a half times (Chester, 1983, p. 16). Thus the average receipts from home League matches of the 10 First Division clubs during the 1981–1982 season were 21 times those of the 10 Fourth Division clubs (Chester, 1983, p. 16).

It is, perhaps, worth speculating as to why attendances have fallen at League matches and why, in particular, this has affected the lower divisions disproportionately. The extraordinarily high attendances which were recorded in the 1940s are certainly partly explicable by the relative lack of leisure amenities for the working class during the years of austerity. This austerity began to disappear from the late 1950s during the long post-war boom and the Keynesian post-war settlement. The new leisure pursuits offered by affluence, many of which were centred around the (relative) luxury of new homes, began to make the 'football' terrace unattractive as a Saturday afternoon pursuit. However, what seems crucial in the decline and bias in attendance was the gradual enfranchisement of the population with the car.

The effect of the car and new roads which facilitated easy and rapid travel to football clubs has been noted by Sloane (1980) and Bale (1989). Sloane argues that the opening of a new motorway in Lancashire (the M6) in 1973 changed the proportion of supporters watching matches involving the two Manchester and two Liverpool clubs. The road facilitated the development of support from a wider geographical area for the big teams, while draining support away from local town teams (Sloane, 1980, p. 27). Bale confirms the point (Bale, 1989, p. 93). In 1951, there was a recorded total annual attendance of 7 million in Lancashire, of whom 40 per cent watched the four biggest clubs – Manchester City, Manchester United, Everton and Liverpool. In 1961, there were 6 million attendances, but 50 per cent were now at the big clubs and by 1971, a full 66 per cent of Lancashire's 5.5 annual football attendances were of fans watching these four clubs (Bale, 1989, p. 96).

Alongside the car, the rapid growth in television ownership constituted a profound cultural transformation in the 1960s and this had a significant, though not easily quantifiable, effect on attendances at Football League grounds. Television coverage tended to concentrate on the top clubs (Department of Education and Science, 1968, p. 123) and, thereby, dovetailed with the developing use of the car, because the television provided the opportunity for the big clubs to establish identifying links with individuals across the country, while the car provided those individuals with the means of attending the big city grounds rather than their local club (Chester, 1983, 4–5). The car offered fans the choice of a day at a glamorous event of national importance, shared with tens of thousands, instead of an afternoon at the half-empty ground of a local town team.

The decline of attendances at Football League grounds between 1948 (with the exception of the post-World Cup bulge in the late 1960s) and 1985 is an archetypically organic development. It was the unintended outcome of a long period in which the actions of a host of individuals acting more or less independently, without central control or overarching knowledge, produced a very important development; the increasing but differential economic pressure on English professional football clubs. The abolition of the maximum wage would have a similar effect.

The Maximum Wage

From the establishment of the League in 1888, the contracts between players and clubs were regulated by three Football League rules: the maximum wage (which ruled that no player should be paid more than a wage set by the League), and the retention[1] and transfer systems.[2]

Although the retention and transfer systems were important to the organic political economic development of the League, in that the eventual removal of these rules and the creation of complete freedom of contract by 1978 facilitated an inflation in transfer fees (which favoured the biggest clubs), the abolition of the maximum wage was the decisive rule change. The abolition of the maximum wage had the immediate and continued effect of inflating players' wages, thereby pressurizing the clubs economically but also, and significantly, differentially. The clubs in the lowest divisions with the smallest attendances and revenues suffered worst from the new pressure initiated by the abolition of the maximum wage.

Although restrictive, the rationale behind the League's labour regulations was comprehensible. The rules were designed to create stability in the League. It was difficult for players to move under the retain and transfer system and clubs could, therefore, rely on the fact that they would have a stable team throughout a season, because poaching by other clubs was rendered impossible. Furthermore, the maximum wage minimized the costs of football and, therefore, maintained at least some parity between the big city clubs, which were financially advantaged by the large attendances they could attract, and the small town clubs. The Football League regarded at least some degree of equality as desirable, since it enhanced competition within the League.

It is important to be historically specific about the origins of these rules. The League's rules were originally forged, like the US Constitution, in historical conditions completely different from those in which they were subsequently employed. The League's restrictive rulings to reduce the cost of football and to maximize the equality between clubs were entirely understandable and workable in the context of the last decades of the nineteenth century. In 1888, when the League was inaugurated, there were only 12 professional clubs. These rules, which were originally drawn up to administer 12 clubs of reasonable economic parity, were maintained into the next century, even though the League expanded into two and eventually four divisions.

The maintenance of the League's redistributive rules throughout the twentieth century up until the 1980s, even though, from the 1950s, the biggest city clubs were growing rapidly in financial independence, can be explained, at least partially, by the establishment of a Keynesian national economic framework at the time when the League's rules were beginning to be stretched. Just as the Keynesian consensus prioritized economic and social universality, employing governmental methods of ensuring that universality, the League abided by the corporatist principles of its foundation and attempted to sustain all the clubs in the League, despite huge discrepancies in income, through the redistribution of revenues, the suppression of wages and the restriction of transfers. In other words, just as the Keynesian state stepped into the economy, sustaining full employment through methods of demand management, the Football

League sought to restrain economic activity in the League in order to ensure the continued economic viability of the smaller clubs. Alan Hardaker, the autocratic secretary of the League from 1956 to 1979, revealed his own (and, by extension, the League's) corporatist orientation in the post-war years in his autobiography. Significantly, Hardaker drew a parallel between the proposals for the reformation of the League which were being suggested during his years as secretary and the Beeching report on railways which was, in effect, a precursor to the policy of concentration which has been typical in post-Fordist Britain. Demonstrating his commitment to corporatism and universality, Hardaker wrote: 'At that time [his appointment as Secretary] Dr Beeching was heavily pruning our railway system, the point was made that football needed similar treatment. I disagreed then and I disagree now' (Hardaker, 1977, p. 65). Later in this autobiography, Hardaker described the abolition of the maximum wage and his opposition to it. He believed that the maximum wage should have merely been raised in order to prevent the excessive inflation which would follow the rule's abolition and which would (and did) put many clubs in financial difficulty (Hardaker, 1977, pp. 77, 78). Hardaker concluded his discussion of the abolition of the maximum wage forcefully, noting the deleterious economic effect of the rule's abolition: 'Once there were 3,500 players registered by the ninety-two clubs of the League. Now there are fewer than 2,500. Freedom is a word with two faces' (Hardaker, 1977, p. 89).

For Hardaker, the corporatist and universalist maintenance of the League through the operation of potential restrictive labour regulations was a greater good than player freedom, which would erode the entire structure of the League and, therefore, also the less gifted players' livelihoods. Thereby, Hardaker demonstrated the Keynesian orientation of the post-war Football League. Moreover, during this Keynesian period, the economic divide between the biggest city and smaller town clubs was not invested with the importance which it later came to have. During the middle of the century, from about the 1920s to the 1970s (Taylor, 1984; Fishwick, 1989; Chapter 11), football was not primarily seen as a site of capitalist accumulation but rather as a place for the public provision of leisure. Hardaker, again, demonstrates this attitude with absolute clarity:

> Is professional football a sport or an industry? Is it an enterprise whose only profit to itself is the pleasure it gives to millions or – and I cannot imagine any club directors subscribing to this opinion – is it a business which is fired by dreams of financial gain? (Hardaker, 1977, p. 65)

The striking difference between Hardaker's view of professional football in the post-war period and the understanding of football in the 1990s highlights the corporatist (and Keynesian) ethos which was the central principle in the administration of the game between at least the end of World War II and the 1980s. Since football was not considered to be a business in these decades, the restrictiveness of these rules and their potential conflict with the realities of an economically divided League were not as important as they subsequently became in the 1980s, when football clubs began to see themselves as businesses.

The abolition of the maximum wage rendered this corporatist administration of the League increasingly unworkable, because the abolition introduced an inflationary economic climate into professional football, which considerably strained the finances of clubs. However, these inflationary pressures had differential effects on the League, as the big city clubs were financially better equipped, with their larger attendances, to cope with the new economic climate. The abolition of the maximum wage created the horizon of possibility for the development of the Premier League, because this transformation initiated the economic divide between the big city clubs and the rest of the League. As I shall attempt to show in Chapter 6, that informal divide was gradually formalized throughout the 1980s, until the economic interests and financial independence of the bigger clubs became so great that they could contemplate and effect a financial separation from the League.

Under-the-Table Payments and European Competition

Although the principal effects of the abolition of the maximum wage were organic, the abolition of this rule was itself a conjunctural moment, which can be analysed by means of the theoretical framework laid out in Chapter 2. From the mid-1950s, it became apparent that it was not uncommon practice for the chairmen of professional football clubs to breach the maximum wage regulation informally by making under-the-table payments to their better players to induce them to stay at the club and to perform at their best. The extent of these illegal payments was revealed with particular clarity in 1957. In that year, the Football League charged six Sunderland players with accepting illegal payments which breached the maximum wage. The players were threatened with expulsion from professional football, and in an attempt to prevent this punishment, Jimmy Hill, who had just been voted chairman of the footballers' union, visited clubs across the country in order to obtain as many signatures as possible from other professional footballers, admitting that they, too, had accepted illegal payments (Hill, 1961, pp. 14–15; Harding, 1991, pp. 270–3; Wagg, 1984, pp. 104–5). In the end, Hill collected 250 signatures in just under a week (Hill, 1961:15) and he presented these to the League. The revelation of the widespread abuse of the maximum wage rendered any punishment which the League might mete out to the six Sunderland players unjust, since it was indefensible to prosecute only six individuals when the League had knowledge of more than two hundred others who were guilty of the same crime. The case of the Sunderland Six demonstrated the contradictory (if not hypocritical) position of the chairmen and ultimately undermined their stubborn support of the maximum wage. As Matt Busby, the famous manager of Manchester United from 1945 to 1969, noted, the illegal payments by chairmen to players made a mockery of the wage system in the late 1950s (Douglas, 1973, p. 59).[3]

Under-the-table payments were made not simply to prevent players from going to other clubs in England but, more importantly, to prevent them from being signed up by European clubs. European clubs, and particularly large Italian clubs, looked to the English Football League for potential players, and since these clubs could offer players far greater wages than could English clubs, they were a serious threat to English football clubs from the late 1950s; John Charles was a notable signing at that time. If English clubs were to retain their players, the chairmen (and the Football League authorities overseeing the game) had to counter this serious threat from European clubs (Jimmy Hill, personal interview; March 1994). The recognition of the informal breaching of the maximum wage by the chairmen in the light of the threat posed by the European transfer market gave rise to the conjunctural moment in which the abolition of the maximum wage was possible. Jimmy Hill, the chairman of the Professional Footballers' Association (PFA) between 1957 and 1961, was a central figure in this conjunctural moment and his arguments were fundamental to the abolition of the maximum wage.

Jimmy Hill's Arguments Against the Maximum Wage

The maximum wage was finally abolished as a result of the wide acceptance that this rule was increasingly incompatible with social developments. Hill successfully highlighted the anomalous character of the maximum wage in the context of the increasing affluence of Keynesian society (Wagg, 1984, p. 71; Walvin, 1986, p. 32), making three central claims. First, under the maximum wage, football players had fallen behind average working-class earnings; in other words, they earned less than the bulk of the people who watched them. Second, Hill argued that the maximum wage was illegitimate because footballers should not be regarded as members of the working class but rather as professionals in the entertainment business. Finally, Hill argued for complete freedom of contract for the football player, the significance of which we will see below.

In conducting the players' opposition to the maximum wage, the historical anomaly of the maximum wage was a central tenet in the argument which Hill skilfully publicized in the press. Professional footballers, who were, by and large, drawn from working-class back-grounds, had traditionally earned a little more than other members of that class. Yet this wage was small enough to ensure that players remained as well-known and respected local figures, living in the same neighbourhoods as supporters, and the professional footballers' larger wage-packet was seen as legitimate, in the light of the manifest skill of the footballer and the fact that his employment was extremely uncertain, entirely dependent on form and fitness. By the mid-1950s, the professional players' earnings began to slip below those of the average worker. The average player in the pre-abolition era earned £2 less than the average industrial wage (Harding, 1991, p. 256). The long boom of the post-war period, combined with the Keynesian commonsense that workers had to be encouraged to consume, had brought about a rise in workers' wages, which had, in turn, dramatically increased the affluence of the working class from the late 1950s. This new affluence of the workers left professional footballers underpaid.

Hill argued that professional footballers had effectively subsidized the game for the working class for many years by facilitating the persistence of low admission prices through their acceptance of the maximum wage (Hill, 1961, p. 129). However, since the average industrial wage was £14 in the late 1950s, whereas it had been only £3 before World War II, Hill argued that admission prices should be increased to three shillings to support an increase in players' wages; no one could complain about paying three shillings a fortnight when they earned £14 a week,[4] reasoned Hill:

> In all fairness, just think a moment and work out how much your football costs you on a Saturday afternoon. I know how much you might pay on London Transport or local Corporation transport going to the ground. If you call in at the local on the way to the match and you've got two or three pals with you, it's going to cost you a few shillings. (Hill, 1961, p. 129)

Hill concludes:

> if you are honest you will admit that the three shillings which you pay to stand on the terracing represents only a small part of the amount of money you spend in connection with attending a football match. (Hill, 1961, p. 130)

The new affluence of the working class rendered the maximum wage anomalous in Hill's eyes, because fans could now afford to pay more and, indeed, these individuals were quite willing to pay more for other indulgences such as beer, travel and food. In other words, Hill's argument for the abolition of the maximum wage was that football had become a commodity like any other. Since the working class had become wealthy enough to afford other luxury commodities, the price of football should be brought into line with other prices.

However, Hill did not merely want better salaries which would bring footballers back into line with the affluence of the new working class. On the contrary, Hill envisaged a new position for the footballer in English culture which was related to the type of commodity which he believed football had become in post-war Britain. Hill insisted that the footballer was an entertainer and football was part of the entertainment business, whose market equals were television, cinema and theatre. As entertainers, producing commodities whose price accorded with the rest of the entertainment industry, Hill suggested that footballers should not only be far better paid than they were under the maximum wage, but that they should be accorded the respect which was due to other entertainers as professionals. Hill reveals this demand for the improvement in the status of players at various points in his account of the dispute over the maximum wage:

> Occasionally, however, I am left with a nasty taste in my mouth, eating in a train or an hotel and it's not from the food. A waiter, who obviously doesn't think much of the social status of a professional footballer, shows it in the service that he gives. (Hill, 1961, p. 136)

Hill's anger at these social slights is significant because it demonstrates his belief that footballers should not be seen as members of the working class but as professional entertainers. In particular, Hill made strategic use of the fact that, by the late 1950s, many of the players were employed by companies to advertise their goods. In his book, there was a double page of photographs which showed Johnny Haynes advertising Brylcreem, Mel Charles advertising Remington, Tommy Banks advertising Gillette and Bobby Charlton promoting the rather more prosaic Flour Advisory Bureau. The point for Hill was that these players, although constrained by the maximum wage within the confines of their own profession, were bound by entirely different contracts away from the sport. While the market decided their (substantial) worth when it came to advertising, a very restrictive set of laws which were drawn up in 1888 still determined their employment contracts within football.

Hill's strategic use of the employment of players in advertising (regulated by labour contracts which clashed fundamentally with the maximum wage) led directly to the final but very significant strand in Hill's argument. As we have noted, the advertising contracts which the players received from various companies were unregulated and determined simply by free-market considerations; companies offered players contracts by reference to the amount which they thought they were worth and to the amount which would equal or better offers from other companies. Significantly, Hill drew heavily on this need for the players' contracts to be decided by a free market to determine their labour contracts in football. Hill argued that the players were pursuing two basic freedoms (Hill, 1961, p. 36), although, as he noted in his book, this notion of two basic freedoms was, in fact, hit upon rather coincidentally when he had to justify his threat of a strike to journalists (Hill, 1961, p. 26). Nevertheless, although the term originated as a rhetorical trope, serving to legitimate the player's claims so they were not seen merely as money-grabbing, the term had a deep significance, demanding that the market should decide players' wages and that the players, like professional entertainers rather than working men, should be free to negotiate the most favourable contracts possible.[5]

Hill's three arguments for the abolition of the maximum wage were accepted. Faced with the threat of a strike organized by Hill for 21 January 1961 and overwhelmingly hostile public opinion, the chairmen finally agreed to the PFA's demands and rescinded the maximum wage on 19 January 1961. This abolition was formally entered into the Football League handbook at the AGM on 3 June 1961.The abolition of the maximum wage set the Football League on an organic trajectory of development which would culminate in the conjunctural crisis of the mid-1980s, when the increases in wages would create an informal division in the League between the top city clubs and the rest, since it was only the bigger clubs which could cope adequately with this inflation in labour costs. For instance, Sir Norman Chester's *Report of the Committee of Enquiry into Structure and Finance* (Chester, 1983) recorded that whereas the wage bills of the First Division clubs amounted to 56.4 per cent of those top clubs' gate receipts, the wage bills of the Third and Fourth Division clubs exceeded their gate receipts. This economic division between the solvent and insolvent would necessitate the reformation of the League.

The maximum wage was abolished because Hill successfully demonstrated that this rule was in contradiction with organic and informal developments; it was breached by chairmen in the light of the increasingly competitive and Europeanized player market, and was anomalous in the affluence of Keynesian Britain. Thus, the abolition of the maximum wage was justified because this regulation was out of kilter both with the realities of football itself and with the emergent social conditions.

The abolition of the maximum wage demonstrates a further very interesting sociological feature. One of the principal rhetorical tropes Hill employed to promote the players' position to the fullest was to demand 'freedom of contract' for players; Hill called this freedom of contract and freedom to negotiate wages the 'two basic freedoms'. As noted above, this demand for 'freedom of contract' was very much motivated out of a desire not to be seen as merely money-grabbing. However, the appeal to freedom and the free market in order to set wages was actually quite radical and, indeed, antithetical to the Keynesianism which informed British social life at that time. As noted in Chapter 3, Keynesianism emerged in the 1930s as a response to the collapse of the *laissez-faire* capitalist world system. Keynes himself insisted that the free market in and of itself was not sufficient to guarantee the wealth of nations. Yet Hill successfully employed a free-market argument in order to achieve very important reforms of labour contracts in football. In other words, Hill's arguments, which were widely accepted by the public, actually contravened the central Keynesian and corporatist premises on which the League was based in the late 1950s and which Hardaker defended.

The abolition of a corporatist labour regulation and its replacement with a free-market rule meant that the everyday (organic) payment of players was informed by a principle which was in opposition to the Keynesian framework of the League. The introduction of this idea was the seed which set political economic developments on a course whereby they would outgrow the social form in which they had their origin. Hill's argument for a free market in wages constitutes a moment when new conditions were implemented. This set the Football League on a line of organic transformation which would eventually necessitate the complete replacement of the League's political economic structure. Yet, as Gramsci maintained, this transformation was not primarily material, although it certainly has political economic effects, but rather, in the first instance, ideological and cultural. Within the formally recognized corporatist framework of principles, Hill introduced a set of values which were directly contrary to those principles and whose implementation in everyday action put the League's political economic condition in contradiction with its overarching corporatist framing principles. The framing ideas which are proposed and accepted in conjunctural moments have overwhelming importance in determining the trajectory of organic change. The idea of the free market for wages contravened the original framing principles of the League, and its employment in practice over the two decades between 1960 and 1980 was to effectively undermine the entire corporate structure of the League.

Notes

1   The retention system was intrinsically bound up with the transfer system. However, although the two systems were intimately related in practice, they were, at the same time, formally separate. The retention system ruled that all clubs had to send the registrations (contracts) of every player to the Football League by the closing day of the season (Football League, 1959, p. 103). At the same time, the clubs submitted a list of players who were available for transfer to the League. The League sent this list out to all the clubs in the League, who would apply to the League for further details if they were interested in procuring the registration of any player on the transfer list

(Football League, 1959, pp. 103–4). The difficulty with the retention system arose when a player wanted to leave a club but that club refused to put the player on the transfer list at the end of the season. Under the League's retention rule, the club was able to keep the player on and register him, against his will. Furthermore, even if a player was put on the transfer list, he had no say in the destination of his transfer. The club had the final say in whether a player was retained or transferred and, if transferred, to which club he should go. The retention system was reformed between 1963 (with the famous Eastham *v.* Newcastle United case) and 1974. I do not discuss its reformation here, as it is the least economically important of the three rules and its eventual abolition became part of the same developments which I will describe at length here anyway (see King, 1995c).

2   The transfer system ruled that if a club wanted to register a player from another club, then the former club would have to pay a compensation fee for the removal of that individual's services from the club. The idea behind this rule was to protect smaller clubs from having their best players poached by bigger clubs. For reasons of space, the final reformation of the transfer and retention systems are not discussed in the text (see King, 1995c). These systems were reformed in 1978, when 'freedom of contract' was introduced. So far as this study is concerned, the important point about freedom of contract and the reformation of the retention and transfer systems was that the chairmen adopted a free-market system for the regulation of the transfer fee (Inglis, 1988, pp. 282, 279; Harding, 1991, p. 315). This created an inflationary market which had the same organic political economic effect as the abolition of the maximum wage: the differential increase in economic pressure across the League which favoured the biggest clubs (see Department of Education and Science, 1968, p. 79; Rippon, 1982, p. 102; Dougan, 1981, pp. 25–6).

3   See also Eamonn Dunphy's *A Strange Kind of Glory: Matt Busby and Manchester United* (Dunphy, 1994),where he describes how it was impossible for a manager, of even Matt Busby's standing, to avoid being drawn into under-the-table payments.

4   There is a slight discrepancy here between Harding and Hill's figures. Harding suggests that the average wage was £10, whereas Hill suggests it was £14. The precise figures are not so important as the fact that professional footballers' pay had dropped behind the working-class average.

5   Hill found widespread support at important sites in British society. For instance, Mr Goodhart, Conservative MP for Beckenham, argued that apprentices in the Middle Ages would have rejected professional footballers' contractual conditions 'with a snort of contempt' (*The Times*, 22 November 1960). *The Times* was equally dismissive, although its reasonings were more complex (*The Times* 6 February 1960, 6 December 1960).

5

Sponsorship

Debates about Sponsorship

By the late 1970s, as a result of the political economic changes which I discussed in the last chapter, professional football could no longer support itself solely through its traditional means of gate revenue. In response to this economic pressure and the need to find new sources of revenue, Derek Dougan, the Kettering Town manager and the former PFA chairman, took the important historical step of introducing shirt advertisements in 1977. He justified his decision to introduce sponsorship in a book he subsequently wrote:

> I knew how sports in other countries had benefited from sponsorship schemes, while deep-seated Puritanism and suspicion had prevented similar schemes being embraced in Britain. Die-hards were still insisting that commerce and sport should not mix, that if sport became dependent on commercial involvements it would lose its independence. My own view was that if it remained aloof and tried to go it 'alone', it would lose its lifeblood. (Dougan, 1981, p. 47)

Dougan continued: 'It seemed to be good sense to attract sponsors, thereby guaranteeing funds when the turnstiles cannot click enough to wipe out overdrafts and debts' (Dougan, 1981, p. 47). Significantly, Dougan argued that the FA's stance on shirt advertisements was anachronistic (similar to Hill's objections to the maximum wage). For Dougan, then, the game's administrators were out of touch with contemporary economic conditions within football and their ideas were irrationally rooted in the past. Furthermore, the English League was out of line with the rest of European sport in not having sponsorship. This appeal to Europe was significant because, as discussed in Chapter 4, the English League clubs were being brought into ever closer competition and contact with the European clubs with the internationalization of the transfer market. If English clubs were not to fall behind, then, in large part, European economic practices had to be adopted. For Dougan, football required sponsorship to sustain itself in the post-abolition period and in the light of increasing European competition. However, behind this claim lay a more radical assumption that football needed to transform itself into a business. Dougan's proposal of sponsorship actually implied a quite radical transformation of the consumption of football, away from its original position as a site of solidarity between the local bourgeoisie and working class.

Although Kettering Town was historically the first club to have shirt sponsorship, the real force for the move to sponsorship came from the chairmen of the big city clubs of the League. John (later Sir John) Smith, the chairman of Liverpool in the 1980s, was particularly vocal in his promotion of sponsorship. After Liverpool had signed a sponsorship contract with Hitachi, against League rules, he commented: 'We felt somebody had to show initiative over this. Football is hard-up as an industry. From an income of £2,400,000 last season we showed a meagre profit of only £17,000' (*The Times*, 25 July 1979). The representatives of these clubs were in an exceptionally privileged position in this debate over sponsorship, because not only were they prominent figures whose arguments were likely to gain publicity and receive attention, but they could back their arguments up with economic influence. The League was heavily dependent on these clubs for its revenue, since they were the central source for funds which were redistributed across the League and especially of television revenue.

The FA and League opposed shirt sponsorship, insisting that the gate was the appropriate and adequate form of revenue for professional football. Those who opposed the introduction of sponsorship viewed the game as a traditional working-class leisure activity which should be witnessed from the terraces. Consequently, the gate revenue was seen as the most important and, indeed, only legitimate, form of revenue, which had to be protected from the threat of new forms of consumption and from television in particular. Rather than look to new means of raising revenue, these individuals argued for ultimately reactionary defences which would protect the gate as the traditional and 'authentic' source of revenue. Furthermore, the administrators were well aware of the deleterious effect which the introduction of new forms of revenue would have on the smaller clubs and on the viability of the League. These administrators effectively opposed sponsorship in a more or less vain attempt to protect the corporate body of the League.

In the course of the debate with Dougan over Kettering Town's shirt sponsorship, the FA effectively put itself in a contradictory position because it allowed the England tracksuit to have its manufacturer's name, 'Admiral', in clear view but opposed clubs having shirt advertisements. Ted Croker, the FA's secretary, argued that the presence of Admiral's logo on the England tracksuit and Kettering Town's shirt advertisement were as different as chalk and cheese. He explained that it was like Borg using a racket with the manufacturer's name on but not being able to wear SAS on his shirt (*The Times*, 10 September 1976). Dougan was not slow to pick up on the weakness of this distinction. However, the apparently indefensible pedantry of Croker's distinction between these two kinds of shirt sponsorship belied an understandable and logical argument against sponsorship. Croker was really concerned that if football clubs became too dependent on sponsorship this would have a profound effect on the League, for companies would only be interested in televised matches and clubs which could deliver that coverage (*The Times*, 10 September 1976). Sponsoring companies' demand for television coverage had two serious drawbacks. Those opposed to sponsorship argued that its demand for television coverage would threaten football's gate money, since fans would be less inclined to attend games (in the cold and wet) if they could watch them on television. Since the gate was by far the most important source of revenue for football in the late 1970s and early 1980s, sponsorship threatened to reduce professional football's lifeblood without sufficiently replacing that form of income. Of course, it was the smallest clubs which would suffer this loss of revenue the greatest, as noted in Chapter 4. Furthermore, as Croker realized, since the television favoured the big city clubs, they would be able to negotiate the best sponsorship deals. Croker regarded this concentration on the biggest clubs and the financial benefits which would come from it as damaging to the corporatist framework of the League.

In effect, administrators like Croker were arguing from within a similar framework to that of Hardaker, whose position was noted in Chapter 4. They sought to protect the corporatist organization of football which had developed in the post-war period, and the apparently pedantic appeals which these administrators made really referred to their understanding of what developments were appropriate to the main-tenance of the corporatist League. Thus when Harold Thompson, the FA's chairman, argued that, 'nothing can be worn that may be regarded as distasteful or morally unethical' (*The Times*, 4 June 1977), he was, in fact, making more coherent claims than this apparently anachronistic statement seemed to propose. These administrators rightly recognized that shirt sponsorship was, in the end, another nail in the coffin of corporatist football.

Despite the opposition of the Football League and FA to sponsorship, the demands of the big clubs finally had to be met. In 1983, a group of big city clubs threatened to sign an independent television contract away from the Football League, if the League did not approve shirt advertisements. Since the League's television revenue was almost solely based on the attraction of these clubs, the League had to capitulate, allowing 32-square-inch advertisements on team shirts (*The Times*, 6 July 1983).

The success of the big city clubs in forcing the introduction of sponsorship was significant, because that success depended on the political economic position which these clubs had attained as a result of the organic developments initiated by the abolition of the maximum wage and the decline of attendance. The introduction of sponsorship in this conjunctural moment consequently fed back into those organic developments which had given rise to the conjunctural moment in the first place. The introduction of sponsorship furthered the financial independence of the top clubs at the expense of the lower leagues.

The Political Economic Effects of Sponsorship

Sponsorship helped the financial situation of the big city clubs in relation to the smaller clubs of the League, since the bigger clubs have been able to capture sponsorship contracts far in excess of those obtained by clubs from the lower divisions. For instance, Liverpool and Everton's sponsorship deals were worth some £50,000 in the early 1980s (*The Times* 15 March 1980). By 1993, Liverpool's sponsorship as a whole, including royalties and ground advertising, was worth some £3.2 million (Liverpool Football Club and Athletics Grounds plc, 1993, p. 11). The club's shirt sponsorship alone was worth £200,000. In 1988, the First Division clubs made £12.8 million on shirt advertisements, in deals which ranged between £90,000 and £1.5 million, while the Second Division clubs made £2.8 million, the Third Division clubs £1.6 million and the Fourth Division clubs £900,000 (*The Times*, 8 November 1988).

We have noted the role of television in highlighting the big city clubs in public consciousness and, with the aid of the car, focusing interest on and support for these clubs. Television played a second and equally crucial role in the political economic division of the League. Since the television companies concentrated on the big clubs,[1] the latter offered their sponsors more exposure and could consequently demand more money. The favourable coverage which television gave to the big clubs, especially during the 1980s, made those clubs more valuable to their sponsors.[2] Television coverage, therefore, added momentum to the big clubs' drift away from the lower divisions, which sponsorship, in itself, assisted.

Furthermore, the fact that Kettering Town under Dougan initiated the sponsorship debate was an anomaly as, by and large, sponsorship trickled down the League. The biggest clubs were able to get sponsors far more quickly than the smaller town clubs and were the beneficiaries of much larger contracts. The introduction of sponsorship into the League, then, has meant that the smaller clubs have effectively had to run only to fall ever further behind the big clubs. Echoing Hill's arguments for the abolition of the maximum wage, Dougan demanded that clubs should be free to make money in whatever way they thought fit. Yet, like Hill's demand for freedom of contract, Dougan's appeal to freedom ultimately improved the position of the big clubs in relation to the small, spelling the end of the corporatist settlement on which the League was based.

These free-market principles, on which the demands for sponsorship were based, reflected the wider historical transformation of British society at this time, which increasingly looked to the free market to resolve the crisis of the corporatist post-war settlement. The application of those free-market solutions to the wider economy and society from the late 1970s had resulted in the liquidation of unviable industries and the laying off of the workforce employed in them. Similarly, the application of the free market to football in the form of sponsorship (as well as the abolition of the maximum wage) resulted in the increasing impoverishment of the smaller clubs and the redundancies of professional players employed at these clubs.

By appealing to a set of ideas which came from beyond and effectively opposed the corporate meanings which informed the Football League's structure, Dougan effectively (although unknowingly) contributed to a line of organic development which would entirely undermine the League's structure. By demanding the right to be free to make as much money as possible, Dougan was also providing the bigger clubs with the opportunity to point up the illegitimacy of the redistribution of funds. If these clubs had made profits in an open free market, then they had no duty to surrender that revenue to clubs which were equally free to compete in that market. The introduction of new framing principles in conjunctural moments such as the sponsorship debate or the abolition of the maximum wage were themselves responses to organic transformations but, having been accepted as a central framing principle, the notion of the free market precipitated the Football League along a historical trajectory which took it yet further from its corporate origins.

The development of sponsorship exacerbated a process which was already under way from the 1960s in which the big city clubs were becoming increasingly differentiated from the rest of the League. This economic division made the creation of the Premier League both possible and logical, because the economic division separated the interests of the top clubs from the rest, so that a breakaway might be beneficial to them. Moreover, the growing economic independence of the big clubs, and the perception that the lower divisions were a mere impediment in the new financial climate, provided the big clubs with a growing political influence in Football League meetings and a reason for exploiting that influence. In the arguments for freedom on which the introduction of sponsorship was predicated, the seeds of a new social order were inexorably sown in the framework of the old, and everyday, organic transactions which were informed by these new ideas brought social reality into ever greater conflict with the principles which supposedly underpinned that reality.

Notes

1 John Bromley, ITV's head of sport in the 1980s, confirmed the widely held view that the television companies did indeed favour the big clubs as a matter of policy, since the latter delivered better audiences (personal interview, 23 June 1994).

2 The connection between television coverage and the profitability of sponsorship deals is highlighted by the attempts of Liverpool's sponsor, Carlsberg, to reduce the value of their sponsorship as a result of the BSkyB deal with the Premier League in 1992, which reduced Liverpool's coverage on television (*Marketing* 11 February 1993).

6

The Big Five

In the Chapters 3 and 4, the transformation of the political economy of football over the last three decades has been described, and it was proposed throughout that these political economic changes aided the financial situation of the big city clubs, while increasingly jeopardizing the financial viability of those clubs in the lower divisions. This long-term and organic division of the League was recognized before the 1980s. The Commission on Industrial Relations report of 1974 argued that a 'superleague' had already come into *de facto* existence in the post-war period. In the 28 seasons from 1946–1947 to 1973–1974, a handful of clubs dominated the championship; Manchester United and Liverpool had won the championship four times each, Arsenal and Wolverhampton Wanderers three times each and four other clubs twice each (Commission on Industrial Relations, 1974, p. 8). There was an informal distinction between the top (and biggest) clubs and the rest of the League. This informal distinction was formally recognized in the 1980s when the top clubs demanded what they regarded as an acceptable share of the television revenue.

This chapter examines the conjunctural moment when organic developments of the *longue durée* (in this case the emergence of the financial distinctiveness of the biggest city clubs) stimulated arguments which demanded the transformation of political economic relations. The organic developments not only opened up the opportunity for self-conscious re-negotiation of relations, but privileged certain clubs in those arguments. In the case of the political economic debates of the 1980s within the Football League, the long-established bias towards the biggest clubs favoured their position in the debates about the transformation of the game and the redistribution of revenue.

The biggest clubs, which emerged as a distinct interest group in the 1980s, came to be known as the 'Big Five' and consisted of Arsenal, Everton, Liverpool, Manchester United and Tottenham Hotspur. It is important to avoid the reification which the slightly grandiloquent term, the 'Big Five', suggests. The five clubs in question commanded the best attendance figures in the First Division by some few thousands. For example, of the five clubs, Tottenham Hotspur had the lowest average attendance during the 1980s with 26,157, but this figure was over five thousand more than that of the Big Five's nearest rival, Aston Villa. The Big Five were also established on the grounds of their success; Aston Villa was the only non-Big Five club to win a Championship between 1980–1981 and 1990–1991. The two cup competitions, the League Cup and FA Cup, did offer non-Big Five clubs the chance to break the oligopoly of the Big Five but, even then, the Big Five clubs featured heavily in the honours lists. Of the 10 FA Cup finals between 1981 and 1990, Big Five clubs won seven of them and featured in every single one, and five League Cup finals were won by Big Five clubs. The term the 'Big Five' is historically specific to the 1980s, when the success of these clubs on the pitch or in terms of popularity endowed them with pre-eminence. However, the unity of the Big Five lay in nothing more than this temporary commonality of political economic status and interest, and it should be noted that the concept of the 'Big Five' is wholly irrelevant to the comprehension of the internal politics of the Premier League in the 1990s, even though it is occasionally and erroneously employed, with different clubs (such as Blackburn Rovers or Newcastle United) conveniently filling the places of the likes of Tottenham Hotspur or Everton.

Yet the distinctiveness of the Big Five did not lie only in their financial and footballing pre-eminence. It was also established by both the print and television media. The newspapers themselves coined the term the 'Big Five', and, in that sense, established them in public consciousness as separate from the rest of the League.[1] The informal division of interests that the organic political economic transformations created within the Football League was recognized by the naming of this division by the press, and was extended by television's response to this division of the League. Throughout the 1980s, both the BBC and ITV focused very heavily on the five clubs, widening the divide between these clubs and the rest. Financially, the Big Five were best rewarded, but they also came to demand more and more of the television revenue as they delivered the best audiences. The unerring presence of the Big Five on television throughout the 1980s was in that sense something of a self-fulfilling prophecy. These clubs were favoured by the television companies *because* they delivered the best audiences but, because of their regular coverage, they came to be seen as the most important clubs and therefore commanded the most national attention.

Alongside, and substantially as a reaction to the Big Five, a second interest group of Football League clubs arose in the 1980s. This group consisted principally of those clubs in the First and Second Divisions which were not part of the Big Five coalition but which could command substantial attendances and would win the occasional trophy. For several reasons, this coalition was much more nebulous than the Big Five. Since it was a bigger group, its interests were never as unified as those of the Big Five's. Furthermore, certain clubs within this group dropped out of the

Second Division and into the Third Division. Alternatively, the more successful of these clubs sporadically aligned themselves with the Big Five and, finally, this group did not have the benefit of being named and, thereby, of establishing an identity which would have provided it with a sense of distinction and unity. The clubs' alliance as an interest group remained patchy and only partly conscious. In the 1990s, however, this group has been named (partly because these clubs established a distinctive set of interests in their negotiations with the Big Five over the development of the Premier League in 1991–1992), and it is convenient to use this name here, with the important proviso that the use of this name is not intended to reify its members' interests and identity as a group. The name, introduced by Fynn and Guest, is the 'Bates–Noades axis' (Fynn and Guest, 1994, pp. 25, 53)[2] and I shall use it to describe this amorphous group of big clubs in the 1980s and up until the establishment of the Premier League.

By reference to these two loose coalitions of clubs – the Big Five and the Bates–Noades axis – this chapter will attempt to trace the sometimes convoluted path which led to the development of the Premier League. The complexity of this path to the Premiership resulted from the fact that changes to the League's rules and structures had to be voted for by a democratic majority of three-quarters of the League's full and associate members. Each of the clubs in the top two divisions had the status of full members of the League and therefore had a single vote, while those clubs from the lower leagues, who were only associate members, were represented by four votes for both divisions. Any decision which came before the League was voted upon and implemented if the reform in question attained three-quarters of the 50 possible votes at a meeting of the League's members.

The democratic principles of the League informed the course of developments during the 1980s because the votes of the members were decided by the members referring to their short-term financial self-interest[3] and by the fact that, although the Big Five were in the dominant political economic position, the Bates–Noades axis actually held the balance of votes. The Premier League, although desirable for the Big Five clubs, could not be brought into existence by the fiat of these clubs. Rather, the potential voting block of the Bates–Noades axis had to be obviated by appealing to the self-interest of those clubs. The history of the Football League in the 1980s and the development of the Premier League is, at one level at least, a history of political economic compromises between the Big Five and the Bates–Noades axis.

The principal reforms with which this chapter will be concerned are the debates and votes over television deals in the 1980s. In particular, I will focus on the television deals of 1986 and 1988, when the Big Five were able to wring substantial concessions out of the League and create the conditions for a breakaway. The examination of these debates and reforms will culminate in a discussion in the final section of the chapter on the creation of the Premier League by the votes of the old First Division. The creation of the Premier League was critical to the new consumption of the game because its increased revenue financed the renovation of grounds.

The Rejection of the 1983 Chester Report

In the early 1980s, the FA and the Football League commissioned Sir Norman Chester, who had previously presided over the Department of Education and Science's report into football in 1968, to produce a second report, which would recommend reforms in the League's structure and finances to improve the League's economic viability in the face of the economic conditions discussed above. Chester's second report echoed much of what had already been recommended not only in his first report but in four other policy documents; Hardaker's *Pattern for Football* (Hardaker, 1963), Political and Economic Planning's 'English professional football' (Political and Economic Planning, 1966), the Commission on Industrial Relations' report (Commission on Industrial Relations, 1974) and the Football League Management Committee's own report (Football League, 1981).

Chester's second report situated its recommendations, like the first, within the context of political economic developments since the 1960s. Consequently, the report argued that the emergence of a distinctive group of clubs at the top of the League was both well established (Chester, 1983, p. 28) and had to inform any recommendation of policy, although Chester deprecated the use of the term 'superleague'. Chester's report supported the interests of the big clubs, since they were best able to cope and thrive in the difficult political economic environment of the 1980s. Chester demonstrated the logic of strengthening the already strong when the report discussed the reallocation of pools money:

> Thus the purpose of the pools payments has never been to make the presently poor clubs financially viable. They have helped to keep such clubs in existence irrespective of the reason for their penury. Is this a good enough reason for directing money from other clubs? (Chester, 1983, p. 38)

In the context of these broader organic economic developments and the poor financial management of the lower-division teams – which Chester implies in the reference to the reason for these clubs' penury – the report suggested that it would be better to allocate funds to those clubs which are best able to use them and who would therefore further the interests of English football generally. Consequently, Chester recommended a reduction in the size of the First Division from 22 to 20 clubs (Chester,

1983, p. 29), a return to regionalized lower leagues[4] and an end to the sharing of home gates with visiting clubs. This last recommendation was aimed at redressing one of the Big Five's major grievances, which is explicable if we consider a hypothetical example which demonstrates the amount of revenue which the biggest clubs lost through the redistribution of the home gate. If Manchester United were to play Coventry City at Highfield Road 21 times, Manchester United would receive £60,000, but if Coventry City played Manchester United at Old Trafford the same number of times, Coventry City would receive £250,000 (*The Times*, 10 February 1983). In other words, as this theoretical example reveals, the League's redistributive rules effectively meant that the bigger clubs were subsidising the rest of their division through the redistribution of gate revenue. The Chester report was against this cross-subsidy as it weakened the strongest clubs while supporting those clubs which were weak, principally because they were poorly managed.

Yet, despite the financial superiority of the Big Five and the League's dependence on these clubs as a major source of revenue, the balance of any vote lay with the Bates–Noades axis. Consulting their immediate self-interest, they opposed Chester's recommendations. In response to the Bates–Noades axis' opposition to Chester's recommendations, the Big Five similarly consulted their own self-interest and, determined to implement what they saw to be highly beneficial recommendations for them, they threatened a breakaway from the League (*The Times*, 27 April 1983).[5] This threat carried some weight because, even by 1983, it was becoming apparent that the Big Five's ability to command television audiences rendered the League significantly dependent on them. The mutual dependence of the Big Five on the Bates–Noades axis for votes and of the Bates–Noades axis on the Big Five for television revenue resulted in the abolition of the redistribution of the home gate revenue, although all of the Chester report's other recommendations were rejected. The Bates–Noades axis was forced to concede the ending of home gate redistribution for the greater good of preventing a breakaway (*The Times* 27 April 1983) and thus the Bates–Noades axis grudgingly contributed to the growing financial independence of the Big Five.

Television Deals

The spiralling financial independence of the Big Five informed debates over the television deals and the distribution of television revenue between clubs in the 1980s. During that period, there were four television deals, which ran from 1983 to 1985, from January 1986 to the end of the season, from 1986 to 1988 and then from 1988 to 1992. I will concentrate on the two final deals, made in 1986 and 1988, as it was in the debates over these deals that the Big Five were able to bring their threat of breakaway to bear most effectively. Crucially, the debates originated in the division of interests between the Big Five and the Bates–Noades axis, and the television deals which were eventually struck were invariably compromises between these two interest groups, but ones which favoured the organically given superiority of the Big Five.

1986: Heathrow and the 10-Point Plan

In May 1985, there was a fire at Bradford's Valley Parade ground, a serious disturbance at Birmingham City's ground and a riot at Heysel; in these disasters over ninety people were killed. These disasters further worsened the quite desperate financial position in which many clubs already found themselves, and the big clubs were particularly squeezed, since, due to a series of disputes between the Football League and the BBC and ITV, no agreement was reached before the beginning of the 1985–1986 season on the coverage of football. Some of the failure to agree terms was due to the fact that the television companies did not want to cover football in the same year as the disasters, since they did not want to be associated with a sport whose public image was so thoroughly tarnished. The immediate origins of the Heathrow meeting and the 10-point plan lay in this dispute between the television companies and the League in Autumn 1985, when there was no coverage of football on television whatsoever. This put the Big Five under particular stress, as their sponsorship deals were heavily reliant on their regular television appearances. The Big Five's impatience was reflected in some of the comments of the chairmen of those clubs:

> The big clubs are very, very impatient for many reasons. We are suffering financial hardship because there is no television agreement, we are not in Europe, gates are declining and altogether the state of our national game is in disarray. (John Smith, chairman of Liverpool FC, quoted in *The Times*, 16 October 1985)

> We cannot continue forever and a day to divide our money among 92 clubs. Under the new format we must concentrate on the senior clubs. The third and fourth divisions will be concerned about the situation. We are starting on a long road of change and there will be financial problems for some clubs. (Philip Carter, chairman of Everton, quoted in *The Times*, 12 November 1985)

Pressed by these economic concerns, the Big Five pushed for reformation of the structure and distribution of revenue within the League.

Consequently, a committee of 10 leading figures in football was appointed and, in December 1985, a 10-point plan was submitted to the clubs for their consideration. The major points of the 10-point plan were that the First Division should be reduced to 20 clubs by 1988, there should be play-offs in the lower divisions for the final promotion place, the First Division should receive 50 per cent of the rewards to be gained from television and sponsorship, the Second Division 25 per cent and the lower divisions 25 per cent between them, the League's levy of 4 per cent on the gate for redistribution across the League should be reduced to 3 per cent, and there should be reform of the voting system[6] (*The Times*, 29 April 1986).

The proposals which this committee suggested were backed by the serious threat of a breakaway by the top clubs if they were not accepted (*The Times*, 19 December 1985):

> If we [the Big Five] do not get the support then the First Division clubs will have to look at their future again. We hate bringing out the idea of a Super League or a breakaway. But if things stay the same there is no way the major clubs will allow themselves to be dragged down into obscurity. (Philip Carter, quoted in *The Times*, 18 February 1986)

Following Carter's threat, the clubs of the First Division met at Villa Park in March to agree that unless the 10-point plan was approved at the AGM in April they would break away: 'Make no mistake, the big bang will happen unless the rest of the league give us their backing' (Martin Edwards, chairman of Manchester United, quoted in *The Times*, 25 March 1986). Martin Edwards' use of the term 'the big bang' was significant, because it revealed that the deregulation which the Big Five envisaged (and which would favour the largest and most concentrated clubs) consciously replicated and drew legitimacy from the Thatcherite reform of the City in 1986, which similarly assisted the biggest capitalist institutions. However, in order to ratify the 10-point plan (and to effect a deregulative explosion), the Big Five had to overcome the potential blocking votes of the Bates–Noades axis. That blocking vote could be obviated if the Big Five offered incentives to enough other clubs in the top division so that the latter would cast their votes with the Big Five. The Big Five employed the convenient distinction of the First Division as a method of spiking the blocking vote of the Bates–Noades axis, and the whole of the First Division was offered a share of the benefits which the Big Five intended to earn for themselves. The use of the First Division as a means of obviating the voting structure of the League was, as we will see below, a strategy which was employed again in the eventual creation of the Premier League in 1991. At the Heathrow AGM in April 1986, the 10-point plan was ratified by a vote of the full and associate members of the League. The concessions which the Big Five forced from the League at the Heathrow meeting in April 1986 temporarily satisfied their financial needs, but when the television deal was up for re-negotiation in 1988, the League again returned to a state of undeclared war between its two principal factions as each attempted to gain the greatest proportion of the television revenue on offer.

The 1988 Television Deal

The BBC and ITV had operated an uneasy cartel since the late 1960s, when they had shared the coverage of League football. The BBC had broadcast *Match of the Day* on Saturday nights, while ITV had screened *The Big Match* for the Sunday afternoon audience. That cartel eventually broke down in 1988, as a result of the growing competitiveness in television for ratings. In the first 20 years of television coverage of the game, recorded highlights had been able to deliver very good audiences, but by the early 1980s the interest in recorded football was dwindling. From 1983, the BBC and ITV had insisted on incorporating some live television in their contracts with football. This desire for live football was substantially responsible for ITV's breach of its cartel with the BBC. Within the cartel, ITV had to share the coverage of live football with the BBC but, since live football delivered the audiences, this restriction became more and more intolerable. ITV wanted a greater share of live football in order to increase its audiences and in order to attract advertising sponsorship. It should be noted that, although clubs have accepted the idea of live coverage in the 1990s, there was still concern in the 1980s about the effects of live coverage on attendance. In the 1980s, the fees which clubs received from television for live coverage were not necessarily large enough to offset the drop in attendances at the ground which a live broadcast might cause. These concerns became irrelevant in the 1990s, with the huge Sky contract.

In addition to the demand for live football, the development of satellite networks threatened the viability of the cartel as a strategy for the BBC and ITV. In 1988, the newly established British Satellite Broadcasting (BSB) set out to revolutionize football coverage by taking over the BBC and ITV's exclusive rights to League football (*The Times*, 14 May 1988). The threat which BSB posed rendered the cartel between ITV and the BBC obsolete. ITV was determined to broadcast live football and, in the light of the competition from BSB, ITV decided to negotiate for a contract with the Football League independently. ITV did not join the BBC in the initial rounds of negotiations, as it had done when the cartel had been in operation, but talked directly to the Big Five.

In this way, ITV precipitated another confrontation within the League between the Big Five and the Bates–Noades axis. The Big Five made an alliance with five other clubs to form a potential superleague which would be exclusively televised by ITV in return for £32 million to be shared equally between them over four seasons (*Financial Times*, 16 July 1988; *Daily Telegraph*, 11 July 1988). Meanwhile, BSB, now ironically allied to the BBC, offered the whole League £35.8 million for four seasons' coverage (*Guardian*, 14 July 1988). This offer was recommended by the Football League Management Committee but, since it was concerned by the Big Five's threat of a breakaway, which would render any television deal a dead letter, the Committee suggested a further amendment to the redistribution of television money. It proposed that the First Division should get 80 per cent of the BSB–BBC deal (compared with 50 per cent from the previous deal),while the Second Division should get 10 per cent and the lower leagues 10 per cent between them (*Financial Times*, 16 July 1988). The final decision on the television deal would be made at the AGM on 8 August. By that time, BSB had withdrawn from the proceedings on the grounds that it did not like the way in which the football clubs operated[7] (*The Times*, 3 August 1988). Despite its eventual failure, the BSB offer had broken the cartel between the BBC and ITV and it also raised the price of football, as the BSB's counter-bids eventually raised ITV's offer to £44 million.

In order to prevent the Big Five and their five allies from creating a superleague which had an exclusive contract with ITV, the League offered the First Division as a whole 75 per cent of the £44 million which ITV had offered for four seasons' coverage; the Second Division would receive 12.5 per cent and the lower divisions 12.5 per cent between them (*Financial Times,* 9 August 1988). This offer was substantially less than what the Big Five and their five allies had been offered directly from ITV (although it was more than these clubs were offered when the BSB–BBC deal was on the table) but they accepted this compromise at the meeting on 8 August 1988. There is no available record as to why the Big Five accepted this compromise, which was substantially less lucrative than their initial negotiations with ITV suggested, but it is possible to make some informed speculations as to why the Big Five withdrew from the grand plan which they suggested in the high summer of 1988 to an acceptance of nothing more than a greater proportion of the television revenue.

Three potential reasons for this retreat can be inferred. First, the Big Five's proposal of a superleague was purely strategic. These clubs had no real intention of breaking away from the League, but merely used the threat, as they had done throughout the 1980s to promote their own interests over those of the Bates–Noades axis. Once that axis had conceded a sufficient proportion of the television revenue, the Big Five were content to sweep their threats under the carpet. A second possibility is that the so-called Big Ten of 1988 had doubts about the viability of 10-club League when they were actually faced with the prospect of this development. The establishment of such a league was actually fraught with uncertainty. In the light of this uncertainty, it was rational for the Big Five to opt for the security of the League but to demand a greater proportion of the television revenue. This solution was the one which offered the line of least resistance, maximized returns and minimized the risks. This course of action may have been especially attractive because it can be assumed that the Big Five knew before they eventually agreed to the television deal that they would feature almost exclusively on the ITV's new Sunday programme, *The Match*, for the next four years with all the benefits that that would provide in terms of sponsorship and appearance money. Finally, the Big Five might have abandoned their attempts at a superleague in 1988 because they simply could not obviate the blocking vote of the Bates–Noades axis with the votes of only 10 clubs. As pointed out in the previous section, the most successful strategy for the Big Five was to create an alliance with the whole of the First Division and thereby undermine the potential obstruction of a majority vote for the Bates–Noades axis. The Big Five followed one or, perhaps, even all of these potential lines of reasoning and it decided to remain within the structure of the League for another four years. Whatever the particular reasons for the Big Five's acceptance of this very substantial proportion of the television revenue, the importance of the 1988 television deal lies in the fact that its outcome was informed by the growing dominance of the Big Five and reinforced that dominance, improving the Big Five's political economic position yet further and thereby precipitating the eventual move to the Premier League.

The Premier League

Throughout this chapter, we have noted how the debates between the Big Five and the Bates–Noades axis were principally directed at the distribution of television revenue, and that in the 1980s the appeals to a superleague were invariably made as the League was about to negotiate a new television deal. The ITV deal ended in 1992 so it was no surprise that the rumblings concerning a Premier League began in the previous year. As with every other 'attempt' at a breakaway, the object of the Big Five's demands for the creation of the Premier League in 1991 was to maximize their income from television. We saw above how the financial independence of the Big Five enabled them to improve their share of the television revenue in 1988. These clubs could only want a further improvement of that share when the 1992 deal came around and they were in a better position to demand it in the light of their growing independence and prominence.

Since ITV substantially favoured the Big Five, whatever their actual League position, broadcasting these clubs almost exclusively,[8] then any redistribution of television revenue to the smaller clubs of the League under the 1988 deal, in which the First Division received 75 per cent of the moneys, became increasingly intolerable. The Big Five believed that since the television audiences were interested primarily in them, they deserved almost exclusive rights to the television moneys. Furthermore, the 1988 deal provided the Big Five with the experience of how to initiate a division of the League. More particularly, it demonstrated to the Big Five the need to take the whole of the First Division along with them, if they were to gain sufficient votes for a breakaway. Consequently, by the early 1990s, the Big Five were in a position where they could realistically, rather than merely rhetorically, propose a breakaway Premier League.

Throughout this chapter, the obstructiveness of the League's voting system to the implementation of reform has been emphasized. In the light of the anarchy of self-interest which the League's voting system created, the move to the Premier League had for practical reasons to be carried out under the auspices of an overarching administrative structure. It was admittedly conceivable that the clubs of the First Division, spurred on by the Big Five, could have established themselves independently, but without at least some nominal organization to bring order to the potential anarchy of the clubs, such a venture was fraught with risks. The debates between the Big Five and the Bates–Noades axis over the distribution of revenue, and the patent inadequacy of the League's structure to deal with contemporary political economic circumstances from the 1980s impelled the two administrative bodies of the game, the Football League and the FA, to propose schemes by which the superseded League structure could be reformed. These administrative bodies had always operated distinctly and, indeed, had often been in open confrontation. The debates over the reform of the League brought these confrontations to a head, because the body which failed to establish itself at the head of any new structure which might administer the biggest clubs was doomed to marginalization.

In the early 1990s, both bodies published blueprints, by which they staked their respective claims to the leadership of the game. The Football League published *One Game, One Team, One Voice* in October 1990 (Football League, 1990), while the FA published the *Blueprint for the Future of Football* in June 1991 (Football Association, 1991). Both documents argued for much the same things; both suggested a smaller, more autonomous Premier League administered by a unified body, comprising elements of the Football League and the FA. Of course, each blueprint had a different notion of which body should be senior within the proposed unified administration of the national game. The details of the blueprints are not relevant here because they were never implemented, but the declaration by the FA that it would administer a Premier League was important to the eventual creation of that institution. The Big Five could scarcely look to the Football League to administer a new League, whose whole point was to separate itself from the inconvenience of the corporatist organization of the League, so the FA's announcement that it would oversee a breakaway acted as the final stimulus for the new league; it provided the necessary protection against the potential risks of a new league. The FA initially wanted to create an 18-club Premier League (*Daily Telegraph*, 6 April 1991) but, in the end, the whole of the First Division had to be separated from the rest of the League. If the FA tried to take only 18 clubs, then those clubs in the bottom half of the First Division would have logically voted against the Premier League's development, as it was likely that they would be excluded from the new league. The initial development of the Premier League had to follow the course which had proved successful for the Big Five throughout the 1980s; the whole of the First Division had to be included, thereby obviating a blocking vote from the Bates–Noades axis.

During the summer of 1991, this inclusion of the whole of the First Division in the breakaway expedited the creation of the Premier League, which was brought into existence very quickly. The FA's blueprint was unveiled on 19 June 1991 (*Daily Telegraph*, 20 June 1991), although the clubs already knew of the contents of that document. On 28 June, 15 of the First Division clubs resigned from the League and the seven remaining ones were expected to follow (*Daily Telegraph*, 29 June 1991). The Football League appealed to the High Court that this departure from the League was unlawful and was against the Football League's regulation 10 (*Daily Telegraph*, 1 August 1991) but Justice Ross ruled against the League, declaring that the Football League's regulation did not operate over the FA (*Daily Telegraph*, 1 August 1991). In response to this ruling, the 22 clubs of the First Division formally left the League on 16 August 1991 (*Daily Telegraph*, 17 August 1991) and the Premier League then held its inaugural meeting on 10 October 1991 (*Daily Telegraph*, 10 September 1991).

Despite it being more logical for the lesser clubs of the First Division to vote for a 22-club Premier League, whereas they would reject an 18-club league, as the risk of their not being part of it was too high, there was a substantial risk in voting for even the 22-club Premier League. There was a high probability of getting relegated from even this larger league, in which case the relegated clubs had effectively voted against their self-interest. Four clubs, whose chairmen I interviewed, did exactly this; they voted for the Premier League and were either relegated the season before the League was established (West Ham United) or in following seasons (Oldham Athletic, Sheffield United, Norwich City). Ian Stott, the chairman of Oldham Athletic, and Peter Storrie, West Ham United's managing director, revealed the logic behind their potentially damaging decisions to vote for the new league:

Obviously, as one suspected all the commercial income and the TV income went that way – all the big income – so, therefore, you couldn't be outside that division. As a general basis now, you would have to say that the difference between a Premier Division side and a Division One side is at least £2 million a season. (Peter Storrie, managing director, WHUFC, personal interview, 25 July 1994)[9]

Not one of the people in the First Division volunteered not to be in the Premier League. Now you can't blame them. There was great heart-searching for me because I have great allegiance to other Divisions really but how can I tell my players or my supporters that we're going to stay down a league for a principle? You've got to give your players and supporters the opportunity to be in the top league. So we went for it. (Ian Stott, chairman, Oldham Athletic FC, personal interview, 21 July 1994)

Storrie's comments demonstrate quite clearly the logic of the lesser teams within the First Division in voting for the Premier League. Despite the potential risk of falling off the Big Five's gravy train, they could not merely stand at the platform edge and allow that train to depart, especially since their place would simply be taken by another club. Stott is rather more oblique about Oldham Athletic's decision to join the Big Five but, although we must assume that he was being sincere in his concern for the players and fans, it seems impossible that Stott was uninfluenced by the revenue which the Premier League promised, especially since he realized that all the other clubs decided to join the Premier League principally on the grounds of self-interest. In the face of a situation in which Stott could either vote for the Premier League, from which Oldham Athletic would benefit financially, or voluntarily renounce these benefits (which would be enjoyed by a club which would take Oldham Athletic's place), it was ultimately impossible for Stott to do anything but vote for the Premier League, despite his own affection for the lower leagues.

Conclusion

The aim of Part II has been to demonstrate how certain organic political economic changes created a horizon of possibility in the 1980s for the development of a breakaway league, by creating both financial independence among the top clubs and also exerting increasing financial pressure on those clubs so that they sought to use their financial independence to wring ever greater concessions from the rest of the League. I have argued that the development of the Premier League can be understood only by appreciating the direction of certain organic developments which were very substantially determined by framing concepts established in certain conjunctural moments. The adoption of certain free-market principles in the organization of labour relations in the early 1960s initiated a course of development which by the 1980s demanded the reform of football in line with the new political economic realities which those free-market principles had brought about. Those free-market reforms recognized the concentration of capital and demanded the (relative) financial independence of the clubs from the formerly corporatist framework of the League.

This examination of the development of the Premier League accounts for the development of the new league as a political economic institution. However, although this transformation is relevant in itself, the real importance of this institutional change lies in the fact that the increased revenue and its new redistribution to the top clubs in the Premier League has facilitated the transformation of football as a site of consumption in the 1990s. The development of the Premier League as a political economic institution has improved the cultural position of the game because the increased revenue of the clubs has financed the building of new stadia and has enabled these clubs to attract top overseas players who have improved the standard of the League. Both of these developments have improved the game's public image and, therefore, its market value.

Notes

1   The first reference I have found to the Big Five was made in *The Times* on 9 April 1983.

2   Ken Bates is the chairman of Chelsea and Ron Noades the chairman of Crystal Palace. Both teams have substantial support but it is unlikely they will ever be capable of commanding the attendances or the success of Manchester United and Liverpool.

3   The fact that clubs vote according to their self-interest is revealed by Storrie and Stott's statements in the fourth part of this chapter, where they argue that they could not countenance not being part of the Premier League.

4   From the 1920s until 1958, the two lower Leagues were divided into two regional divisions (the Third Division, North and South). In 1958, these two regional divisions became the national Third and Fourth Divisions.

5   As noted in Chapter 5, the Big Five also threatened a breakaway because of the Football League's opposition to shirt sponsorship.

6   Up until the 10-point plan, the voting structure of the League consisted of 46 full member ballots (one vote for each club in the First and Second Divisions) and four associate member ballots (which represented the interests of the two lower divisions). Any rule change required three-quarters of the vote (37 votes). The 10-point plan sought to obviate the blocking vote of the Bates–Noades axis by recommending that the First Division clubs should have two votes each and that the decisive majority should be reduced from three-quarters of the vote to two-thirds. The Bates–Noades axis rejected the doubling of the First Division's votes, but Jimmy Hill proposed a compromise of one-and-a-half votes for each of the First Division clubs, which was accepted (*The Times*, 18 April 1986).

7   In fact, BSB's explanation was certainly untrue and covered the real reason for its withdrawal; it was incapable of broadcasting anything and would

soon be effectively liquidated in a merger with Murdoch's Sky television (Chippendale and Franks, 1992).

8   In a personal interview, John Bromley, head of ITV sport throughout the 1980s, revealed that the ITV did indeed concentrate their coverage on the biggest clubs because they delivered the best audiences: 'There are only about eight teams in the First Division which are attractive to the nation' (John Bromley, personal interview, 23 July 1994). Since ITV could only cover relatively few matches a season, they could only afford to televise those clubs which commanded the best audiences, especially since the television audiences consisted not so much of the committed fans of one team but of individuals with much looser affiliations to the game; these viewers preferred to see the famous teams and players in action, even though a single game between two minor clubs might actually produce the best football. Whatever their League position, the Big Five clubs invariably promised better audiences.

9   'The difference between a Premier League and First Division team is now £4 million to £5 million pounds a year and West Ham United's current turnover is £15 million' (Peter Storrie, personal communication, 4 February 1997).

PART III

CONJUNCTURAL ARGUMENTS FOR THE REFORM OF FOOTBALL

7

The Strong State and the Crisis of 1985

The political economic transformations discussed in Part II were central to the creation of the Premier League, which facilitated the new consumption of football in the 1990s. However, the connection between the organic political economic developments which gave rise to the Premier League and the new consumption of football were not direct or simple. The new consumption of football only came into existence in so far as football was highlighted as an area of concern by the government, the media and the judiciary, and their recommendations for the transformation of football were implemented. Obviously, there were other agents which contributed to the debates about football, such as the amorphous and differentiated but, nevertheless, very significant 'public', but I want to concentrate on the government, media and judiciary, as they were in a particularly privileged position of definition in the conjunctural crisis of football from 1985 to 1990. In the next three chapters, I will argue that these three agents specified a set of reforms which informed the new consumption of football and that, despite a degree of incompatibility between the reforms proposed by these different agents, there were dominant themes in their arguments, which these chapters are designed to highlight.

In Chapter 2, I argued that the transformation of society would necessitate the reform of its rituals, so that the meanings which informed the wider society as it transformed were appropriately expressed. The crisis of the 1980s can certainly be understood partly in this way. By the mid-1980s, football was increasingly anomalous in the light of wider social changes. However, these arguments for reform also emerged in response to the inadequacy of the organization of football with respect to its own political economic and organic development. The judges, journalists and politicians only self-consciously set about solving the problem of football when organic developments had both demonstrably indicated the inadequacy of the game's organization with respect to its own development and also suggested a line of reform by which that inadequacy could be overcome. The arguments which were made by these agents prescribed the particular transformation of consumption practices for football in the 1990s by insisting that football be transformed in line with other changes which British society was undergoing as it moved towards it own peculiar post-Fordist settlement.

Although I want to emphasize the coherence of the various arguments which I examine in the next three chapters, it is important to remember the actual complexity of the social process. It may be heuristically necessary to simplify and abbreviate for reasons of clarity, but that does not imply a theoretical affiliation to mechanistic and reductivist ideas of social change, in which complexity is ignored. Indeed, the extensive discussion of the debates about the emergence of the Premier League in the last chapter were intended to highlight the sometimes convoluted path of historical change. In practice, the arguments of the three sets of agents, which I will discuss in the next three chapters, were shifting, overlapping or even in opposition to each other and their implementation into policy was similarly complex.

The Disasters

The moral panic about the behaviour of young male fans at football grounds had been expressed in the media since the 1960s, when hooliganism became a regular feature of an English Saturday afternoon (see Ingham, 1978; Dunning *et al.*, 1988). However, this panic came to a head with the disasters of 1985. On 11 May 1985, the main stand at Bradford City's Valley Parade ground was incinerated during the course of the last home game of the season; 55 people died. On the same afternoon, there was a riot at a game between Birmingham City and Leeds United, in which one innocent teenage boy was fatally crushed by a falling wall. On 29 May, before the European Cup final at the Heysel Stadium in Belgium, 39 Juventus fans were killed when Liverpool fans charged them. They were crushed to death when a wall collapsed as they tried to escape. The responses to these events were informed by understandings which were becoming increasingly 'commonsensical' as Britain reformed itself along Thatcherite lines. That the special quality of the disasters of 1985 and the position they attained in public consciousness was not inherent in those events but was the result of the dominant understandings of the time is demonstrated by a brief consideration of other disasters that occurred within a few years of May 1985.

During the mid-1980s, it seemed that Britain was a society plagued by disaster; the footballing tragedies at Valley Parade and Heysel were only two among several other equally fatal accidents. Within a few years of these disasters, there was a fatal fire at King's Cross underground station in November 1987, and a serious crash at Clapham Junction during the rush hour in December 1988, while on the water, the Herald of Free Enterprise capsized while leaving Zeebrugge in 1987, drowning hundreds of passengers, the Piper Alpha oil-rig exploded in July 1988, and the Marchioness, a Thames pleasure boat, was rammed and sunk by a larger boat coming upstream, killing many young people. Furthermore, a plane, taking off from Manchester Airport, caught fire, causing substantial loss of life in August 1985 (see Taylor, I., 1989, p. 108). None of these disasters, which in terms of loss of life were far more serious than those of May 1985, spawned nearly as much commentary, criticism and opprobrium as the footballing tragedies.

The special treatment of the football disasters cannot be taken as being inherent in those disasters themselves. Rather, the extraordinary level of coverage which the disasters received, both in the media and in Parliamentary discussions, was due to the social perception of football. In their work, *Policing the Crisis*, Hall *et al.* (1978) examined the statistical evidence on mugging in the early 1970s to see whether the moral panic about mugging reflected an actual increase in this type of crime. The statistical evidence about the occurrence of street crime suggested that the extent of the moral panic in the early 1970s was not justified, since there was no sudden increase in the crime rate. Consequently, Hall *et al.* suggested that the moral panic about mugging was in fact the expression of wider anxieties about changes in British society. Hall *et al.* asked the rhetorical question which is relevant to this analysis of the crisis of football in 1985: 'Could it be possible that a societal reaction to crime could precede the appearance of a pattern of crime?' (Hall *et al.*, 1978, p. 182). In relation to the disaster of 1985, it is worth asking the same question. In the light of the more measured reactions to the disasters at King's Cross, Zeebrugge, on the Thames and in the North Sea, could it be possible that the crisis in which football found itself in 1985 was due to the perception of the game before that date and that the societal reaction to football's crisis preceded the actual appearance of that crisis in the form of the disasters at Bradford and Heysel? The perception of football before 1985 ensured that the disasters were taken as evidence of a crisis. Thus, although Bradford and Heysel were particularly shocking because they were transmitted live on television, even if these events had not been broadcast at all, football would still have been considered to have been in crisis by the mid-1980s. We might go further and say that, even if Heysel and Bradford had not happened at all, some other event would have been highlighted as evidence that football was in crisis. The point is that, given the state of football at that time, the government and press had ample evidence that football was an increasingly intolerable anachronism. It was this incompatibility with wider social and economic developments which was the professional game's real crisis. The disasters at Bradford and Heysel merely confirmed that crisis.

The special significance of football and, therefore, the special outrage which was saved for it is attributable to the fact the game is a ritual. It is a charged arena in which meanings and values are debated and relations re-negotiated. The importance with which football has been endowed by large sections of society, as a principal site of identity and meaning, ensured that the disasters of Bradford and Heysel were not merely incidents of fatality but rather brought into question the values which were expressed in football and informed the lives of many individuals. In particular, the outrage which Bradford and Heysel stimulated can be explained by the fact that football was increasingly coming to be regarded among certain agents (the media, government and judiciary) as deeply anachronistic. It had failed to implement the reforms which, under Thatcher's leadership, were being widely instituted across social relations and institutions in Britain. Whereas the other disasters were regarded (rightly or wrongly) as either freak accidents (The Marchioness) or progressive disasters in which a risk had been taken in the name of modernization (Piper Alpha), the disasters of 1985 were catastrophes which were the result of football's backwardness. Since football was an important site of the creation of identity, it was particularly inappropriate that it should communicate a set of meanings which were increasingly regarded as old-fashioned and discredited. Moreover, the serious problem of hooliganism up to the disaster of 1985 emphasized the inadequacy of football's administration, and the extensive public debates since the mid-1960s about hooliganism were a vital precondition to the crisis of football in 1985. After Heysel, hooliganism, and therefore the kind of football in which that violence was possible, became rightfully intolerable.

In a recent article in defence of the Leicester School's use of Elias's concept of the 'civilizing process' in explaining hooliganism, Dunning (1994) has argued along similar lines to those which I am advancing here. Dunning suggests that during the 1970s and 1980s the media amplified the hooligan problem because they were generally dissatisfied with the state of football and, in particular, its poor economic condition. However, during the 1990s, despite the fact that hooliganism was still a feature of football (see Dunning, 1998), the press has de-emphasized the problem by under-reporting it, because it is generally much more content with the economic state of football:

> The effect of the combined ditching of Part 1 of the Football Spectators Bill, the Government's support for re-entry into Europe and the more optimistic mood regarding the English game seems to have been to make the issue of football hooliganism less newsworthy. As a result, it started to be under-reported, particularly in the national press. (Dunning, 1994, p. 133)

Dunning goes on to cite examples of football violence in the 1990s and, in particular, a disturbance at Filbert Street between Leicester City and Newcastle United fans, concluding:

I think it is also reasonable to surmise that, had the moral panic over football hooliganism of the 1970s and 1980s prevailed, at least some of these incidents would have received the 'mindless morons', 'smash the animals and thugs' headline treatment by the national tabloids and that, in that way, the moral panic would have been reinforced. (Dunning, 1994, p. 134)

Although Dunning might have to qualify his argument in the light of the eagerness with which the press has pursued stories of 'sleaze' and misconduct in football (especially in the 1994–1995 season),[1] suggesting that the press did not sweep every unfavourable facet of football under the carpet in a bid to render the game as commodifiable as possible, Dunning's line of argument is plausible and echoes my position here. The arguments for reform were the conjunctural responses to certain organic political economic developments, which had left football's structure inadequate with respect to the level of its own political economic developments and to that of wider social developments. The crisis of the 1980s was not objectively caused by the disasters but rather the disasters exemplified a deeper problem in football. Football's real crisis was that it had not begun to transform itself in the light of emergent Thatcherite realities.

Disciplinary Arguments

Although the political economic backwardness of football stimulated the special outrage which was widely expressed in response to the disasters of 1985, the arguments which predominated immediately after those disasters were primarily authoritarian, arguing for the imposition of greater discipline onto the football crowd and, in particular, its containment into fenced pens (Taylor, I., 1989, p. 97). The authoritarian argument involved two essential claims: families had to be introduced into football, as they were disciplined entities, and violent young male fans had to be controlled, by either containment, surveillance, exclusion or punishment. In particular, I want to focus on Thatcher's demands for reform, which eventually culminated in the ill-fated Football Spectators' Bill, and the Popplewell report, which constituted the judicial manifestation of the authoritarian argument.

In Chapter 3, I discussed Thatcherism, arguing there that Thatcherism is best seen as a political and interpretative response to the collapse of the post-war settlement and that Thatcherism consisted of two essential ideological strands: the strong state and the free market. Although it is important to avoid oversimplification, since Thatcher's attitude to football was shifting, her reaction to the disasters of 1985, and her recommendations for the reform of football in consequence, principally drew on her ideological and political commitment to the strong state. Almost certainly influenced by the media's amplified representation of the hooligan, Thatcher's principal response to the problems of football emphasized the authoritarian themes of family discipline and the control of hooligans.

After the Heysel disaster, Thatcher made a speech in the House of Commons on 31 May which highlighted her notion of the strong state. Speaking of hooliganism, Thatcher argued that, 'these violent people must be isolated from society' (*Guardian*, 1 June 1985). She went on to make very interesting claims about her perception of post-Fordist British society. She linked the violence of the terraces with two other types of violence in the country, that on the picket line and terrorist violence in Northern Ireland,[2] and she went on to argue that violence in the young was the 'disease of prosperous society' in which the young had more money but less responsibility. Thatcher suggested that an increase in mobility (presumably both social and geographical) was linked to the increased use of drugs, violence and terrorism (*Guardian*, 1 June 1985). Elsewhere, Thatcher made it clear how these individuals should be controlled: 'There is violence in human nature and there are three ways of trying to deal with it: either persuasion, prevention and punishment' (*Guardian*, 4 June 1985).

It is worth considering Thatcher's statements in some detail, as they highlight her notions both of the individual and of the solution to the apparent problem of order which post-Fordism posed for the state. For Thatcher, the affluence of post-Fordism was a threat because it had loosened the constraining boundaries of the previous social order, freeing individuals from their social bonds and allowing them to indulge in the violence and nameless other vices which are inherent in human nature. For Thatcher, the only solution to the increasing dissolution of social, geographical and behavioural boundaries was the isolation of those individuals who had succumbed to their instincts. By isolation, I infer that Thatcher wanted to identify these individuals and separate them from society through imprisonment. By means of the strong state, which Thatcher avowed as a method of decontaminating society of these individuals, she hoped to re-inscribe the social boundaries which hold back the bestial essences within them.

However, Thatcher's application of the strong state was not directed at all individuals – not all individuals have succumbed to their bestial human nature. Rather, her disciplinary reforms were directed at quite specific groups which were seen to threaten post-Fordist society: trade union pickets, terrorists, drug users, hooligans and, more generally, the dangerous young. In Chapter 3, I suggested that post-Fordism is characterized by the development of a 'two-thirds, one-third' society. The individuals on Thatcher's list of the damned were either from those groups which opposed and threatened Thatcher's post-Fordist project or formed part of the one-third who have been excluded from that project's benefits. Of course, both groups were closely related, since those individuals who picketed in the hope of preserving their jobs in industry have been substantially relegated to the growing underclass. Thatcher's response to the disasters of 1985 accorded with her understanding of how British society had to negotiate a passage to a post-Fordist settlement. It was, perhaps, not insignificant that on 17 May 1985 – six days after Bradford – a government White Paper was published which was designed to curb mob violence on the picket lines and at soccer matches and which later became the 1986 Public Order Act (*Daily Telegraph*, 17 May 1985).

In the passage which I have cited above, Thatcher defined what kinds of individuals needed to be isolated from society, but she did not clarify what she meant by society. Her understanding of the latter is implied in a separate statement about football: 'We have to have grounds that are safe for our families to go and safe from hooligans' (*Daily Telegraph*, 20 May 1985). Hooligans must be separated from 'families', and if we follow Thatcher's syllogism (that hooligans must be isolated from society, and that families should be safe from hooligans), we can infer that for Thatcher society consisted of families. Indeed, this is exactly what she has claimed explicitly, when she famously declared that 'there was no such thing as society – only individuals and families' (*The Times*, 19 January 1985; Morgan, 1990, p. 440). In other words, for Thatcher, the family constituted a critical site of social control, especially in the potentially dangerous affluence and mobility of post-Fordist society. Consequently, the family as a central disciplinary force had to be upheld and supported by the additionally repressive force of the state; where the family could not impose order, the state had to intervene by isolating those individuals who threatened decency. The state could then leave the field free again for the respectable discipline of the family. As we shall see below, Thatcher's main attempt to apply repressive state measures to football failed. However, her argument for the introduction of disciplined families into the game was highly significant and dovetailed with the arguments for free-market reform which were more successfully applied to football.

Thatcher's own arguments were not idiosyncratic but were typical of a wider Conservative argument which was expressed throughout the 1980s. Roger Scruton, the Oxford philosopher, was an important figure in this argument and insisted on the centrality of the family as a site of social order: 'It hardly needs saying, in the light of all that has gone before that the support and protection of this institution [the family] must be central to conservative outlook' (Scruton, 1980, p. 144). The Conservative press followed a similar line,[3] although there is not room here to examine those particular arguments more closely. The point is that at certain key points of definition, in the press and in government, social control by means of the state and the family was highlighted as the solution to football's crisis.[4]

The Popplewell Report

There had been other government-sponsored reports about football since World War II,[5] usually following a fatal disaster, but the context in which the Popplewell report was written – a football 'crisis' and an overarching authoritarian response to that crisis – was unique and, as I shall argue below, influenced the recommendations of the report. The disciplinarian framework of the Popplewell report was apparent even in the very form of its commission by the government. After the disasters of May 11 at Bradford and Birmingham, Thatcher ordered a single judicial inquiry into both of these quite separate and very different events. This decision that Popplewell should examine both these events conflated the issues of safety and control and allowed the disciplinarian argument to gain ground. There can be no doubting that the two issues are closely interrelated at a football ground, as a poorly controlled or violent crowd is necessarily dangerous and, therefore, a threat to public safety. Yet, as the fire at Bradford demonstrated, the issues could be quite separate, where a perfectly well-behaved crowd might be in a situation of danger because of the negligent management of the ground. In the 1990s, reforms of football grounds emphasized the need to improve the grounds, which would encourage the attendance of less violent people. After the disaster of May 1985 and up until the Hillsborough disaster of April 1989, the disciplinarian argument was dominant and it stressed the repressive control of the crowd above the architectural safety of the ground. As Ian Taylor has argued, the disciplinary issues of control 'overdetermined' (overruled) all other safety and crowd issues (Taylor, 1989, p. 97) and the Popplewell report itself 'finished up reading like a contribution to the debate, which was then current in England, on the Police and Criminal Evidence Bill and the extension of police powers of search' (Taylor, 1989, p. 99). This disciplinary argument was only finally discredited by the deaths of 96 individuals at Hillsborough, when it became obvious that the caging and constriction of the crowd, which the disciplinarian argument demanded, was potentially lethal.

The conflation of the issues of safety and control initiated by the decision to commission a report which dealt with the two very different disasters continued to feature as a central interpretative motif in the Popplewell report itself. After the fire at Bradford, there was quite extensive debate in various newspapers about the cause of the fire. Significantly, many accounts blamed the fire not on the criminal negligence of the club, although the evidence for such neglect was overwhelming, but on certain male fans on the terraces at the ground. Furthermore, newspapers continued with these unfounded accusations even after they were in possession of the real reasons for the fire. Initially, the cause of the Bradford fire was widely believed to be a smokebomb.

Assistant Chief Inspector Domaille claimed that the fire had been started by a smokebomb (*Sunday Telegraph*, 12 May 1985) and by 14 May the police had still not 'ruled out the possibility that a smokebomb may have been lobbed from a nearby terrace' (*Daily Telegraph*, 14 May 1985). In order to denote hooliganism as the central issue on 11 May, which was suggested by the dominant disciplinary argument, newspaper articles highlighted other cases of hooliganism around the country and specifically tried to link hooliganism with fire-raising.

Thus the *Daily Telegraph* (14 May 1985) contained an article about smokebombs as part of the hooligan's armoury, thereby emphasizing the connection between hooliganism and fire and promoting that connection as being primary to the understanding of Bradford. This link was made elsewhere when the paper highlighted arson at football grounds as a issue of national concern. For instance, the *Daily Telegraph* (16 May 1985) reported the attempted arson of a stand at Fareham Football Ground. Normally, an event of such minimal interest would never have featured in the pages of the national press, but the dominance of the disciplinary argument in 1985, in the light of Bradford, rendered this bungled arson meaningful. It seemed to confirm that since certain individuals, described in the *Daily Telegraph* piece as 'mindless morons', were capable of burning down a stand in Hampshire, it was also conceivable that other individuals could also have been responsible for a similar (but more successful) conflagration some three hundred miles north in Bradford.

The dominance of the disciplinarian argument as the interpretative framework for football in the middle years of the last decade is most acutely demonstrated by the fact that discussions of smokebombs and hooligans continued even after the real cause of the fire was known. On 14 May 1985, the newspapers were already in possession of the real reason for the Bradford fire – the build-up of combustible material under the stand due to decades of club negligence. For instance, the *Daily Telegraph* published extracts of letters which had been sent to Mr Terence Newman, Bradford City's secretary, by the council concerning this potentially dangerous accumulation of detritus beneath the seats of the stand on 11 and 18 July 1984 and on 30 April 1985 (*Daily Telegraph*, 14 May 1985). Tragically, the final letter informed the club that a visit by the fire safety inspectors had been arranged for the week following the disaster. Despite the fact that the *Daily Telegraph* knew the reason behind the fire, that reason was subscripted (on page 3) below the titled theme of hooliganism and arson.

The Popplewell report itself operated within this interpretative framework. The first task of the report was to identify the cause of the fire, which it did with efficiency and accuracy:

1.35   The answer to the question of how the fire started, is that it was due to the accidental lighting of debris below the floor boards in rows I or J between the seats 141 to 143. (Popplewell, 1985, p. 6)

Justice Popplewell surmised that an individual (who subsequently died in the fire) had dropped a match or cigarette through the floorboards onto the debris below. Furthermore, not only had Popplewell identified the immediate cause of the fire but he was also fully aware of the quite staggering level of negligence at the club. The club failed to reply to a letter dated 18 July 1984, which pointed to the hazardous build-up of waste below the main stand. Only when the club gained promotion to the Second Division at the end of the 1984–1985 season did they arrange a meeting with the county council's safety inspectors for 15 May 1985, because the higher division required better facilities (Popplewell, 1985, pp. 20–1).

However, despite Popplewell's identification of both long-term and immediate causes of the fire and the fact that they had nothing to do with hooliganism, one of the principal recommendations of his findings at Bradford was that the police should have greater freedom to search crowds entering a football ground and that the possession of a smokebomb in the ground should be outlawed:

3.41   I am minded to recommend, therefore, that in England and Wales the police be given unfettered right of search before entry to football grounds by Statute.

3.42   Smoke bombs may do no actual damage but the panic which they are likely to engender among spectators is very great. I recommend that consideration be given to making it a criminal offence in England and Wales to have a smoke bomb or similar device at sports grounds. (Popplewell, 1985, p. 16)

Although there have been incidents of hooligans throwing smokebombs, Popplewell focused his judicial expertise on an issue which had not claimed the life of a single person at any Football League ground in the history of English professional football and, more importantly, had nothing to do with the Bradford fire or the Birmingham riot which were the putative concerns of the Popplewell report. Consequently, Popplewell deflected his expertise away from the real causes of an event which had actually killed 55 individuals. Such a distortion of judicial insightfulness can only be explained by reference to the wider disciplinary framework that was current at the time. Popplewell's crusade against the mirage of the smokebomb only makes sense within the context of this dominant interpretation for, in the context of the findings of his report, his discussion of smokebombs was itself no more than a diversionary smokescreen.

Beyond the banning of smokebombs, Popplewell's report did little more than re-emphasize the rulings of the Green Guide, which had been instituted after Wheatley's report into the Ibrox disaster in 1971. Popplewell's analysis of the Bradford fire fell unwittingly back onto the disciplinary argument which was dominant at the time, but his examination of the Birmingham riot consciously and knowingly emphasized the repressive measures which Thatcher espoused so enthusiastically:

6.2 There seem to me to be four ways, apart from abolishing football altogether, in which hooliganism can be prevented at football grounds. They are:
1. Physically preventing hooligans who are in the ground from disturbing football matches.
2. If that is not possible, to prevent them attending football matches.
3. When they do behave like hooligans, to identify them.
4. When they are identified, to apprehend and punish them severely. (Popplewell, 1985, p. 41)

Popplewell's identification and isolation of the hooligan from football and society more generally echoed Thatcher's own ideas on how the hooligan had to be combated. His recommendation of repressive techniques accorded with Thatcher's project of the application of a strong state over those individuals who threatened her project of reconstructing Britain.

Popplewell went on to consider the methods which might be employed to identify and exclude the hooligan. Significantly, he discussed the merits of all-seater stadia (Popplewell, 1985, p. 42, para. 6.16) but dismissed them on the grounds that hooligans wanted to stand and would use the seats as weapons. Instead, Popplewell looked to more obviously restrictive measures of control. In order to prevent the admission of hooligans into the ground, Popplewell recommended a membership scheme (Popplewell, 1985, p. 46, para. 6.48). This membership scheme would exclude away fans from the ground and, therefore, necessarily prevent hooliganism; there would be no away fans to fight. Popplewell accepted the marketing loss that this membership scheme would inflict on football:

6.42 It [the membership scheme] has, of course, obvious disadvantages for the club. Firstly, all gates are made up to some extent of visiting supporters; numbers vary from match to match and from club to club, but on average they amount to some 10 per cent of the gate. Most clubs, I would suspect, would be willing to lose the revenue from that 10 per cent if they could have a violence-free game.

6.43 Membership will also effectively prevent the man or woman who on the spur of the moment wishes to go along to a match, the 'casual' visitor, from so doing. That, in my view, is a price which the public and the club have to pay to reduce football violence. (Popplewell, 1985, p. 45)

In his final report, mainly on the advice of the Sir Norman Chester Centre for Football Research under Eric Dunning, Patrick Murphy and John Williams, Popplewell decided to restrict membership schemes to only half the ground (Popplewell, 1986, p. 44).

In addition to excluding the hooligan, Popplewell had to recommend measures by which they might be identified. His principal means of identifying the hooligan was to recommend the introduction of closed-circuit television at League grounds (Popplewell, 1985, 46, para. 6.54). Popplewell also made several recommendations, which were differentially significant; the hurling of physical objects and obscene or racist abuse were both recommended as punishable criminal offences (Popplewell, 1985, pp. 47–8, paras 6.57, 6.67). Finally, Popplewell endorsed the presence of perimeter fences as a means of control:

6.63 In Scotland, they [fences] are uncommon. At Birmingham they proved no obstacle. There is no doubt a limit to the amount of fortification which a club can reasonably introduce. But a standard, efficient perimeter fence with proper exits should not be difficult to design and provide. I therefore recommend that consideration be given to the design of a standard, efficient perimeter fence with proper exits. (Popplewell, 1985, p. 48)

This disciplinary endorsement for the control of the crowd by means of physical restriction was to be revealed as fatally flawed on 15 April 1989.

The Football Spectators' Bill: the Apotheosis (and Nemesis) of Authoritarianism

The disciplinary orientation of the Popplewell report can be substantially attributed to the cultural context in which it was created, and a central element of that culture, as I tried to argue in Chapter 3, was the project of Thatcherism. The Popplewell report was informed by Thatcherite notions of the need for a strong state, but the report itself influenced both the Thatcherite disciplinary argument and the application of that argument into policy measures. Drawing on the Popplewell report, the Thatcher government made many of his recommendations law in the form of the new Public Order Act 1986 (*The Times*, 1 January, 1987). After much negotiation and following Popplewell's final recommendations, the government ruled that from the beginning of the 1987–1988 season all clubs should have a membership scheme which covered at least half of their home support (*The Times*, 9 August 1987; Crick and Smith, 1990, p. 164). This membership scheme was a temporary measure which was intended to precede a much grander scheme for controlling entry into football grounds. After Heysel, Thatcher was determined to create a national identity card scheme in which every single supporter would have an identity card which they would present on admission to the ground. Of course, hooligan offenders would have their cards rescinded and would, therefore, be excluded from the ground – theoretically at least.

The debate over the national identity card scheme raged from the moment the temporary measure was brought in, until the publication of the Taylor report in January 1990. The government formally announced the national membership scheme on 6 July 1988 and tried to introduce it as part of the Football Spectators' Bill, the White Paper of which would be proposed in the autumn of 1988 (*The Times*, 17 June 1988). Significantly, the national membership scheme put Thatcher's focus on the control of the individual into practice, for the scheme operated around the premise of isolating violent individuals from each other and from law-abiding fans by excluding them from the ground and punishing them by the law.

The introduction of a national identity scheme, under the Football Spectators' Bill, was to be the first and one of the few major defeats which Thatcher suffered throughout her premiership. Although her belief in a strong state expressed the sentiments of many sections of British society, the imposition of the national identity scheme was regarded by many as inappropriate and even counterproductive. The police opposed its introduction on the grounds that it would only delay entry into the grounds, thereby exacerbating tension and providing fans with a greater opportunity for confrontation outside the grounds (*The Times*, 19 April 1989, 20 April 1989; *Daily Telegraph*, 19 April 1989; Taylor, 1990, pp. 61–73). All the clubs, the FA and the Football League were unanimously opposed to the scheme, because it seriously threatened their revenue and did not promise to remove hooliganism anyway (*The Times*, 25 January 1989). Furthermore, a large number of football fans rallied behind the Football Supporters' Association (FSA) to oppose the scheme, which they regarded as a threat to football's finances, as a potential infringement of their civil rights and as potentially ineffective anyway (*The Times*, 25 January 1989). Thatcherism did receive some support, however, notably from *The Times*, which regarded the imposition of identity cards as necessary.

Despite the overwhelming opposition which the Bill received from very diverse sections of British society, it was only Lord Justice Taylor's report into the Hillsborough disaster which finally tipped the balance against the national membership scheme. Thatcher could not ignore a (highly regarded and detailed) report into the deaths of 95 supporters, which her own government had commissioned and which dismissed the scheme on practical grounds. The scheme was likely to create more problems than it solved and it was likely to be most easily circumvented by the very individuals whom the scheme was set up to exclude – criminal hooligans (Taylor, 1990, pp. 72–3).

Conclusion

In response to the manifest inadequacy of football's administration with respect to wider Thatcherite transformations and to the sport's own political economic developments, the disasters of 1985 were seized upon as the outward signs of a deeper crisis which required the thorough reform of football. As we have just seen above, however, the authoritarian arguments proposed by Thatcher herself collapsed substantially under their own weight; they could not deliver the law and order which they promised. Furthermore, in the light of the Hillsborough disaster, it was plain that, although the resolution of the hooligan problem would have to be part of any wider reform of football, there were many issues which the authoritarian arguments of the 1980s did not even consider. In particular, authoritarian arguments almost wholly failed to take account of the political economic reforms which were essential to bring football's administration and its guiding principles into line with both the level of its own political economic development and with the norms expected in Thatcherite society.

Notes

1   The 'sleaze' which the media highlighted in football in the 1994–1995 season involved misconduct in the administration of the game (such as the cases of 'bungs' involving George Graham, Terry Venables, Bruce Grobbelaar, John Fashanu and Hans Segers) and violent conduct on and off the pitch by players: notably, Eric Cantona, Duncan Ferguson, Dennis Wise and Paul Ince.

2   This speech substantially repeated the themes of Thatcher's famous 'Barrier of Steel' speech in 1979. See Clarke (1982) for an analysis of the speech.

3   See Peregrine Worsthorne's 'How to bring the mobs to order' (*Sunday Telegraph*, 9 July 1985), Gordon Brook-Shepherd's 'When the mood of a nation changes' (*Sunday Telegraph*, 2 July 1985) and Richard West's 'From great port to piggery' (*Spectator*, 8 July 1985).

4   It should be added that although this authoritarian argument was extensive, it was not universal. For instance (and unsurprisingly), the *Guardian's* analysis of the Bradford fire brought Thatcher's appeal to authoritarian solutions into question (*Guardian*, 13 May 1985).

5   There were seven government sponsored post-war reports into football before the Popplewell report; the Moelwyn Hughes report, 1946 (on the

Burnden Park disaster), the Chester report, 1968 (on finances, see Part II), the Harrington report, 1968, the Lang report, 1969 (both on hooliganism), the Wheatley report, 1971 (on the Ibrox disaster), the McElhone report, 1977 and an Official Working Group on Football Spectator Violence, 1984 (both concerned with fan violence).

8

Free-Market Arguments

Although authoritarian proposals were important to the transformation of football in the 1990s, that line of reform was superseded by free-market arguments, which had, in fact, been expressed through the 1980s, in an admittedly subordinate way. In a single and terrible afternoon, the Hillsborough disaster changed all that, thoroughly undermining the confidence and apparent logic of demands for the containment and control of the crowd. Consequently, after Hillsborough, the free-market argument which had always been a significant element in the demands for reforms was thrust to the fore and became the dominant principle for the reform of football in the 1990s. The free-market argument consisted of three main strands. First, it argued that the Football League should be subject to the forces of the market like any other business; the attrition of football clubs which were poorly run or simply economically unviable was necessary. Second, football clubs should adopt management practices in line with those of successful contemporary businesses; the individuals who managed the finances of football clubs should demonstrate similar abilities and outlooks as the new entrepreneurial capitalist class, which was held up as definitive and symbolic of the 1980s. Finally, football should establish a relationship with its fans which was typical of other businesses; football fans had to become 'customers', while football clubs became leisure services which had to compete for these customers' patronage like any other business.[1]

Attrition

In the 1980s, the free-market argument initially focused on the issue of attrition. Following the fire at Bradford and the riot at Birmingham, the *Daily Telegraph* was the first paper to apply the free-market idea of attrition to the Football League as a means of bringing the game into line with the understandings and practices which were by the mid-1980s establishing themselves as typical in emergent British post-Fordist society: 'The time is fast approaching when only a handful of big clubs, such as Tottenham, Liverpool, Everton and Manchester United, will earn sufficient money to cope with renovation and replacement' (*Daily Telegraph*, 13 May 1985). Significantly, in this conjuncture, the free-market argument promoted exactly those clubs which organic developments had privileged since the 1960s. The solutions to the crisis of football which were hit upon in this conjunctural moment in the 1980s were those suggested by the trajectory of political economic development, which created the conditions for crisis in the first place.

The *Sunday Times* echoed these arguments in a renowned leader, entitled 'Putting the Boot In', published a week after the Bradford fire:

> Reassessment should start from the fairly obvious fact that it [football] must stand or fall on its popularity. If people do not want to watch a match then there is no reason in the world why 22 men should be paid to play it. Football, like any other professional entertainment, is nothing if it does not draw crowds on its own merits. Subsidising entertainment is a contradiction in terms. (*Sunday Times*, 19 May 1985)

Clubs should confront the full force of the market, and those which were incapable of sustaining themselves on their own merits should be allowed to go out of business.

The leader continued in this free-market vein, prescribing a role for the state which was typical in its Thatcherite ideology and argument:

> The perception of the game's health goes very well with what should be the government's important but narrow role. When all the necessary inquiries have been made, the government should lay down strict requirements for the security of all football grounds, from fire to safety to violence. Clubs should be given a minimum period of time to meet those requirements. Those that fail should be closed down. Since improvements are likely to be expensive only those clubs that can attract large gates will be likely to afford them. The rest will go. This would be no bad thing; most of England's 92 'first class' clubs are, in fact, distinctly third rate. (*Sunday Times*, 19 May 1985)

Drawing on a central tenet of Thatcherism, the leader regarded the state's economic role as minimal; the state should do no more than create the boundaries within which market forces would be free to operate. In this case, those boundaries were to be a set of stadium standards, and these stadium standards would accelerate the process of free-market attrition. Only those clubs which were financially viable would be able to afford the necessary renovations, and so by releasing the free market into the game and enforcing the regulations of the strong state, the *Sunday Times* leader recommended a free-market reformation of the League.

The leader concluded with a final argument against protecting the smaller clubs from the forces of the free market: 'Subsidy will do no more than help keep football miserably alive, like a clapped-out

Victorian factory producing a product nobody wants to buy. After Bradford, such an approach would be unforgivable' (*Sunday Times*, 19 May 1995). The leader's conclusion is particularly significant because it extended the terms of reference from the advocacy of a free market in football to a more general project of reform of the whole of Britain in the face of the challenge of post-Fordism. Just as Thatcherism has allowed the inefficient sections of industry to wither away, unprotected by the state from market forces, so should poor football clubs be similarly sacrificed.

Management Practices

The second strand of the free-market argument was the call for proper management practices at football clubs. The demand for the introduction of management practices which were in line with those in contemporary business was, of course, related to the demand that clubs should be unprotected from the force of the market, for, in the free market, only those businesses which were run properly had any chance of survival: 'football clubs will flirt with bankruptcy so long as their financing continues to be unconventional by business standards' (*Financial Times*, 7 January 1984). However, the demands by the press for the introduction of modern management practices had socially significant implications.

The demand for new management practices envisaged a quite explicit change in the personnel who inhabited the directors' boxes at football grounds. In particular, various sections of the press looked to the emergent entrepreneurial fragment of the capitalist class as the necessary successors to the provincial businessmen who had generally been on the boards of clubs up to the early 1980s. The financial incompetence and complacency of these 'traditional' directors, which will be discussed in Chapter 11, was highlighted in various press accounts as a fundamental precipitating factor in the disasters of 1985. The *Sunday Times* responded to Heysel with a leader which echoed 'Putting the Boot in':

> Stern action against violence has been resisted for the same reason that stadiums have been allowed to remain as tinder-boxes: it might hurt the pockets of those who do well out the sport. As long as local worthies in sheepskin coats can sip their gin-and-tonic in the director's box at half-time and gain a bit of status and profit in the process what does it matter what is happening among the masses on the terraces? (*Sunday Times*, 2 June 1985)

The *Sunday Times* sneered at the 'traditional' directors of football clubs. They were pompous 'worthies' who were concerned only with their own status but, more importantly, they were essentially incompetent and amateurish. They were not interested in establishing football on a properly businesslike and profitable basis and were, therefore, responsible for the chaos in which the game found itself in the 1980s.

Various newspapers suggested individuals who might introduce the correct business practices into football and thereby prevent future repetitions of Bradford, Heysel and Hillsborough. The newspapers highlighted the kinds of businessmen which football required and who would replace the 'local worthies':

> The time-honoured characteristics that have marked the way European's great soccer clubs have been run – mindless conservatism and pompous megalomania – have been swept away on a tide of money. As a result, the motley crew of minor entrepreneurs which controlled these clubs is being squeezed out by the captains of multi-national commerce. (*Financial Times*, 5 January 1991)

The *Financial Times* was quite specific, then, about the social location of the individuals whom football required for its reformation. In place of the provincial and backward businessmen, football needed members of the progressive capitalist class who were aware of the workings of the post-Fordist global economy. The *Financial Times* implies that it might have found the kind of figure which it outlined in the article cited above, when the paper published a profile of Martin Edwards, the chairman of Manchester United, some months later: 'He [Edwards] has run the club full-time and looks more like a sober northern businessman than a football manqué: not for him the coifed hair, Riviera tan and tendency to call women "sweetheart"' (*Financial Times*, 22 April 1991).

Creating the Customer

The free market provided two potential and important benefits which would assist in aligning football with the emergent post-Fordist social formation. The free market offered a means of removing unprofitable clubs and of replacing inadequate club directors. However, the free market suggested a third reform. We have already noted that the *Sunday Times* advocated stadium renovation as a method for liquidating the poor clubs, but the demand for stadium renovation implied a second and very significant transformation. Stadium reconstruction would improve the popularity of football, since more people would be attracted to the game, knowing that they did not have to suffer the dangers and indignities of standing on a terrace, but equally importantly this renovation of the grounds would transform the relationship between the club and the fans. Through the provision of better facilities, the club would begin to create a closer relationship with the fans which would accord with that more widely found in the leisure industry. In short, the fans were to become customers. Following Bradford and Heysel in 1985, these demands for the transformation of the fan into a customer were infrequent in comparison to the vehement attacks on the 'traditional' directors and on the need for the attrition of clubs. After Hillsborough, however, the demand for a new relationship between clubs and fans became the dominant free-market principle for the reform of football. This shift from authoritarian to free-market understandings as the dominant interpretation, and this new emphasis on the need to treat the supporters as customer, should not be underemphasized. It is a change of historical importance.

In press responses to Hillsborough, the argument for creation of a customer were intimately bound up with demands for the renovation of the grounds and, in particular, the development of all-seater stadia. For instance, after Hillsborough, *The Times* insisted upon the creation of all-seater stadia: 'But its [Hillsborough's] principal result may eventually be the modernising of Britain's league football grounds into all-seater stadiums where a tragedy such as Saturday's simply could not happen' (*The Times*, 17 April 1989). Or, again: 'I believe we are in sight of an end to standing accommodation which will give way to seated stadiums with better facilities such as cover from the rain, decent lavatories and improved refreshment areas' (*The Times*, 17 April 1989). The *Daily Telegraph* echoed this view: 'It is no longer safe or socially tolerable for football supporters to be packed standing in huge crowds. All-seater stadiums must become the rule' (*Daily Telegraph*, 17 April 1989). Importantly, the demand for all-seater stadia was supported even in liberal interpretations of the disaster:

> Terraces on our big grounds pack in more spectators than the seated areas where no surges can occur. Scrapping the terraces, installing seats, would cost money. So what? The clubs gripped by market forces have never struck a balance between transfer fees and civilised facilities for the millions whose five pounds a time make them possible. (*Guardian*, 17 April, 1989)

Although the *Guardian* rejected the exclusionary implications of the free-market arguments which will be discussed below, their demands for an improvement of public services were effectively recruited into the support of the free-market argument, given the dominance of free-market interpretations at the time.

The argument for renovation of the grounds implied a transformation of the relationship between fans and clubs. Whereas the fans in the past had been treated poorly, fans in the improved grounds of the future had to be treated as customers: 'All-seater stadiums and fewer all-professional clubs may be part of the answer but it is definitely time for the spectator to be treated as a paying customer and not a dangerous nuisance' (*Financial Times*, 17 April 1989). Since football fans became customers when the grounds were transformed into all-seater stadia, the idea of the customer which was widely envisaged by the press after Hillsborough was of an individual who paid more in return for better services at the match.

This apparently simple transformation of fan into customer, which was certainly inspired by a genuine concern for the welfare of football spectators and which seemed entirely commonsensical, actually implied a significant and politically controversial development. The notion of the customer, who paid more for better services, implied a shift of football support towards more affluent sections of society. This shift was explicit in some of the press arguments in the 1980s. One of the earliest examples of this argument for the social relocation of football was Russell Davies' piece published in the *Sunday Times*, called 'Cockpits of Ignobility'. He argued that 'the game drifts slowly into the possession of what we are now supposed to call the underclass; and a whole middle class public grows up without ever dreaming of visiting a Football League ground' (*Sunday Times*, 28 August 1983). In a leader written in response to the Bradford disaster which we have already cited, the *Sunday Times* expounded furiously upon the need for the social relocation of football: 'British football is in crisis; a slum sport played in slum stadiums increasingly watched by slum people, who deter decent folk from turning up' (*Sunday Times*, 19 May 1985). By the derogatory term 'slum people', the *Sunday Times* can only have meant those individuals who had been increasingly confined to the unemployment, crime and poverty of the 'underclass' (Therborn, 1990, pp. 111–12; Burrows, 1991, p. 8; McDowell, 1989, pp. 1–3; Murray, 1990a,b). Significantly, this leader effectively implied that many of football's problems could be solved by replacing these fans from the 'underclass' with 'decent folk', i.e. respectable individuals and families from the more affluent sections of society.

The Economist, 'a key voice of progressive capital' (Taylor, I., 1989, p. 95), was similarly explicit about the need to attract a more affluent audience to football, at the effective cost of excluding the poor:

> Those close to Mrs Thatcher have always seen measures to change the nature of football as guaranteed vote winners. Their convictions reflect a common view that the game is irredeemably tied to the old industrial north, yobs and slum cultures of the stricken inner cities – everything, in fact, that modern Britain aspires to put behind it. (*The Economist*, 22 April 1989)

By 'putting these slum cultures behind it', however, Thatcherite free-market arguments did not refer to the elimination of the poverty in which such cultures have developed but only the social exclusion of the poor. With regard to football, the creation of the customer refers to the exclusion of the urban poor from football and their replacement by the affluent middle classes and white-collar workforce. *The Economist* was explicit about this exclusion:

> What of the fans themselves? American football is a family event, with many women and elderly people in the crowd. Clubs try to encourage parents to bring children by selling cheap family tickets and putting on children's entertainment before a match. Stadiums are organised with middle-class families in mind. (*The Economist*, 22 April 1989)

The idea of the customer refers to the exclusionary remarketing of football away from the periphery and into the core of post-Fordist society. According to free-market arguments, the renovation of football grounds was intended to replace the dangerous poor with 'decent folk'; the respectable members of the white-collar workforce and the professional middle classes. The customer is a useful rhetorical device because, within the context of an emergent Thatcherite hegemony, the benign neutrality of the term conceals the intensely political nature and social divisiveness of the developments which the concept envisaged. We will discuss the political importance of the customer as a rhetorical device in Chapter 11.

The relocation of football into the affluent core of British society, which is implied by the process of turning the football fan into a customer, also involved a feminization of support. In order to broaden football's market and to reduce the level of disorder in the ground, by curbing aggressive masculinity, the free-market argument proposed that women and family groups would be encouraged to attend by the renovation of the stadia. Significantly, this free-market argument for the introduction of women and families[2] (as customers) to football was the point of connection between free-market principles and the authoritarianism discussed in the last chapter. The affluent family, socially located within the core of British post-Fordist society, promised to solve football's crisis because the family was a disciplined social unit which would also spend much more money in the ground than the groups of single male supporters.

The importance of the introduction of families into the game, to replace less affluent masculine support, was demonstrated in a number of statements. For instance, Philip Carter, the chairman of Everton and president of the Football League from 1986 to 1988, argued that 'clubs are already individually helping to bring families and children back to football and the gates are up' (quoted in *The Times*, 3 December 1986). Graham Kelly, then secretary of the Football League, argued that 67 clubs had family enclosures but that 'these must be enlarged and extended, as all clubs must follow this lead' (*The Times*, 2 January 1987).[3] In point of fact, Carter's idea that football was 'bringing families back' was incorrect as whole families had rarely attended football in the past.

Nevertheless, the conscious attempt to attract families to football was one of the most important marketing strategies in the development of the new consumption of football, for, as the free-market argument insisted, the family promised to remedy the problems of football's insolvency and its crowd problems in a single blow. Families spent more money and behaved better.

Conclusion

Although the notion of the customer was part of a wider argument which itself accorded with the understandings and interests of certain class fractions, this does not somehow imply that the notion of the customer was fictitious – a mere conspiratorial invention. On the contrary, the very force of the free-market argument lay in the fact that it was based in social experience, as it was widely interpreted in the 1980s. First, the Football League grounds in England of the 1980s *were*, by and large, a disgrace; they were unsanitary and dangerous. Second, not only were fans provided with poor facilities but they were treated poorly by the club; ticketing and entrance to games was frequently disorganized – often dangerously so.[4] Third, and of paramount importance, there can be no denying the brutishness which often characterized masculine terrace culture from the 1960s and, although free-market arguments were socially exclusionary in intent, so was the aggressive masculine culture which free-market arguments sought to eradicate from the ground. At the very least, these cultures excluded many individuals, especially women, from attending football by the very real threat of violence, and, at certain clubs, ethnic minorities were effectively barred from entry to the grounds by overt and offensive displays of racism. By the mid-1980s, football grounds required thorough refurbishment, and the culture of the crowd required reformation. The free-market argument, with its demands for the creation of a football customer, successfully recognized the deficiencies of English football grounds and their fans and was forthright in their condemnation, while many liberals still maintained a romantic and, in fact, untenable view of the authenticity of terrace culture. Since the free marketeer's interpretation of football in the 1980s was widely recognized across the social formation as the most adequate account of that reality, it was able to command greater support.

The success of the argument was also assisted by its connection to wider social developments. The free-market argument was part of a nascent interpretative framework which was already attaining dominance in British culture by the mid-1980s. The recommendations of the free-market argument paralleled the wider acceptance of the free market as the most acceptable solution to the collapse of the post-war settlement. Moreover, in the light of the dominance of this framework, it became increasingly intolerable to dominant groups in the press, government and business that the free-market understandings which informed their own domination were not expressed in a major public ritual, such as football. Football's anomalous nature was not merely intolerable at the symbolic level, however; as long as football was organized along corporatist and effectively Keynesian principles, it would never be profit-making. The introduction of the free market into football was primarily demanded because entrepreneurs, the government and the press (itself owned by entrepreneurs) wanted to transform football in order to make money from the game. This transformation of the sport into a profitable business would subsequently establish the free-market hegemony in the most convincing of ways – on the balance sheet.

The transformation of football along free-market lines was substantially dependent on the organic trajectory of football's development since the mid-1960s, which was beyond the control of any one group. As emphasized throughout Part II, football was in increasingly open conflict with its own political economic realities from the 1960s. Significantly, the contradictions were very similar to those of the Keynesian post-war settlement in the 1970s. Like the Keynesian post-war settlement, football was coming under increasing political economic pressure due to growing insolvency, while corporatist methods of economic management were becoming increasingly untenable. In the light of the anachronistic nature of the Football League by the mid-1980s, and football's own disjunction with wider society, the free-market argument became the dominant argument for reform because it suggested a way of resolving the crisis of football which was most in line with the organic political economic developments within the game and would bring football back into line with wider historical developments.

Notes

1   Although this chapter analyses the three strands of the free-market argument as if they were coherent throughout the 1980s in the different newspapers, this coherence is only assumed for reasons of space. In fact, it is fully accepted that these debates were complex and often contradictory in the press.

2   It is not being argued here that the family necessarily includes a (patriarchal) husband, wife and children. Rather, I am simply suggesting that the reform demanded by the press envisaged this essentialist notion of the family.

3   Despite the forcefulness of the free-market argument, it was not monolithic; there were other opposing interpretations of the crisis of football. See, for instance, Jeremy Seabrook's piece in the *Guardian* (17 April 1989). However, the opposition to the free-market argument was sporadic within the press throughout the 1980s and it has remained a subordinate argument into the 1990s. See Corry *et al.* (1993) for an example of this counter-argument in the 1990s.

4   See Hornby (1992, pp. 128–9).

9

The Taylor Report and Italia '90

The Taylor Report

On 15 April 1989, 95 Liverpool fans[1] were crushed to death at the Leppings Lane End of Sheffield Wednesday's Hillsborough Stadium at the start of an FA Cup semi-final between Liverpool and Nottingham Forest. The particular circumstances of this disaster – the allocation of tickets, the police's administration of the crowd, the inadequate turnstile arrangements and the removal of critical crush barriers – cannot be discussed here. Rather, I want to examine the Taylor report,[2] which was commissioned by the government in response to the disaster, to try and highlight the connections between this report and the transformation of football in the 1990s.

The primary point which requires emphasis in any discussion of the Taylor report was the unexpected breadth and insightfulness of its recommendations. As Lord Justice Taylor himself commented of football:

> What is required is the vision and imagination to achieve a new ethos in football. Grounds should be upgraded. Attitudes should be more welcoming. The aim should be to provide more modern and comfortable accommodation, better and more varied facilities, more consultation with the supporters and more positive leadership. (Taylor, 1990, p. 12)

In his final report, Taylor outlined how this 'new ethos' might be created in football. Although Taylor made 76 demands in all (Taylor, 1990, pp. 76–82), the report made two fundamental recommendations (both of which were implemented). First, and famously, Taylor recommended the introduction of all-seat accommodation at football grounds:

> **61** There is no panacea which will achieve total safety and cure all problems of behaviour and crowd control. But I am satisfied that seating does more to achieve those objectives than any other single measure. (Taylor, 1990, p. 12)

Taylor's recommendation for the installation of seats was not only an expression of the contemporary climate of opinion in Britain but also reflected the development of European standards concerning the condition of football grounds. Signally, UEFA ruled that by the 1994–1995 season there should be no standing at any European competition. If English clubs had any European aspirations whatsoever, then the thorough transformation of the grounds was necessary, just as the abolition of the maximum wage had been necessary in the early 1960s.

Second, Taylor ruled against the national membership scheme which had been proposed in Part I of the Football Spectator's Act (Taylor, 1990, p. 75) thereby bringing Thatcher's authoritarian arguments crashing to the ground. In addition to these central recommendations, Taylor simultaneously suggested certain measures for the control of the crowd: closed-circuit television should be installed at grounds, and any fencing which did remain should be no more than 2.2 metres high, with sufficient exits; and obscene and racialist abuse, the throwing of missiles and pitch invasion should be made offences. The latter was a mediated method of control, as the type of chanting and aggressive behaviour which Taylor outlawed was likely to precipitate violence in the ground. By banning these practices, Taylor sought to create an atmosphere in the ground which would be less conducive to violence. In addition to these negative measures, Taylor also recommended methods by which better relations might be established with fans; he suggested that fans might be consulted (Taylor, 1990, p. 23) to 'enlist the goodwill and help of the decent majority' and that membership and family areas be extended (Taylor, 1990, p. 23).

Although the recommendations which Taylor made in his final report were related to wider arguments current at the time – the demand for all-seater grounds was, as we have seen, expressed widely in the broadsheets (*The Times*, 17 April 1989; *Daily Telegraph*, 17 April 1989; *Financial Times*, 17 April 1989; *Guardian*, 17 April 1989) – Taylor cannot be linked straightforwardly to Thatcherite arguments for the free market and the strong state. However, the Taylor report can be connected in a circumspect way to free-market arguments by its suggestion that football fans should be treated with the respect due to the customer in other spheres. Furthermore, despite his rejection of Thatcher's identity card policy, he still espoused certain important disciplinarian methods of control. Taylor was not Thatcherite, then, but some of his recommendations brought him close to some of the positions which were on Thatcherite territory. Moreover, Taylor's recommendations could, in the context of 1990s Britain, only ever be implemented by the entrepreneurial and free-market forces, while his concern for the spectator (which actually stemmed from social democratic sensibilities) was interpreted as if it were a mere restatement of all too familiar free-market rhetoric.

Methods of Control

90 I therefore conclude and recommend that designated grounds under the 1975 Act should be required in due course to be converted to all-seating. I do so for the compelling reasons of safety and control already set out. (Taylor, 1990, p. 16)

Taylor's preference for seating stemmed partly from his belief that a seated crowd was more controllable. Seating ordered the crowd, so that the spontaneous surges of the terraces could not occur. The control which seating permits over the crowd should not be overstated, for, as various incidents have demonstrated (e.g. the Luton–Millwall riot in 1985, the Ireland–England friendly in March 1995), hooliganism was possible from seats, and Taylor himself was realistic about the control which seating alone could have over determined troublemakers:

> Put together with progress towards all-seating, improved accommodation, better facilities, improved arrangements for crowd control, and better training of police and stewards, I believe these measures would give the best chance of eliminating or minimising football hooliganism. (Taylor, 1990, p. 75)

For Taylor, then, seating and these other controlling measures could not be guaranteed to eliminate hooliganism, but they were the best available option.

The most attractive aspect of seating was not only that it could architecturally restrain the worst effects of crowd disorder but that it made the identification of fans much easier, especially with the installation of closed-circuit television (CCTV), with its 'detection and evidential potential' (Taylor, 1990, p. 75), which Taylor recommended alongside seating:

> Apart from comfort and safety, seating has distinct advantages in achieving crowd control. It is possible to have disturbances in a seated area and they have occurred, but with the assistance of CCTV the police can immediately zoom in with a camera and pinpoint the seats occupied by the troublemakers as well as the trouble-makers themselves. (Taylor, 1990, p. 12)

In addition to creating a panoptic arena (Foucault, 1979) in which offenders could be easily identified, seating offered a second potential means of control, because it was intended to encourage the attendance of disciplined (respectable) families, in place of more violently disposed young males. For example, in discussing family and membership areas, Taylor argued that family and membership schemes 'had the dual advantage of creating areas of reliable good behaviour and offering discounts' (Taylor, 1990, p. 23). The final report's support for the family echoed some aspects of the authoritarian arguments which were discussed in Chapter 7, for Taylor thought that the attendance of the families would encourage respectable and disciplined behaviour in the ground. However, as Taylor's concerns with the discounts which clubs could offer to families reveal, Taylor's recommendations were premised on a socially inclusive, social democratic framework which was at odds with exclusive Thatcherite free-market thinking.

Although Taylor applauded the attempts of certain clubs to encourage the attendance of families, nowhere did he argue that these families should come from more affluent sections of society, as the free-market argument suggests. On the contrary, throughout his report, Taylor was concerned about the cost of his recommendations and assured the reader in a number of places that the price of tickets would not increase sufficiently to exclude fans who had attended the game in the past; Taylor cited the example of Ibrox, where seats cost only £2 more than standing (Taylor, 1990, p. 13). Football fans should expect the standards typical of the leisure industry more widely but they should not become customers in the manner which the free-market argument envisaged. They should not have to pay significantly more for these services. This concern with the universal provision of football (in line with social democratic and even Keynesian sentiments) positions the Taylor report outside of the free-market argument. Throughout the report, then, Taylor was sensitive to the financial constraints on most football supporters and this led him to argue for the public provision of seating through local authority sponsorship.

The Cost of Taylor and the Premier League

Although the implications of Taylor's report occasionally drew his position close to some Thatcherite ideas (as the framing remedy to social and economic ills), Taylor himself cannot be situated within such a rightist framework. However, the effect of the report was to establish the free-market argument as the dominant principle in the reformation of the game. In the context of 1990s Britain, Taylor's recommendations were only ever going to be implemented by means of the free market and by the initiatives of entrepreneurs who regarded his report as an opportunity for investment. The cost of the ground renovation meant that there was a wide divide between Taylor's social democratic intentions and the eventual implementation of his recommendations in the 1990s.

Taylor was conscious of the potential cost of his recommendations for both the fans and for the clubs themselves, and he therefore recommended methods for funding the reconstruction which flew in the face of much free-market thinking. Taylor proposed that the Football Trust and the Football Grounds Improvement Trust should assist in financing the reconstruction of grounds, as well as recommending that a greater percentage of the Pools money, part of the Betting Tax and a levy from transfer fees should be give back to the football clubs (Taylor, 1990, pp. 17–19). In addition, Taylor approved of strategies such as those followed by St Johnstone, which had sold its ground to the supermarket company, ASDA, who had then paid for the construction of a new stadium on the outskirts of the town. Furthermore, Taylor advocated that some local authority involvement in the construction of new grounds might be possible, citing the co-operation between Millwall and the London Borough of Lewisham, which agreed to pay £70,000 if the club made its ground available to the local community (Taylor, 1990, p. 21).

Taylor acknowledged the limitations of local council or government sponsorship within the political context of the late 1980s: 'I accept that in the current financial climate and with our different approach to communal funding, local authorities are unlikely to be able to provide subsidies for such stadia' (Taylor, 1990, p. 21). Nevertheless, despite Taylor's awareness of the impoverishment of public bodies and the growing role of private corporations in the provision of 'public' goods, a major plank (and, indeed, it might be said, 'the bottom line') of his argument was that the clubs would be able to afford the transformation of grounds. Despite Taylor's provisos, he looked ultimately to public funds to pay for this renovation. In particular, Taylor, as we have noted, did not regard the substantial increase in ticket prices as necessary – an oversight whose significance will emerge in Chapter 12. Taylor's proposal for financing ground reconstruction was the gravest gap in his argument – a gap that would be bridged by the business buccaneers who typified Thatcherite Britain. Moorhouse has highlighted this lacuna in the Taylor report:

> Lord Taylor's idealisation of the Scottish situation is no accident since the flaw in his plan for British soccer is the issue of finance. In his report various European stadiums are held out as examples but Taylor does not indicate how the gap implicit in the different pattern of the ownership of grounds between Britain and the Continent is to be bridged. In most of the rest of Europe the local authority or a sporting federation owns the ground and maintains it. This difference is noted in the Taylor Report but is smuggled out of the limelight since to ruminate upon it too long would bring to the fore the whole problem of football finance and how the facilities which the British Government and EUFA [sic] deem necessary are to be paid for. (Moorhouse, 1991a, p. 215)

The Taylor report suggested that £130 million would be required to renovate all the grounds in the League, but the methods which Taylor suggested were hugely inadequate to that task.

The weakness of Taylor's proposition of public funding was recognized among those who were responsible for implementing Taylor's recommendations. For instance, Ian Stott, the chairman of Oldham Athletic, highlighted the shortcomings of the grants from bodies like the Football Trust and the Football Ground Improvement Trust:

> What people do forget you know, when they say, 'Look what we've done for you' and the Football Trust and the government say, 'Look what we've done for you'. It's all very well giving somebody 50 or 60 per cent as long as they can afford the other 50 or 40 per cent. I mean there are an awful lot of clubs who can't afford 20 per cent of what they might have to spend on a stand so there's no point giving them 50, 60, 70 or even 80 if they can't find the other. (Ian Stott, personal interview, 21 June 1994)

Indeed, Stott believed that Taylor's recommendations 'went over the top' and he was not alone in his reservations about the extensiveness of the Taylor report. For instance, Peter Storrie, the managing director at West Ham United (personal interview, 25 July 1994), argued that the retention of shallow terracing would have been desirable, as did Danny Macgregor, the commercial manager at Manchester United (personal interview, 19 August 1994). Although apparently sensible, in that it would intuitively appear that large open terraces are inherently more dangerous, the lethal Leppings Lane end was, in fact, exactly the kind of terrace which these individuals regarded as safe – presumably after the removal of fencing. It is an open question whether this is the case. Nevertheless, the quite widespread belief among club directors (especially at the smaller clubs in the Premier League) that Taylor's reforms went too far was really an expression of a deeper concern that the reforms were too expensive.

Taylor was wrong to play down the difficulty of raising this £130 million. The public funding which he envisaged could never have nearly covered the costs of the reconstruction of the grounds, and seat prices have risen substantially more than the £2 which Taylor predicted from the evidence he gathered at Rangers. Furthermore, as the free-market argument proposed, the very point of installing seats was to raise the price of admission and, indeed, ticket prices have increased substantially in the 1990s both to pay for ground developments and to improve clubs' finances (see Table 11.1). Despite his socially inclusive intentions, the cost of Taylor's demand for all-seater stadia has had to be borne, at least partially, by the paying spectator.

In Part II, I argued that the transformation of the political economy of football increased the market pressure on clubs but did so differentially, so that the big clubs were relatively better off than those in the lower divisions. This provided a horizon of possibility in which the top clubs could contemplate a separation from the league to maximize their income. Although the informal separation of the top clubs from the rest, which was the essential precondition for a breakaway, was in existence by the mid-1980s, the Taylor report finally made such a breakaway essential in the early 1990s. The huge costs which the Taylor report implied constituted the final push towards the Premier League. Separated from the rest of the League, this elite would both be in a better bargaining position in relation to the television companies, and would no longer have to redistribute any of its earnings. Such a League would be better able to afford the expensive renovations upon which the Taylor report insisted. The financial burden which the Taylor report laid upon the clubs was matched by the ever-increasing pressure from the Europe which stretched the biggest clubs' finances. The need to compete in European competitions and with European clubs for the best players was a particularly apposite point for all the top English clubs in 1990, who were just facing the lifting of a five-year ban from European competition after the Heysel disaster. In order to compete at that level, which offered vast financial rewards, the clubs had to transform their grounds in line with Taylor and their teams in line with Europe's best. This overriding need made the transformation of the political economic structure of the League and each club absolutely necessary.

Italia '90

The Taylor report constituted a vital conjunctural moment in the transformation of the game, and since its recommendations became legal requirements in 1990, it can be assumed that they would have been implemented, whether the World Cup, Italia '90, had happened or not. However, the huge popularity of this tournament (principally as a television spectacle), due mainly to the success of the England team, altered the perception of what football could be as a ritual, facilitating the acceptance of Taylor's recommendations.

Italia '90 demonstrated the inadequacy of English grounds but also the potential market for football if it was properly organized. First, the Italian stadia confirmed both the insights and recommendations of the Taylor report. English League grounds were an embarrassment in comparison with the magnificent architecture within which the World Cup matches took place. Some of the press highlighted this gulf in facilities. For instance, *The Times* published a letter which echoed their complaints about English grounds throughout the 1980s: 'The World Cup gives us a view of modern Italian sports stadiums which put our facilities to shame' (*The Times*, 28 July 1990). *The Times* confirmed this perception elsewhere: 'The stadiums were majestic' (*The Times*, 10 July 1990). Italia '90 provided the Taylor report with momentum because it demonstrated the manifest poverty of English grounds.

Furthermore, the World Cup demonstrated how powerful football could be as a sign value, if it was properly organized and marketed. Italia '90 showed that the transformation of the consumption of football was potentially hugely lucrative. In particular, it opened up the market for football in England. In doing this, the 1990 World Cup echoed the effect which the 1966 World Cup had had 24 years earlier, when there had been a similar increase in public interest in the game. The successful performance of the England team, and especially the role played in that success by Paul Gascoigne, attracted very large television audiences. In the UK, 25.2 million viewers (nearly half of whom were women) watched the semi-final between England and West Germany (*The Times*, 14 July 1994), and Italia '90 led to an interest in football among sections of society which had previously shown limited interest in the game.

This shift seemed to have been particularly successful because of the representation of the World Cup on English television. Italia '90 had employed Pavarotti's singing of the 'Nessun Dorma' aria from Act 3 of *Turandot* (which included the appropriate words 'Vincero! Vincero!' – 'I will win! I will win!') as its anthem, and the BBC used this aria as the theme tune to its own coverage of the World Cup. In addition, the BBC's introductory footage to its coverage featured an opera stage, the curtain of which then rose to reveal some balletic figures dancing around a football to the 'Nessun Dorma' aria, followed by a series of images from the tournament itself. The significance of the BBC's use of this aria and the operatic images that went with it was that it contributed to the transformation of the cultural perception of football. Football was connected with high culture and, therefore, it was being strategically constructed as an appropriate entertainment for classes who were traditionally uninterested in football.

The success of Italia '90, and the BBC's coverage of the event, in attracting new audiences to football was demonstrated in a number of articles in the press. Revealing this new interest in the game, the *Sunday Times* (8 July 1990) described a charity concert held in the ballroom at Buckingham Palace, tickets for which cost £5000, on the same evening as the semi-final between England and West Germany and at which most of those who attended were more interested in the match than the music on offer. The point of this humorous article was to demonstrate the shift in the cultural position of football. There were numerous other examples of the press highlighting the development of this wider market for football. For instance, Laura Thompson, a (non-sports) journalist on *The Times*, wrote a feature on how she, who had had no interest in football before Italia '90, had been beguiled by Paul Gascoigne (*The Times*, 25 August 1990). The particularly significant point about this article was not its content but its timing; it was published on the opening day of the new season after the World Cup. *The Times*, which sold football as a sign-value, was trying to promote this commodity to as wide an audience as possible by reminding its (female) service-class readers of Italia '90 as the new season began. Confirming this strategy, the well-known columnist, Julie Welch, wrote a similar article about Gascoigne in the following month, 'A hero of our dinner time' which announced a new topic of conversation on the London professional-class dinner circuit: 'I can hardly believe this but I have just spent an entire evening talking about one footballer' (*The Times*, 3 September 1990). Anthony Giddens, Professor of Social and Political Science at Cambridge, expounded on the same theme in the *Times Higher Education Supplement* (21 December 1990). These articles addressed a new audience for football among those sections of the professional classes which might not have taken much interest in football before 1990.

Furthermore, various reports confirmed the new popularity which the sport commanded or should command. In an article entitled, 'A chance not to be missed', David Lacey, the *Guardian*'s football correspondent, argued that 'The 1990–1 Football League programme opens today on a strident note of optimism which will quickly become a lost chord if players, managers and coaches, not to mention club chairmen, fail in their duty to catch the public mood' the (*Guardian*, 25 August 1990). Colin Malam wrote 'In the dark days after Bradford, Heysel and Hillsborough, it was hard to imagine that football would ever be greeted with the anticipation which heralds the 102nd League season' (*Daily Telegraph*, 25 August 1990). Italia '90 played a crucial role in the realization of the Taylor report and the free-market demands for reform by attracting the more affluent, familial support to football which these arguments proposed as remedies to both football's financial and crowd control crisis.

Despite the fact that Italia '90 itself, and particularly the success of the England football team, could not have been planned and was entirely contingent to the course of developments in football, the representation of that World Cup was not somehow a matter of luck which happened to support the free-market arguments for reform. On the contrary, the representation of the World Cup was the interpretative achievement of the media. In other words, the very agencies which argued for the reform of football constructed a World Cup in 1990 which seemed to confirm the veracity of those arguments; that football could be a valuable commodity, when played in the correct surroundings and when it attracted more affluent customers than those who had attended the game during the 1980s.

Conclusion

Throughout this study I have argued that the solutions which are accepted at conjunctural moments when society submits itself to self-conscious examination reflect the direction of organic developments which have brought that society to a state of crisis and that the guiding frameworks which are established reflect the dominant interests in a society, albeit in contested ways. The Taylor report demonstrates the way in which organic developments, themselves precipitated by the adoption of certain framing ideas which inform practice, influence the outcome of conjunctural moments favouring solutions in line with those organic developments and the dominant interests of a society. Although Taylor argued against any simple application of the free market, the interpretation of his report and its eventual application to football was informed by the free-market ideas which had been at the root of football's outgrowing of its corporate structure. In the end, then, the Taylor report, despite its own intentions, did little more than provide judicial legitimacy to the free-market arguments which proposed the easiest line of reform for football in the light of the organic development of the sport, on the one hand, and the transformations of British society, on the other. In the final part of this book, I want to analyse the particular application of these free-market arguments to the transformation of football and to consider their contestation by various fan groups. The point of analysing the contestation of the new consumption of football is not simply to provide an adequate empirical account of the transformation of football in the 1990s but to make the important theoretical point that conjunctural moments (and, indeed, organic developments) are not monolithic and simplistically unidirectional but are always and everywhere the result of complex negotiation, although organic developments will always favour particular groups whose arguments seem to reflect emergent social reality most adequately.

Notes

1   The number of Hillsborough victims rose to 96 in March 1993 when Tony Bland's life support machine was turned off.
2   Taylor wrote an interim report which dealt with the specifics of the Hillsborough disaster itself and was published on 1 August 1989, and a final report which was concerned with laying out his wider understandings and was published in January 1990. This chapter concerns itself with the final report.

PART IV

THE NEW CONSUMPTION OF FOOTBALL

10

Sky Television and the Premier League's New Deal

In the 1980s, the chairmen of football clubs frequently complained about the way in which the BBC–ITV duopoly forced down the price of football, and many of the debates between the television companies and the Football League in that decade can be understood as an attempt by the League to demand its full worth in the context of this cartel. Robert Maxwell was, perhaps unsurprisingly, the most outspoken of the League's chairmen in deploring the television companies' strategy of suppressing the value of football, insisting in the mid-1980s that he could get the Football League £50 million for television rights. Maxwell's outspokenness on this issue earned him some respect among other League chairmen; Ken Bates, for instance, suggested that Maxwell's position on the television coverage of football meant that he was not 'unlamented' (personal interview, 10 October 1994). The television contract between BSkyB and the Premier League in 1992 constituted a moment when Maxwell's prophecies eventually came true and football finally gained a price which it was certainly worth. In political economic terms, the profitability of this contract was very important, since it furthered the financial independence of the biggest clubs.[1] Furthermore, the influx of this capital from BSkyB was central to the financing of the new consumption of football, since the new television moneys constituted a substantial form of financial assistance towards the reconstruction of the stadia demanded by the Taylor report.

The significance of the BSkyB contract went well beyond this fairly straightforward political economic effect, however, for this television contract was an important symbolic moment. In particular, BSkyB communicated notions of the free market which were central to the reformation of post-Keynesian British society. Thus the coverage of football on television was not simply an economic settlement of importance but a meaningful symbolic conjuncture in which football came to be irretrievably associated with free-market ideas since, it was broadcast by a satellite company which embodied Thatcherite ideals. As a ritualistic arena, football's transmission came to highlight those free-market ideas. Before discussing the meaningfulness of the BSkyB contract, a brief account of the eventual adoption of this contract by the Premier League is necessary, and this effectively concludes the account of the debates between the Big Five and the Bates–Noades axis which was given in Chapter 6.

The Vote for BSkyB

The Premier League was created to prevent the loss of income to the lower leagues which the top clubs had found increasingly intolerable throughout the 1980s, but the League was also established to maximize the bargaining position of the top clubs in their re-negotiation of a new television contract which was due in 1992. The decision in favour of BSkyB over the rival bid from ITV followed the Byzantine course which typified financial settlements in professional football in the 1980s, involving a complex compromise between the Big Five and the Bates–Noades axis.

In May 1992, the FA, which now administered the Premier League, invited television companies (ITV, BSkyB and the BBC[2]) to make secret offers for exclusive coverage of the new League which would be voted on by the clubs in a final meeting on 23 May. That meeting was surrounded in controversy, as it was widely alleged that Rick Parry informed Alan Sugar, the chairman of Tottenham Hotspur but also the owner of Amstrad,[3] that ITV had bid £262 million for exclusive coverage. BSkyB had not yet made its final bid but Sugar, concerned that BSkyB would be outdone, rang Murdoch's company and was heard to conclude his conversation with the memorable phrase 'get something down here quickly to blow them out of the water' (Chippendale and Franks, 1992, p. 322). BSkyB (with BBC) subsequently raised its bid to £304 million and was voted for by a majority of clubs.

The government played an important role in the eventual success of BSkyB's bid. ITV was furious about this deal, declaring that it did not accord with the standards of fair trading, and threatened to take BSkyB and the Premier League to the High Court. However, David Mellor, the new National Heritage Secretary, rejected calls for an inquiry (Chippendale and Franks, 1992, p. 323), arguing that Britain had to accept that commercial satellite broadcasting was here to stay and that there would be no intervention in the BSkyB deal (*Daily Telegraph*, 16 June 1992).

Within the context of the new Premier League, the choice of the BSkyB bid over the ITV bid was finally the decision of the Bates–Noades axis, as they enjoyed the balance of the votes. Fourteen clubs voted for BSkyB, six voted for ITV and two abstained.[4] The six clubs which voted for ITV were Arsenal, Everton, Liverpool, Manchester United (i.e. the Big Five clubs, except for Alan Sugar's Tottenham Hotspur), Aston Villa and Leeds United. These clubs favoured the ITV deal, as the terrestrial company, following previous practice, promised to concentrate on them, and so they would make the most money from the ITV deal, receiving the bulk of the substantial appearance money and benefiting indirectly from the increased sponsorship which more television coverage would command. Tottenham Hotspur voted for the BSkyB deal because Alan Sugar, the club's chairman, was more or less formally allied to Murdoch: Amstrad made satellite dishes for BSkyB. He declared his interest at the meeting but the Bates–Noades axis, which needed him on board in order to have a majority, supported the motion allowing him to vote.

Although the particularities of this deal are certainly interesting in and of themselves, the important thing about the deal in so far as this account is concerned is that it followed the course laid out in Chapter 6. The crux of the matter came down to a fraught compromise between the Bates–Noades axis and the Big Five, and, in this case, the Bates–Noades axis was successful. The Bates–Noades axis was resentful of the way in which the 1988 deal had been negotiated. In 1988, ITV had consulted only the Big Five, who had then been able to wring political economic concessions from the rest of the League as a result of this collusion. Ian Stott, the chairman of Oldham Athletic, revealed the bitterness with which the Bates–Noades axis viewed this deal and the fact that this bitterness had partially motivated the vote for BSkyB:

> It was certainly to their [the Big Five's] benefit when the television deal [with ITV in 1988] was done, of course. That scandalous side-letter television deal was done with the Big Five because they probably couldn't justify it and that was totally contrary to the spirit of the negotiations and one of the reasons why, in my view, ITV stood very little chance of getting the later contract – nobody trusted the fellow from ITV [Greg Dyke]. (Ian Stott, chairman of Oldham Athletic, personal interview, 21 June 1994)

The Bates–Noades axis' choice of the BSkyB contract was not motivated out of a blind sense of vindictiveness alone, however. The ITV deal and the subsequent coverage had robbed these clubs of a significant amount of revenue.

The vote for BSkyB was an attempt to redress that loss of revenue and the vast increase in television revenue which BSkyB offered to all the clubs was the critical factor in the support for their bid: 'As soon as the small clubs knew that 50 per cent of Sky receipts were to be shared equally between all the Premier League clubs, the deal was irresistible' (*Guardian*, 24 May 1992). The more equitable distribution of both revenue and coverage promised by BSkyB ensured that the satellite company gained the support of the financially weaker clubs of the Bates–Noades axis. BSkyB's strategy of promising the same downpayment to all the clubs and to provide at least some coverage for the lesser teams was a conscious plan designed to obviate the potential problems of gaining a balance of the votes:

> We think their [ITV's] strategy was wrong. They were guilty as ITV have been in the past of getting the contract and concentrating, perhaps, on the big five or six clubs and only giving coverage to those clubs. A lot of the other clubs in the old First Division didn't trust ITV. They thought it might be the same again – look after the big clubs. Their strategy was to woo the big clubs and hope that they would carry all the clubs. Our strategy was not that. We negotiated direct with the chief executive of the Premier League, Rick Parry, and we made certain promises, guarantees that we would share the coverage around. (Vic Wakeling, BSkyB, head of sport, personal interview, 24 May 1994)

The BSkyB contract was essential to the new consumption of football, because the new contract was a major source of finance for the required renovation work:

> The money which we put into football meant that the stadium improvements which were demanded by the Taylor Report – nothing to do with us – have been undertaken and the price of tickets, for the real fans who want to go to the game, has not gone through the roof. The clubs have been able to contain the price of all that development as well as paying wages and signing stars and stopping too many people going to Italy or wherever because they've used our money. If you were the bad old days of the BBC and ITV the money would not have gone up to the £304 million that has been quoted and the fans would be paying for all these improvements. Where else would they get the money from? (Vic Wakeling, personal interview, 24 May 1994)

Through providing a substantial part of the finances with which stadia have been rebuilt, BSkyB has assisted in transforming the game, but satellite television has also played a crucial part in announcing this transformation across the social formation. BSkyB's coverage has broadcast the new stadia to a wide football audience: 'What we have done by our coverage is to shown that stadia are safer, more comfortable places to go to on a Saturday afternoon or a Sunday afternoon or a Monday night' (Vic Wakeling, personal interview, 24 May 1994). Thereby, BSkyB has both contributed to the improvement of the perception and market position of football and also, through its coverage of the grounds, simultaneously communicated the meanings which informed the renovation of the stadia. Thus the coverage of football on satellite television has been symbolically important, because it now shows football which is played in a league and in grounds which are the expression of Thatcherite notions of the free market.[5] As we have seen in Parts II and III, free-market principles, which envisaged a solution to football's crisis in line with organic developments, have informed the move towards the Premier League and the new consumption of football in the 1990s. The communication of these free-market ideas by BSkyB's coverage of football was a significant symbolic moment which contributed to the establishment of a free-market hegemony, for the free-market meanings which football communicated, as an arena of meaning, were now beamed into front rooms and public houses across the nation.

Yet the meaningfulness of BSkyB's coverage of football has resided not only in the transmission of grounds and a league which embody free-market ideals. BSkyB is not merely a transparent medium which communicates meanings which are established elsewhere; the very political economic constitution and technology of BSkyB embody certain meanings and values. Consequently, through its transmission of football, the values which BSkyB itself expresses are irretrievably associated with the game. Unsurprisingly, BSkyB's political economic organization embodies those same free-market ideas.

Thatcherite Broadcasting Policy

Primarily, Thatcherite broadcasting policy was vigorously opposed to the licence fee and to the heavily regulated system of television broadcasting which had existed in Britain since the founding of ITV in 1955. In place of this she wanted to establish a free-market broadcasting system which centrally insisted upon the need to increase consumer choice.

At the simplest level, the demands for a free market in broadcasting were founded in a desire to stimulate economic growth in the broadcasting industry which would bring the obvious economic benefits of more employment, would assist business by providing more advertising space[6] and would also guarantee more revenue for the government in the form of tax. However, Thatcher's free-market broadcasting policy was heavily ideologically motivated. The duopoly of the BBC and ITV was incompatible with the principles which she regarded as essential to the regeneration of Britain. The BBC–ITV duopoly was symbolic of the post-war consensus, constituting a balance between the state (in the form of the licence fee) and the market (in the form of independent television). In particular, the licence fee was regarded by Thatcher as inappropriate to contemporary realities, since it was founded in Keynesian notions of universalism and paternalism whose supersession Thatcher regarded as essential. The licence fee was premised on the belief that every citizen in Britain should have access to the television, as every citizen had access to education, health care and welfare support, in return for a universal flat-rate charge whether that individual actually used that public service or not. For Thatcher, such a universal charge was inefficient, unfair on those who never intended to use that service (principally because they had money to spend in the private sector) and supported a middle-class public sector professional who, sheltered from the buffeting of the free market, developed unacceptable political views. In particular, Thatcher highlighted the importance of extending consumer choice, which she believed the licence fee limited. This commitment to choice was revealed in various policy statements by the government, over which Thatcher, herself, had much say:

> It [government] should enable, not dictate, choice. (Home Office, 1988, p. 5)

> Wherever possible the Government's approach to broadcasting should be consistent with its overall deregulation policy. It should help enterprises and meet the needs of consumers. (Home Office, 1988, p. 6)

For Thatcher, the licence fee symbolized all that was wrong with British television and, indeed, Britain more generally. It limited both entrepreneurial activity and consumer choice.

Sky Television and the Free Market

Significantly, Sky television drew on Thatcherite notions of the free market to define (and legitimate) itself. When Sky television was launched on 5 February 1989, the new station announced itself in significant terms: 'This is the television revolution! A revolution in quality! A revolution in quality and choice!' (Chippendale and Franks, 1992, p. 96). Furthermore, when Murdoch announced the launching of Sky television to the national press, he declared:

> We will be bringing for the first time real choice of viewing to the British and European public, particularly the British public. (*The Times*, 9 June 1988)

> We are seeing the dawn of an age of freedom for viewing and freedom for advertising. (*The Times*, 9 June 1988)

Sky television's concern with consumer choice was confirmed by Vic Wakeling, the head of sport at BSkyB, in a personal interview: 'Sky television is all about choice. It's about people who want to tune in and watch the news whenever they get in during the day or night. It's about people who want to watch a selection of movies' (Vic Wakeling, personal interview, 24 May 1994).

Perhaps Murdoch's most important statement of the meanings which he attached to Sky television and the ideals which he thought his new broadcasting company embodied were expressed in his McTaggart Lecture, 'Freedom in broadcasting', in August 1989, in which Murdoch demonstrated his support for the free market and its competitive pressures: 'Competition is much to be preferred to monopoly' (*The Times*, 26 August 1989). For Murdoch, British broadcasting was an effective monopoly which was therefore inefficient and reduced consumer choice. In place of that restrictive monopoly, Murdoch viewed his Sky television as a liberating force: 'Why should television be exempt from the laws of supply and demand, any more than newspapers, journals, magazines books or feature films?' (*The Times*, 26 August 1989). For Murdoch, then, television should be subject to exactly the same market pressures as publishing.[7] This pressure would produce more choice for the consumer because television companies, forced from the comfortable duopoly, would have to attract audiences or they would sink. Murdoch was convinced, or at least he wanted to convince others, that this competition would increase consumer choice because television companies would have to diversify and seek particular niches in the market, like publishing houses, in order to survive. For Murdoch, a multi-channel satellite future guaranteed better and more diverse programme quality.[8]

The fundamental transformation which Sky television embodied was a move away from the licence fee to payment by subscription. The licence fee was typical of the ethics which had informed the post-war settlement. It was a universal and relatively small payment which then ensured universal and free access to a public good at the point of delivery. However, the cost of that relative cheapness and universality was a (putative) lack of consumer influence over the productions; the relationship between the consumer and the BBC was indirect.

Subscription was founded on a different set of ethics, which were intimately related to Thatcherite thought and therefore in line with the direction of social transformation in the 1980s. The indirect relationship between the licence fee and the BBC was replaced by a direct payment to Sky corporation from the consumer. With Sky television, consumers decided what kinds of programmes they wished to watch and paid only for those programmes. They would not, as occurs with the licence fee (and with taxation more generally), pay for programmes which they would never watch. Free-market discourse insists that this system is not only fairer, as consumers pay only for what they receive, but is also economically more efficient. Through subscriptions, companies receive direct market information about which programmes or channels are successful. This also means that those channels which deliver the most subscriptions are also rewarded automatically with the biggest budgets. Sky television, then, consciously attempted to embody the principles of the free market, insisting that it offered greater choice and a greater say for consumers over the productions which they wished to consume; they could vote directly with their subscription fees.

Sky's subscription television, then, replicates wider free-market reformations, which have been typical in Britain throughout the 1980s and 1990s. However, the emergence of Sky television has done more than merely replicate wider transformations. Its emergence is emblematic and symbolic of those transformations, since Sky television embodies the values of the emergent hegemony. The important symbolic role which the television has played in this reformation of British society is revealed by the political importance which Thatcher herself invested in television. For Thatcher, it was important that Britain should have a broadcasting system which adequately reflected its social formation, since the television is a central element in the communication of society's interpretive framework.

Both Thatcher and Murdoch went to great lengths to establish the free-market credentials of Sky television. Murdoch insisted that the development of Sky television amounted to a revolution in British television, in which market forces opened up consumer choice for viewers who would be better placed to choose the kinds of programmes which they wished to view. This rhetoric was indissolubly associated with Sky television, but the relationship which the consumer has had with this new broadcasting company may be different and actually more complex than the free-market ideology envisages. There are serious questions, which emerge when we interpret Sky television's claims critically, over whether Sky television has extended competition in British television and whether it has extended choice for the consumer, and there has been extensive public debate about these issues. However, since Thatcherism has attained a hegemonic position in contemporary British culture, the interpretation of Sky television as the embodiment of free-market ideals has been allowed to triumph over counterclaims – although this triumph is continually contested and never conclusive.

Sky television's more or less successful construction of itself as an example of free-market values is important to the consumption of football in the 1990s, since its transmission of football has reinforced and widened the expression of free-market ideas in the 'metasocial commentary' around football. Sky television adds its own free-market meanings to those already embodied in the meaning and transmits these along with its broadcast of live Premier League football. The football fan might well reject Sky television's notion of itself but the viewer is nevertheless presented with persuasive free-market arguments which carry with them important social implications. The development of Sky television and its contract with football ensure that ideas of consumer choice and enterprise are central to debates in the ritual consumption of football.

The 1996 BSkyB Deal and the Confirmation of the Free Market

The contract which was signed between BSkyB and the Premier League in 1992 was for five years of coverage and was due to end in 1997. Consequently, in the summer of 1996, there was a new round of bidding for the Premier League contract. Having delivered four years of successful and lucrative coverage to the clubs, BSkyB had little difficulty in winning the contract in 1996, although it did face competition from the Mirror Group and Carlton Communications and United News and Media (*The Times*, 7 June 1996). Consequently, BSkyB raised its bid (with the BBC) from the £304 million of 1992 to £743 million for a further four years of coverage, through until 2001. It is unwise to speculate beyond this contract, but it would seem that BSkyB has ensured its coverage of football for the foreseeable future and that, therefore, the transmission of football will be irretrievably linked to ideas about the free market. Furthermore, the transformation of the clubs in the Premier League along free-market lines will be substantially aided by this huge influx of television revenue.

In addition to maintaining its control over the Premier League, BSkyB continued its imperialistic policy towards the coverage of sport on television by buying up the rights to the rest of the Football League, which meant in effect the coverage of the First Division (the old Second Division). After the 1992 deal, independent regional companies around England broadcast local First Division matches on Sunday afternoon in order to counter BSkyB's Premier League coverage. It is uncertain whether this had much effect on viewing figures for BSkyB, but it certainly meant that some viewers could choose not to buy a BSkyB dish and still watch live football on television. The purchase of the Football League contract will obliterate that avenue of choice when it comes into effect in 1998, rendering it ever more imperative for football fans to subscribe to BSkyB if they wish to see live football. Channel 4's popular coverage of Italy's Serie A will then be the only live football broadcast on a weekend on terrestrial television. BSkyB's purchasing of the rights to the Football League and the extension of its contract to broadcast the Premier League affirms the position of BSkyB as a major force in British broadcasting with an increasing stranglehold over sporting events.

Conclusion

The 1992 BSkyB contract was a crucial moment for the transformation of the top level of English professional football because it linked the game to Thatcherite developments: the new contract was a central means by which the renovation of the grounds was financed and, since these renovations were heavily informed by Thatcherite ideas, BSkyB, in effect, assisted in promoting these Thatcherite ideals into a central position in the ritual of football. BSkyB then communicated these new meanings through its week-long coverage of the game across the social formation. Furthermore, the satellite station was itself constructed in Thatcherite arguments as the embodiment of the very values which were central to those arguments. BSkyB itself, as a political economic organization, was interpreted as a free-market institution whose subscription fees introduced a new and improved set of relations between customer and the company. As we shall see in the following chapters, BSkyB's emphasis on the idea of the customer and of freedom of choice was entirely in line with the transformation of football more widely in the 1990s.[9]

Notes

1   The importance of the increased television revenue to the Premier League's growing financial independence is revealed by Deloitte and Touche's survey of professional football. Substantially as a result of increased television revenue, the Premier League's turnover constituted 62.4 per cent of the entire turnover of professional football in the 1993–1994 season, and this figure rose to 68.9 per cent in the following season (Deloitte and Touche, 1996, p. 8).

2   The BBC joined BSkyB, contributing a relatively small amount to BSkyB's offer in order to gain recorded highlights which would be broadcast on Saturday evenings on *Match of the Day*.

3   Alan Sugar and Rupert Murdoch were in close alliance over their mutual interest in satellite television and there has been some suggestion that Murdoch sponsored Sugar's takeover of Tottenham in 1991 in order to ensure that he had an effective vote in the Premier League through Sugar (*The Times,* 30 November 1992; Horrie, 1992, p. 263; Scholar, 1992, p. 344).

4   Extraordinarily, considering their vocal opposition to the Big Five throughout the 1980s, Ken Bates, the Chelsea chairman, and Ron Noades, the Crystal Palace chairman, were the two who abstained from this vote.

5   The cultural effect of the transformation of the coverage of football is important and is a clear line of research which sociologists of football would be well advised to explore, if the research is carried out in the rigorously theoretical manner suggested in Chapter 1. For a discussion of some aspects of the new coverage of football, see Taylor (1995).

6   Businesses lobbied strongly for more advertising space on television throughout the 1980s (*The Times*, 17 December 1984). For a longer discussion of the meaning of Sky TV, see King, 1998a.

7   The analogy between television and publishing was first drawn in the Peacock report into the licence fee (Home Office, 1986, p. 125).

8   Murdoch dismissed the often-made claim that extreme competition in television produced not better television but the reduction to the lowest common denominator, where companies rationally choose to broadcast cheap programmes (such as soap operas or game shows) because they are most likely to deliver the biggest audience for their cost.

9   As a general footnote to this entire chapter, it is worth commenting on an argument which has featured in the press that the BSkyB deal brought about the disenfranchisement of the football fan (e.g. *Guardian*, 23 May 1992); all-seater stadia have priced fans out of the grounds and the BSkyB deal threatened to price them out of watching live football on television. This argument exaggerates the extent of live television coverage of football in the 1980s. The first League game to be transmitted live was in 1983, and even after that date the number of games transmitted live was restricted.

11

The New Directors

In his contemplations on the Hillsborough disaster, Taylor (1989) noted the failure of progressive capital to become involved in football in the 1980s. The signal shift in the 1990s is that football has become a central site of commercial development for progressive and entrepreneurial capital in many regions of England. Significantly, this capital has been most obviously at work in those very areas which have suffered the worst as a result of economic restructuring and, in particular, the rapid and dramatic decline of manufacturing; in other words, the north of England. This transformation has been particularly striking in the north-east. Over the last five years, Newcastle United has completely rebuilt St James' Park, while Middlesborough and Sunderland have built entirely new grounds. The football club in these cities is increasingly becoming a central part of the economy of signs and space (Lash and Urry, 1994). Through capitalist investment, the football club has become a very important symbolic value which is sold on the post-Fordist market and which attracts capital to these regions. Significantly, the new grounds at Middlesbrough and Sunderland are situated on derelict docklands and the site of the now closed Wearmouth colliery, respectively, which were once the economic core of this region. The football club has become a capitalist enterprise which is increasingly replacing old forms of heavy industry with the production of new symbolic commodities which facilitate the creation of identity rather than the fulfilment of material function.

The Distinctiveness of the New Directors

The new directors are those entrepreneurs who emerged after the collapse of the post-war consensus and have, since the early 1980s, but more particularly in the 1990s, become involved in football, exploiting the meaningfulness of this ritual in English society for commercial ends. There are two principal defining features of the new directors and their involvement in football. The first is that the new directors operate in the interstitial markets at the regional level below that of the concentrated multinational companies, which has given the transformation of English football in the 1990s a distinctiveness in comparison with other European countries.[1] English football clubs have not been incorporated into larger capitalist companies. Rather, the new directors have merely added the football club to their capital interests or have put all – or a substantial part of – their capital into a single club. For the entrepreneurs who have become new directors, the football club is an independent and profitable business.

The business career of Alan Sugar and his involvement with Tottenham Hotspur Football Club, in north London, near where his original business was based and in the area in which he was brought up (Thomas, 1990), is instructive here. He achieved phenomenal business success in 1986 when he marketed a personal computer, the Amstrad PCW 8256, with which Amstrad gained a 60 per cent stake in the British home computer market (Thomas, 1990, p. 199; *The Times*, 1 January 1997), but after the collapse of the stock market on Black Monday in 1987, Amstrad's fortunes declined dramatically (*The Times*, 15 February 1992, 10 December 1992). Moreover, Amstrad has faced increasingly difficult competition from the global computer multinationals. As Amstrad has failed, Sugar has diversified his interests into football, buying the majority shares in Tottenham Hotspur in 1991 until, in 1995, Sugar announced his intentions to sell Amstrad completely and put all his business concerns into the football club. For Sugar, then, Tottenham Hotspur has become an independent business venture which has replaced Amstrad as his prime concern.

Although Sugar's route to Tottenham Hotspur has been complex, it is representative of the way in which entrepreneurs have looked to football clubs as regionally situated investment opportunities. From this fact follows a second crucial defining characteristic of these new entrepreneurial football directors. Since the football club is regarded as an investment opportunity in itself – a business operating in its own right in different niches from the multinationals – it is essential that the football club is profitable. Here the new directors in England are distinguishable from both their predecessors and from many football club owners in Europe. For the very reason that football clubs are integrated within larger capitalist interests in many parts of Western Europe, immediate losses are acceptable in the footballing subsidiary,[2] if the club provides the parent company with an international profile and assists in easing relations between capital and labour. Although it is the particularly innovative entrepreneurial figures, such as Hall, Sugar, Gibson, Dein and Edwards, who have insisted most forcefully that football clubs in the 1990s are profit-making businesses, many club directors who have administered clubs in a 'traditional' way in the past have adopted the strategies of the new directors and have accepted the central understanding of these businessmen that football clubs must be profit-making.

The 'Traditional' Chairmen

To appreciate the historical specificity of the new directors' project in football, it is necessary to be aware of the style of football proprietorship which was in existence before the new directors became involved in the game. Although I have entitled this style of administration 'traditional', this terminology should be treated with some care. As Hobsbawm and Ranger (1983) have demonstrated, the appeal to 'tradition' is more often than not an attempt to legitimate a contemporary and relatively recent practice by inventing a fictitious heritage for that practice. I will suggest below that the 'traditional' style of directorship might actually be historically specific to the period between World War II and the 1970s.

Traditional chairmen administered and financially assisted clubs out of a sense of obligation to provide a service for the city or town in which their business interests lay: 'A football ground was in many ways as much part of a burgeoning corporation as a public library, town hall and law courts and was certainly used by more people' (Inglis, 1991, p. 12). The traditional directors of football invested in clubs out of a similar notion of public utility which informed the capitalist class's funding of various public services, such as libraries, museums, parks and baths. For instance, Denis Hill-Wood, who went on to become chairman of Arsenal, created a League team in Glossop, his home town, in which he owned some mills, and his son, Peter, explained this creation of a football club as an example of bourgeois philanthropy: 'I suppose my father felt it was his duty to give the townspeople something. They had schools and a hospital, so I suppose he said he'd give them a football club' (Hopcraft, 1990, p. 153).

For traditional directors, the football club was a public utility and, in line with the logic of this provision of a public good, these directors did not regard the football club as an appropriate or possible site of capitalist accumulation. This unprofitableness of football was revealed by Peter Hill-Wood's remarks about the accession of David Dein, who, as I will argue below, was one of the new directors: 'Some rich men like to buy fast cars, yachts and racehorses but Dein is more interested in Arsenal. I'm delighted he is but I still think he's crazy. To all intents and purposes, it's dead money' (*The Sunday Times*, 8 August 1991). As the transformation of football in the 1990s has revealed, Dein was certainly not 'crazy' for investing money in football, and Hill-Wood's delighted incomprehension at the interest of a successful businessman in Arsenal neatly illustrates the decisive divide between traditional directors and the new directors.

Although the notion that football was a public utility in the past has become commonplace in historical and sociological accounts of the game (e.g. Taylor, 1984, p. 110; Fishwick, 1989, pp. 42, 150), I want to suggest that this tradition is, perhaps, somewhat fabricated. Although I cannot fully sustain the suggestion that the notion of the traditional director is invented, since the empirical evidence required for such an argument is beyond the remit of this book, it is possible to trace a different style of chairmanship at the beginning of the century. For instance, in the early years of the League there were complaints that football was 'too much of a business' (Inglis, 1988, p. 16), while William Macgregor (one of the architects of the League) 'paraded that fact with satisfaction' (Inglis, 1988, p. 19) and 'confirmed that professional football was an expanding, thriving industry' (Inglis, 1988, p. 19).

It would be unwise to read too much into this scanty historical evidence, but it does suggest that the so-called traditional style of directorship emerged in the twentieth century. Following Fishwick's claim that from the 1920s until the 1950s football could be seen as 'the Labour party at prayer' (Fishwick, 1989, p. 150), it might be suggested that the 'traditional' directorship of football clubs which saw the proprietorship of that institution as the non-profit-making provision of a public good could be linked more to the wider development of Keynesianism and therefore to the period between about the 1940s (perhaps 1930s) and the 1970s. In line with the Keynesian commonsense of the time, the 'traditional' directors consented to the corporatist redistribution of revenue across the League and believed that football should be, in effect, a public good which was cheap enough to be almost universally affordable. In this, they concurred with Alan Hardaker's views, which were outlined in Chapter 3.

However, whenever this style of directorship emerged, it came under serious assault in the 1980s from free-market arguments, as Chapter 8 revealed, although there had been complaints about the style in which these traditional directors ran clubs since the late 1950s, when the directors' own anachronistic and hypocritical attitude towards their players was revealed in the debates about the maximum wage and freedom of contract. In the 1980s, the pressure which was exerted on the traditional directors by the press was matched by the financial pressures discussed in Part II. These dual developments rendered the traditional directors' amateurish administration of football clubs inadequate and anachronistic. In the light of the demands for the reformation of the administration of the game and the replacement of the individuals who run it, the first representatives of the new directors began to emerge in football in the early 1980s.

The New Directors' Emergence in the Game

In 1982 the regulation which restricted the maximum dividend for any shareholder in a football club to 7.5 per cent was rescinded. This rule was designed to prevent clubs attracting unscrupulous owners who were concerned only with the profits of a club and thereby demonstrating that the Football League was more concerned that football should be a universally available public good than a profit-making industry. The Football League abandoned the rule in the face of recommendations from various reports and the demands from sections of the press which argued that the rule discouraged the very entrepreneurs who could most effectively assist the finances of football clubs from investing in them.

The abolition of the maximum dividend encouraged the investment of entrepreneurs because they could now hope to get a decent return on their shares. It was at this point, in the early 1980s, that Dein (Arsenal),[3] Edwards (Manchester United),[4] Bates (Chelsea)[5] and Scholar[6] (Tottenham Hotspur), who were all entrepreneurial businessmen, established themselves on the boards of major clubs. Significantly, the lifting of the maximum dividend transformed the football club from being effectively a privately owned public utility into a profit-making concern in its own right at a stroke. The pursuit of profit through the commodification of football was the distinguishing feature of the new directors and marked them out from their predecessors. Of course, many have failed to achieve this end and many clubs still have difficulty maintaining solvency.[7] However, that solvency, minimally, and profit-making, ideally, must be the aims of a football club has become the dominant understanding in the 1990s. This transformation of football clubs from effective public utilities into profit-making companies is fundamental to the comprehension of the new consumption of football in the 1990s.

That the profit motive is the decisive defining and differentiating feature of the new directors' involvement in football was revealed in the interviews I carried out with the directors of football clubs. Ian Stott, the owner of Oldham Athletic, had originally become involved in the club in the 1970s and had now moved all his capital interests into it; the club was now his full-time occupation (personal interview, 21 June 1994). The inference here is that his very livelihood was at stake if Oldham Athletic failed to make a profit. Ken Bates, the chairman of Chelsea Football Club, was typically outspoken about the need for football clubs to recognize that they had to make a profit, and he usefully distinguished himself from more traditional directors:

> I can remember arguing with the late chairman of Gillingham, Dr Grossmark. Again, fifteen, twenty years ago and he turned round and said, 'Oh, you don't understand football. It's not like any other business.' I said, 'That's rubbish'. I said 'The plumber down the road writes a cheque and there's not enough money in the bank and it will bounce.' I said, 'At the moment, you don't think banks will dare to do anything but one day they will, they will bounce your cheques. (Ken Bates, personal interview, 10 September 1994)

The belief that football is a business and must therefore prioritize profit-making (or at least solvency) is a practically universally held belief by the new directors[8] and this belief differentiates these entrepreneurs from their forbears at football clubs.

Although profit is central to most of the new directors, there have been examples where these directors' involvement in football has not been motivated out of a concern with short-term profit and, in this, these new directors are more similar to their European counterparts than to their English rivals. Sir John Hall, the chairman of Newcastle United, and Steven Gibson, chairman of Middlesbrough, are key examples of this kind of financial strategy, which does not prioritize immediate profit but regards the football club as part of a much larger and more integrated strategy of capital accumulation. I will discuss the specifics of their projects but, for now, it is necessary to note only that, although these new directors do not prioritize short-term profit, over the long term they are concerned with the profitability of their clubs, as we shall see below.

Furthermore, although these football clubs are themselves loss-making at the moment, their effectiveness as sign values for the new directors and sponsoring companies is that they connote profitability and wealth, *despite* this fact of immediate loss-making. Clubs like Newcastle United and Middlesbrough are able to embody the free-market principle of profitability because, unlike the traditional directors, Gibson and Hall insist that profit-making is the dominant norm. This false embodiment of an entrepreneurial norm which is central to the sign value of the clubs is very significantly assisted by the fact that other clubs in the Premier League do make substantial profits, and the profitability of these clubs effectively redounds onto Middlesbrough and Newcastle United, endowing them with a vicarious appearance of financial success. Effectively, the strategies of Hall and Gibbon are intended as self-fulfilling prophecies, where the communication of wealth and profitability (even in the absence of the latter) is intended to attract investment which will eventually ensure that profitability.

The New Directors in the 1980s

The project of the new directors in the 1980s was not generally unified or coherent. Only in the 1990s, after the Taylor report, have the new directors set about the serious reform of the game. This failure of the new directors in the 1980s can be explained by the fact that it was more logical to take a piecemeal approach to this reform in the 1980s than to take the risk of implementing expensive strategies individually, until compelled by the government after the Taylor report. In addition, after the disasters of 1985, football was financially disadvantaged by its poor public image. Consequently, there were insufficient funds in the game to finance the extensive reform which would be achieved in the 1990s.

However, although the cultural and economic climate of the 1980s was not conducive to the transformation of the game, the new directors realized that football was in need of reform (as various quotations in Chapter 6 revealed) but it was impossible in the context of the mid-1980s to late 1980s to implement these schemes fully. Indeed, those entrepreneurs who attempted to implement wholesale reform, forcing the pace of change beyond wider social conditions, and along the lines which would be undertaken in the 1990s, failed. Yet, although the new directors did not aim at the total reform of the game in the 1980s, their modest projects of reform were essential to the new consumption of football in the 1990s. The piecemeal projects of the new directors in the 1980s involved two particular strategies; the attempt to increase television revenue and the attempt to gain greater control over the football crowd.

Television Revenue

It is unnecessary to discuss this project at length, as Chapter 6 was almost solely concerned with the debates over television revenue in the 1980s. In that chapter, however, the debate between the Bates–Noades axis and the Big Five was highlighted as the dynamic which precipitated the development of the Premier League. Here, it is necessary to emphasize not the divide within the League *per se* but rather the fact that, whatever may have been the debates between clubs over the distribution of revenue, all the chairmen were unanimous in their determination that football should command a higher price than it had under the duopoly of the ITV and BBC.

Those new directors who presided over the Big Five clubs (Edwards at Manchester United, Scholar at Tottenham Hotspur, Carter[9] at Everton, Dein at Arsenal, Smith[10] at Liverpool), attempted breakaways throughout the 1980s and, as I have shown in Chapter 6, these attempts created the conditions for the eventually successful breakaway in 1991 with the establishment of the Premier League. Since the Premier League enabled all the First Division clubs to increase their incomes exponentially, with which money they could finance their self-transformation, the new directors of the Big Five clubs in the 1980s who had been instrumental in both raising the price of football on television and in creating the Premier League played a significant part in the eventual success of the new directors' project in the 1990s. Of course, these individuals did not intend to assist the projects of other chairmen, but their demands for a redistribution of football's revenues in the form of a breakaway league certainly aided those clubs involved in that breakaway to implement the necessary reforms.

Crowd Control and the Football Spectators' Bill

The new directors had two main responses to the problem of crowd control in the 1980s; the erection of fences and the opposition to Thatcher's national identity scheme. Both of these strands contributed to the development of the new consumption of football, albeit unintentionally. First, the installation of fences was a cheap and relatively easy method of limiting the worst excesses of crowd disorder inside grounds. However, it was also an extremely dangerous method of preventing pitch invasions, as the Hillsborough disaster demonstrated. Through the installation of fences, the new directors unknowingly facilitated the eventual new consumption of football in the 1990s, because the fences demonstrated that the terraces could not be made both safe and controllable. Consequently, the fences precipitated the eventual move towards all-seater stadia, since the latter seemed to be the only solution to hooliganism. It was ironic, then, that a strategy which the new directors adopted to minimize financial outlay on grounds should, in the end, ensure that the complete renovation of the grounds at quite astronomical expense was necessary.

Although the new directors did attempt to control the crowd through cheap and clumsy fencing, the most important contribution which the new directors in the 1980s made to the new consumption of football was to oppose the Football Spectators' Bill. Despite the new director's affiliation to Thatcherism, due to the ideological and practical political support which Thatcherism provided with its affection for free-market doctrine and policy, the new directors opposed Thatcher's attempted implementation of this authoritarian measure. It has already been suggested that, in general, Thatcher's demand for a strong state was not in conflict with her espousal of the free market; the strong state created the conditions for the free market and defended business interests against the unions. However, the proposal of a national identity card scheme was plainly against the interests of the new directors. The identity card scheme promised to reduce attendances at a time when attendances were already poor. Furthermore, the card scheme did not promise to rid the game of hooliganism for, as Lord Taylor noted, the scheme merely threatened to create congestion outside the grounds which would increase the likelihood of fan confrontation there.

In the 1980s, the new directors were among the most vocal of chairmen to oppose the Bill. For instance, Martin Edwards publicly condemned the scheme, citing the chaos at an FA Cup tie between Queens Park Rangers and Manchester United as an example of the effect which the scheme would have (*The Times*, 25 January 1989). Scholar was also vociferous in his opposition, giving a speech on 24 January 1989 to the Lords which highlighted the shortcomings of the scheme (*The Times*, 25 January

1989). He argued that the scheme would reduce attendances and increase disorder outside the ground, and added that the new Bill was superfluous in the light of the Public Order Act of 1986 (*The Times*, 25 January 1989). As we have seen, the national identity card scheme was finally condemned in the Taylor report, but the new directors' opposition to the scheme can only have assisted in that judicial rebuttal by contributing to a general sense of opposition to the scheme. In this way, the new directors assisted in establishing the free-market argument as the dominant interpretation which would inform the transformation of football in the 1990s.

The Visionaries

The new directors of the 1980s were generally pragmatic in their attempts to reform the game, attempting only piecemeal reforms which were designed to maximize the revenue of the game with the minimum of outlay. The fences were symbolic of the new directors' project in the 1980s – they were clumsy stop-gap methods of achieving some crowd control without ever resolving the root of the crowd disorder problem or of football's financial crisis. However, there were some new directors who attempted to apply coherent projects of reform to football, some of which would be adopted successfully in the more amenable cultural and financial environment of the 1990s.

Irving Scholar

Scholar attempted to transform Tottenham Hotspur as a football club along entrepreneurial lines, employing the marketing methods typical of progressive (post-Fordist) capital to improve the financial position of the club. The extent of Scholar's vision for the transformation of football was revealed in his speech at the launch of the Rothman's Football Yearbook in 1984, in which he laid out a series of radical but, in his eyes, wholly necessary reforms for football (Scholar, 1992, pp. 52–3). In line with the projects which he laid out in this speech, Scholar implemented three specific and original strategies to improve Tottenham Hotspur's financial position: the extension of the fan base, the public floating of the club and diversification.

Scholar employed Alex Fynn of Saatchi and Saatchi, the advertising company, to develop strategies by which Tottenham Hotspur might promote itself. Scholar had apparently been impressed by Fynn's work for the Health Education Council (Alex Fynn, personal interview, 11 August 1994) and hired Fynn to assist the club in marketing itself. In 1983, under Fynn's guidance, Tottenham Hotspur released the first ever television advertisement for League football when they broadcast a commercial which announced its first League match of the 1983–1984 season against Coventry City. The advertisement was particularly significant, since it explicitly promoted football as a potential leisure pursuit for those individuals who were not associated with the sport in the early 1980s. The advertisement attempted to attract the attention of potential fans other than the 'traditional' constituency of white, young, working-class males.

Scholar's second strategy was to float Tottenham Hotspur on the Stock Exchange. The initial share issue on 13 October 1983 was a success; 3,800,000 shares were sold at £1 each. Beyond the £3.8 million that this share issue raised, it was also meaningful in other ways. Symbolically, it announced the transformation of Tottenham Hotspur as a football club. The club, and by extension football itself, had become a business like any other in a way which Hardaker would have rejected completely. Tottenham Hotspur Football Club was subsumed under a purely financial holding company, Tottenham Hotspur plc (Horrie, 1992, p. 38).[11]

Finally, Scholar diversified into a range of leisurewear goods. In 1985, he signed a four-year deal with the leisurewear company Hummel for replica shirts and obtained the right to the franchise brand in the UK (Horrie, 1992, p. 100). Hummel expanded into leisurewear for adult football fans more generally and, in an attempt to brand this new commodity, Glenn Hoddle, the gifted Tottenham Hotspur player and now England manager, was persuaded to model the new garments (Horrie, 1992, p. 101). Tottenham plc also purchased two other clothing companies, Martex and Stumps, a ladies' fashionwear distributor and a cricket clothes manufacturer respectively. The plc's strategy of diversification, although in principle logical (and successfully implemented by Manchester United and Arsenal in the 1990s), was flawed. Hummel faced too much competition from Adidas and Umbro, which were already successfully established in the football leisurewear market (Horrie, 1992, p. 101), especially considering the poor market position of football in the 1980s. Furthermore, Scholar diversified into ranges of goods which the club was incapable of branding with its own distinctive identity, since these goods were not related to football.

The significance of Scholar's project lies in the fact that, while his specific first project of reform failed, the methods which he sought to implement were exactly those which *would* be successful in the 1990s; a new market for football, share issues and diversification (into leisure commodities). Scholar's failure demonstrates that the success of new directors was substantially determined by wider historical circumstances. In the 1980s, the financial position of football was so weak, due to its poor cultural position, that the ambitious strategies which Scholar sought to implement were unlikely to succeed; football itself was not yet an attractive commodity, ready for market expansion.

Maxwell and Bulstrode

Scholar was not the only casualty of the historical circumstances of the 1980s. David Bulstrode, the chairman of Queens Park Rangers, and Robert Maxwell, the chairman of Oxford but with links to Reading (and later chairman of Derby), also failed in their attempted merger schemes. In 1983, Maxwell attempted to merge Oxford and Reading into the 'Thames Valley Royals', while Bulstrode sought a similar amalgamation in 1987 of Queens Park Rangers and Fulham, whose ground his company, Marler Estates, owned. The merger scheme accorded with the logic of the free market; both teams were financially struggling but their amalgamation would both combine resources and enhance their support, since both sets of fans would theoretically be drawn to the new club:

> The two clubs had no alternative, with costs going up and neither side receiving sufficient support. Supporters must realise that they have to move with the times. I hope the new club, the Thames Valley Royals, could eventually get into the First Division and they will carry on the great traditions of Oxford and Reading. Otherwise, there will be no League football in this area. (Maxwell, quoted in *The Times*, 19 April 1983)

Bulstrode's justification for the merger of Fulham and Queens Park Rangers involved a similar line of argument based on financial viability:

> There are too many clubs chasing too many customers. The implication for football is the same for any business. (Bulstrode, quoted in the *Financial Times*, 28 February 1987)

> Fulham was going nowhere. This had been a working class area, people walked from their cottages to the game. Those cottages now sell for £250,000. There is no local following left. There is no football solution for Fulham. It has to be a property answer. (Bulstrode, *The Times*, 25 February 1987)

The proposed merger schemes foundered in the face of opposition from the fans[12] and the Football League itself.

However, the significance of these projects was that they drew on arguments which would inform the new consumption of football in the 1990s. The new directors in the 1990s would then use the free-market principles which Bulstrode and Maxwell employed to legitimate their projects. In particular, football was to become a business, in which clubs were subject to attrition, and fans were to become customers. Bulstrode and Maxwell took this free-market argument to its logical conclusion and sought to concentrate the capital of the football clubs through mergers. However, although Bulstrode and Maxwell were ahead of their times – their explicit appeal to the free-market discourse would become commonsensical in the 1990s – their project would still have failed in the 1990s, as it went against the fans' understanding of themselves too forcefully.

These radical new directors attempted to apply free-market projects to the reformation of the game. Although some of these strategies were to be successful in the 1990s, they failed in the context of the 1980s because these new directors attempted to implement particular conjunctural projects which were not privileged by organic conditions. Neither the interpretative framework nor the level of economic development had been reached at which the projects of Scholar, Bulstrode and Maxwell could be accepted.

The New Directors in the 1990s

The new directors consisted of those certain entrepreneurial individuals who had attempted piecemeal reformations in the 1980s and other individuals (such as Alan Sugar, Sir John Hall and Steven Gibson) who became involved in football for the first time in the 1990s, looking upon the game in a very different way from the traditional directors. Not every club had a change of clientele at the boardroom level in the 1990s, but the persistence of individuals who, in the 1970 and 1980s, might be regarded as 'traditional' does not undermine the case which is being put here. For the most part, even 'traditional' directors transformed their styles of management to bring them into line with the activities of the more dynamic new directors. For instance, Derek Dooley, the chief executive of Sheffield United Football Club, demonstrated a belief in the need to make football into a business (personal interview, 17 August 1994), even though he would not fit easily into the same category as entrepreneurial figures like Hall. Moreover, this self-transformation of traditional directors was especially notable at the large clubs in the top two divisions. Clubs at this level could not afford to look on themselves as public utilities which existed as islands washed by the tides of the free market. The project of the new directors involved three central and interrelated projects; the installation of proper club administration, the maximization of profit (along with the belief in the attrition of those clubs which were incapable of turning a profit) and the transformation of the fan into a customer. It will, of course, be noted that all three strategies featured as elements in the free-market discourse which had been expressed in response to the crisis of the mid-1980s to late 1980s.

Club Administration

As I have already argued, the fundamental project of the new directors was to transform the game into a business; football should no longer be run as a public utility but should make a profit. As we shall see below, this transformation of football into a business by the new directors has not been a purely instrumental matter, but rather the creation of profit-making clubs has depended primarily on the re-creation of the meaning of the club in the popular imagination. This interpretative change has involved the intervention of the press, the government and the judiciary in establishing a new framework of meanings which highlights the free market and, in particular, which successfully convinces the football fans that football is a profit-making business. In the following pages, some of this complex and interesting social negotiation over the meaning of the football club will be analysed but there have also been straightforward instrumental changes which have been important in the transformation of football and, in particular, in turning football into a business.

Primary among these instrumental transformations has been the reformation of the administration of the clubs in line with contemporary management practice:

> Football has to be a business. We have to pay the VAT. We have to comply with the Inland Revenue Regulations. We have to comply with the very sophisticated safety certificates and rightly so. There is as much skill at managing the football business today as there is playing on the pitch. (Robert Chase, chairman of Norwich City, personal interview, 18 October 1994)

> I think you have to [think of football as a business]. I mean, I think that has probably been one of the problems with clubs over the years. They've been growing and growing and still been treated very much as the football industry. But West Ham is a £9 million turnover business. That is a reasonable size business. That is not a small business anymore. That has to be run professionally. You have to get all your income levels. (Peter Storrie, managing director of West Ham United, 25 July 1994)

Since football is business, clubs have to be run in accordance with contemporary management practice. The renovation of club's administrations to bring them into line with contemporary management practice has involved the transformation of the club's financial arrangements. These financial arrangements have been transformed on two levels. First, the revenue of the club is more closely accounted for; professionals, usually accountants, have often been employed on a full-time basis to oversee these finances. For example, Manchester United appointed Robin Launders, a fully qualified accountant, as finance director. Second, at the level of the board, the club has also transformed itself in accordance with modern business practice. Traditional boards which featured chairmen and major shareholders have often been formalized, so that clubs now have chief executives, chairmen and managing directors in line with company practice. Although the reform of clubs' administrations is initially instrumental, the appearance of new, formal bureaucracies within clubs has an important interpretative role, for it announces that clubs are now profit-making businesses and thereby, in effect, legitimates the very state of affairs which new forms of administration were designed merely to assist technically.

Methods of Accumulation

The purpose of the reform of club administration has been to maximize profits. Poor administration resulted in costly financial inefficiency which no club could afford in the competitive political economy of the 1980s and 1990s, but proper administration cannot in and of itself ensure the financial viability of the clubs, but can only prevent the wasteful loss of revenue which the club is earning from other sources. The transformation of the clubs into profit-making concerns necessitated the introduction of new techniques of accumulation as well as the development and extension of old methods of money-making. The increased capital accumulation from these developed sources would then be efficiently processed by the reformed administration of the clubs to maximize that new revenue.

One of the primary elements of the new profit-making ethic was that clubs should be independent of each other. They should be allowed to develop their own strategies of accumulation. Ken Bates was explicit about the need for financial independence.

Now the moment you said that home clubs could keep their own gates then that meant that every club could run their business according to the way they thought best. Some people let unemployed people in, some people don't, some people do special deals with schools, others don't. You can vary your prices. For example, Chelsea did lead in one thing which is 'eventing'[13]; i.e., we charge more if Manchester United or Arsenal come to the game, come to here, than if you want to watch Ipswich or Coventry. People pay more for Barbara Streisand than Barbara Dickson. Same principle. But it means that every club can run their business accordingly, it also means they can adapt to their local community or area more than if you legislate at the national level. (Ken Bates, personal interview, 10 October 1994)

For Bates, the clubs' financial independence is crucial to the new directors' project of making football profitable, for that autonomy liberates the clubs, presenting the opportunity of developing their own strategies for maximizing income. Significantly, Bates' approval of financial independence must also mean that not only are clubs free to adopt strategies which will maximize their profits but they must also be free to go out of business if they fail to make profits. To sustain loss-making clubs would involve the redistribution of revenue from profit-making clubs, and such redistribution would imply that clubs are not free to make profit but are constrained by the need to support others. Bates implies this attrition of loss-making clubs in the statement quoted above, when he warned Dr Grossmark that the banks would foreclose on clubs in the future. For Bates, it is essential that clubs make a profit. Otherwise, they are dependent on the uncertain goodwill of the bank.

In Chapter 9, I questioned Taylor's belief that the transformation of the grounds into all-seater stadia was possible within a social democratic framework of public provision. The cost of this rebuilding work was simply too high for admission prices to be restricted in the manner which Taylor cited at Glasgow Rangers, and this is borne out by ticket price rises in the 1990s. For instance, at Manchester United the price of season tickets increased exponentially with the demolition of the large standing terrace, the Stretford End. Thus the cheapest season tickets for seats at Old Trafford in the K-Stand rose from £110.50 in the 1990–1991 season to £228 in the 1992–1993 season (at the end of which season the new all-seater West Stand, formerly the Stretford End, was completed). This rise in prices was partly justified by the cost of the building work, but Martin Edwards and the board at Manchester United (and the new directors who were implementing similar increases at other clubs) justified this quite extraordinarily rapid increase in prices on the grounds that the demolition of standing terraces necessarily reduced capacity, thus reducing the gate revenue which a club might earn. The increased price of each seat was intended to offset this reduction in the numerical capacity of the ground. In addition, and more importantly, the increased prices have been justified because the facilities, which were recommended by the Taylor report, were now clearly better than the basic services which had formerly been offered to football fans. The new directors' reconstruction of the grounds, although in line with the recommendations of the Taylor report, was informed by a very different ethos from the spirit of Taylor's report. Whereas Taylor operated with social democratic sensibilities, according to which universality of provision was important and the inclusion of the poor necessary, the new directors saw the enforced transformation of the stadia as an opportunity to extract greater revenue from the attending fan in line with free-market thought. Although at its most extreme at Manchester United, this explicit policy of using increased ticket prices as a form of increasing capitalization is typical throughout the entire Premier

Table 11.1 Increases in admission prices at clubs which have been in the Premier League

Club	Average admission (£) 1988–1989	Average admission (£) 1994–1995	Percentage increase
Arsenal	6.71	11.92	77.6
Aston Villa	5.39	9.72	80.3
Blackburn Rovers	3.64	10.15	178.8
Bolton	3.10	6.83	120.3
Chelsea	7.30	13.48	84.7
Coventry City	5.72	9.25	61.7
Crystal Palace	6.15	12.50	103.3
Derby County	5.09	6.39	25.5
Everton	4.79	9.71	102.7
Ipswich Town	4.05	9.03	122.9
Leeds United	4.27	9.07	112.4
Leicester City	4.35	10.08	131.7
Liverpool	5.41	10.89	101.3
Manchester City	3.94	7.87	99.7
Manchester United	4.71	16.06	240.9
Middlesbrough	4.48	6.53	45.8
Newcastle United	4.50	12.48	177.3
Norwich City	5.26	9.41	78.9
Nottingham Forest	5.18	9.10	75.7
Oldham Athletic	3.60	9.03	150.8
Queen's Park Rangers	5.82	9.39	61.3
Sheffield United	3.91	6.88	75.9
Sheffield Wednesday	4.50	9.17	103.8
Southampton	4.97	11.95	140.4
Sunderland	4.08	7.12	76.5
Swindon Town	4.35	8.67	99.3
Tottenham Hotspur	6.55	14.25	117.5
West Ham United	6.15	11.26	83.1
Wimbledon	5.77	9.08	57.3

Source: Football Trust (1991, Table 2.4, p. 28; 1996, p. 30)

League (see Table 11.1) and, indeed, throughout professional football. It is at this moment with the development of new facilities at the grounds and the concomitant increase in ticket prices that the notion of the customer has become a central political concept for the new directors, which I shall examine critically below.

Although the revenue derived from gate receipts is clearly very important financially, gate revenue has constituted a declining proportion of the football clubs' revenue with the development of sponsorship but more particularly the growth of television coverage and revenue. In addition to the increasing importance of television and sponsorship revenue to the top clubs, issues which have been discussed in Chapters 6 and 11, the new directors have also sought to expand the range of activities from which the club can raise revenue.

Diversification has been one of the commonest strategies for increasing a club's profits and has involved the retailing of commodities (especially clothing), branded with the club's name or crest. In the 1990s, replica shirts have been the most lucrative strand of diversification for clubs.[14] In branding their commodities with the club's emblem, clubs are effectively providing the fans with the right to consume the symbolic value of the club, but in order to exploit that symbolic value, the club has had to ensure its exclusive rights over it. For example, Manchester United has registered its own name as a trademark in order to establish its property rights over products which draw on the club's identity, to ensure the maximization of profit from such products, by reducing the loss of revenue to independent businesses which, in the past, have used the club's name on T-shirts and other merchandise. In line with this proprietorial concern, Manchester United has made it increasingly difficult for independent traders to operate in the environs of the ground. Thus, the club has franchised certain stall-holders along the Warwick Road to sell official Manchester United merchandise, while unlicensed salesmen are removed from this street and Manchester United's trademark rights are rigorously enforced (Danny Macgregor, personal interview, 19 August 1994). By enforcing its trademark, Manchester United has improved the profitability of its diversification strategies.

The attempt by the new directors to make football clubs profitable has involved grander schemes than merely seeking new ways of increasing the revenue through better administration and diversification. Some of the new directors have employed football as part of a much broader capitalist project, of which football is but a part – albeit a crucial symbolic part. These grand capital projects have been exemplified by the investments of Sir John Hall at Newcastle United and Stephen Gibson at Middlesbrough. Hall's development company, Cameron Hall, has invested some £26 million for ground renovations and an estimated £40 million to £50 million on players at Newcastle United (Williams, 1996, p. 28). There is clearly going to be no immediate financial return on this huge investment. Rather, Hall has employed Newcastle United as a symbol of north-eastern identity and cosmopolitanism designed to attract international capital into Tyneside:

> They say you can't regenerate the UK by shopping centres alone. But you can break into the manufacturing decline of an area by making it an attractive area. Industries won't come just because Geordies are nice people. You have to present them with ambience, lifestyle. (Cited in Gardner and Sheppard, 1989, p. 41)

Newcastle United is being employed by Hall, along with the very large shopping mall, the Metrocentre, which Hall also built, to demonstrate to international capital that Newcastle is an affluent, thriving city in which capital can be invested with a good chance of a return. Hall seems to have been successful in this, as Samsung, the large Japanese electronics company, has decided to set up its European operations on Tyneside, very much due to Hall's intervention (see Williams, 1996, p. 26).

Hall, then, is more radical in his project than the other entrepreneurs involved in English football in the 1990s. By employing Newcastle United as a symbolic representative of the economic and social vibrancy of the area, Hall intends to regenerate Tyneside through attracting international capital which will expedite his own regional, business project there. Hall's use of Newcastle United as a symbol of north-eastern cosmopolitanism and affluence accords with Lash and Urry's (1994) argument that in post-Fordist economies of signs and space, the central economic value is no longer use or exchange value but what they call sign value; that is, commodities whose worth is decided by the identities which they are able to provide. At the same time, it should be recognized that Hall has in no way ignored the strategies adopted by other new directors. For instance, he has increased the club's turnover from £4 million in 1991 to £40 million in 1995, £8.5 million of which is derived from the sale of merchandise (Williams, 1996, p. 30).

Interestingly, in the same region, Stephen Gibson has transformed Middlesbrough along very similar lines to those of Hall.[15] Gibson has invested substantially in the club which has also been dependent on some more or less covert underwriting from the chemical giant (and major local employer) ICI, which is a majority shareholder in the club, is represented on the board (by George Cook), and also formally sponsors Middlesbrough Football Club. Gibson is well positioned for this mediating role, as he used to work for ICI and now has close business contacts with the corporation through his haulage firm, BulkHaul, which specializes in the transportation of dangerous chemicals, especially for ICI.

However, although both Gibson's company BulkHaul and ICI are hugely successful businesses in their own right, Middlesbrough Football Club operates at a loss, due to extravagant dealings in the transfer market, which have included the purchase of 1994 World Cup star Juninho in 1995 and the Italian player Ravanelli in 1996. The acceptance of this running loss by both Gibson and ICI seems to be explicable on two counts (beyond Gibson's own undoubted fanaticism for Middlesbrough). First, the heavy investment into football in the mid-1990s can be seen as a rational strategy of capital speculation. With the influx of hugely increased television revenue for Premier League football through the BSkyB contracts in the 1990s and the promise of much greater rewards if a club is successful enough to compete in Europe, Gibson and ICI might have these long-term rewards in mind, and without accepting initial investment losses, the club (and, therefore, Gibson and ICI) would never have a chance of the kind of rewards offered by the Premier League and European competition. It is likely that Gibson and ICI may be speculating to accumulate.[16]

There is also certainly a second strategy at work which parallels Hall's own project at Newcastle United. Gibson and ICI, in particular, have invested in Middlesbrough not as a profit-making business in itself but rather as a crucial symbolic part of a more integrated strategy. The success of Middlesbrough Football Club creates sign value for Middlesbrough as a city, situating that city in the global economy. In particular, the new Riverside Stadium, which is significantly situated on the once derelict docks which were traditionally the heart of this city's economy, communicates the rejuvenation of the region and the development of new (post-Fordist) service industries which sell sign values. The new Riverside Stadium, like the new St James' Park, communicates an 'ambience' about Middlesbrough. The creation of a successful football club is beneficial for ICI, because not only does it communicate their name, as the formal sponsors of the club across the globe, but the club makes the region more attractive, facilitating the employment of the best staff at ICI and encouraging international capital to invest in the area. The use of Middlesbrough Football Club as a sign value suggests that some new directors are using football clubs as part of an integrated strategy of capitalist accumulation.[17]

The Creation of the Customer

The concept of the customer has become particularly important to the new directors in the 1990s as they have attempted to transform the clubs into profit-making institutions. Ken Bates, for instance, revealed this importance in his thinking about football:

> The customer in any business pays for what he gets. I've been converted to all-seating. I mean the working class no longer go to Blackpool for their holidays, they go to Spain or Madeira and Phuket and the Caribbean they go on cruises. They no longer have Blackpool rock and cloth caps and handkerchiefs on their heads and their stockings rolled up while they're packing in to Brighton. And the other thing is that when they go to the pictures, the working class, they don't go in and stand in the rain with water running down the back of their fucking neck with their cloth cap and a muffler. They go into a warm place where they can sit down. Somewhere to hang their coats up. They can get a cup of coffee or an ice cream or pop corn or whatever and they sit down in two or three hours comfort. (Ken Bates, personal interview, 10 October 1994)

In line with the argument out forward in various parts of the press in the 1980s, for Bates the football fan has had to become a customer. As his eloquent and amusing statement reveals, the customer, for Bates, refers to those individuals in contemporary society who pay more for the goods and services which they consume but who purchase better-quality goods. As Bates demonstrates, this increase in price and quality is linked with quite profound social and cultural changes which go back to the development of affluence in the late 1950s at least. The customer is, then, a historically specific figure in post-Fordist Britain who pays more for better services.

In addition to referring to a more affluent individual capable of paying more for football, the concept of the customer also refers to the fact that an increasing number of individuals taking up these improved and more expensive services will be women[18] and, indeed, whole families. For instance, Peter Storrie (personal interview, 25 July 1994) argued that 'Football is moving towards the family model. There is a strong basis to go forward if we push the family idea.' Robert Chase (personal interview, 18 October 1994) confirmed the need to attract women and families: 'It's life. Women have a greater role in the world than they had in the past. They are 50 per cent of the market. Isolate yourself or improve your facilities.' The improvement of their facilities in order to create a customer relationship with their fans aims at increasing the attendances of women and of whole families at football. By attracting women and families to the ground by turning fans into customers, the new directors will extend the market for football and thereby improve its finances.

At the same time, however, the new directors' use of the notion of the customer effectively endorses and envisages the exclusion of the poor in the same way as the press's use of this concept did. Although the price of tickets has become high for the single fan, to fund the attendance of an entire family (or even part of a family) at a football match in the 1990s renders the attendance of the unemployed or marginally employed impossible. The attraction of affluent families through the improvement of facilities and the concomitant increase in prices necessarily implies the exclusion of poorer sections of society from an important public ritual, in which identities, solidarities and social debates are expressed, but the concept of the customer makes this political exclusion of the post-Fordist periphery appear neutral.

Not only does the attempted introduction of new affluent families to football under the concept of the customer imply socially exclusionary strategies, but the idea of the family as the new customer has also suggested a new method of disciplining the crowd. In this, the notion of the customer, although originally embedded in the free-market discourse, also effectively connects with important authoritarian strands of which Ian Taylor wrote (Taylor, I., 1989). Robert Chase (personal interview, 8 October 1994) has made this disciplinary aspect of the notion of the customer explicit.

In any business, in any walk of life, you have to say sometimes to your customers, 'I'm sorry, you're abusing the service that I'm providing, if you're not prepared to mend your ways or to conduct yourself in a better or more reasonable manner, the service will cease.' Take, for example, the bank. If you open an account and you don't stick to the rules, the manager generally writes to you nicely. The second time, he rings you up and says, 'I think you ought to come and see me' and the third time, he closes the account.

The free-market model carries with it disciplinary implications but, significantly, the free-market argument obviates political debate about these implications. The free-market argument, which Chase uses here, reduces the relationship of the fans and the club to a purely economic one, given by the market. Political debate about the nature of this relationship is, therefore, effectively sidestepped, since the rules which govern market relations are all but commonsensical. Drawing on the market principle, that the owner of a private service must be free to refuse to serve a customer, Chase therefore concludes that football clubs must be equally free to refuse entry to those who go beyond the rights prescribed by the market or who simply cannot afford entry. The political dimension of the issue of discipline is effectively repressed, as the argument is flattened to an economic issue.

Although the seriousness and unacceptability of much of the behaviour on the terraces since the 1960s cannot be ignored (Taylor, I., 1989), the strategy by which the new directors seek to transform this behaviour by reducing political and social issues to economic ones (which are much more difficult to dispute) is significant. In particular, Chase's commonsensical appeal to the analogy of a bank assumes that football clubs are now suddenly private institutions and that, therefore, the rules which frame relations in the market for private services are automatically applicable to football. Yet the crucial assumption that the football club is a private service (to which free-market concepts like the customer are applicable) has not been established through public debate but merely taken as an *a priori* fact by the new directors. Although it is all too easy to accept this assumption, because it is in line with the free-market commonsense which has become dominant in Britain since 1979, this privatization of the football club is a new and radical departure. The traditional directors, as we have seen, viewed profit-making domains but rather as public institutions whose purpose was the provision of an inclusive public good to the working population. Taylor (1971) probably overstated the case when he argued that, traditionally, football clubs were participatory democracies – fans have never had formal entry to the board's decision – but these clubs were democratic in their provision of the leisure service they offered. Entry to the ground was sufficiently cheap to be potentially universally affordable. The notion of the customer is intrinsically bound up with the privatization of the football club and the reduction of the social relations between fans and club to a purely and formally economic one. This reduction has not only facilitated and legitimated the transformation of the football club into a capitalist enterprise but it has undermined the potential for political protests by the fans. According to the market model which the new directors are attempting to implement, the only valid form of protest in the market is the withdrawal of custom, but that is exactly what the fans are protesting against.

The Inadequacy of the Concept of the Customer

Sociological research (Tomlinson and Whannel, 1986, p. 120; Bromberger, 1993, pp. 90–1) and football fan autobiographies (e.g. Hornby, 1992) have emphasized that football fandom is centrally bound up with the process of social identification. Since fans express their identities and self-understandings through the club and, therefore, simultaneously define themselves in terms of football, their attachment to the football club is peculiarly strong. Their consumption of football is radically different from that of the consumer of domestic goods, who will merely go to the cheapest or most convenient shop. Indeed, even in comparison with the fans of pop bands, the football fan shows remarkable monomania. Most fans of pop bands own the records of other bands or see other bands playing, while the dedicated fan of a football club will exclusively attend the matches of that club and purchase only that club's merchandise.

In addition, the consumption of football is curious in a second but equally important way. The standard economic model of the consumer envisages that figure purchasing a commodity at a shop and then using that product away from the shop at a later time. The shop provides the commodity and the service at the time of purchase, and it is for this that the consumer pays. The consumption of football differs significantly from this conventional model, for the football fan does not simply purchase what the club presents to the fans. The commodity which fans buy is not confined to the players whom they watch; the fans also purchase the atmosphere which they themselves create in watching the match. Paradoxically, at the football match, the fans are asked to purchase what they themselves actively and imaginatively create: the spectacle of support. In his account of his life as a fan, Nick Hornby recognizes this interesting feature of football:

> atmosphere is one of the crucial ingredients of the football experience. These huge ends are as vital to the clubs as their players, not only because their inhabitants are vocal in their support, not just because

they provide clubs with large sums of money (although these are not unimportant factors) *but because without them nobody else would bother coming.* (Hornby, 1992, p. 77)

The fans are an integral part of the commodity which the new directors ask them to buy as customers.

The football fan's relationship to the club, although at one level monetary, is complex and much richer than the unidimensionality of the market transaction. The close identification which the fans have with the club, the extraordinary loyalty which they generally demonstrate and the fact that they are an integral part of the very commodity which the new directors seek to sell suggest that the fans' relations to the club cannot be adequately theorized within the confines of conventional economic understandings. Football is a curious product, and fans are extraordinary consumers.[19] Yet the concept of the customer reduces the totality of this complex and significant social process to the greyness of standard economic concepts. The new directors flatten out the interpretative aspect of fandom and the vital and active contribution that the fans make to the commodity.

This flattening out of a complex relationship which implies mutual indebtedness beyond the scale of normal economic transactions is convenient for the new directors, for, by attempting to reduce their relationship with the fans to a purely economic one, they can deflect attempts by the fans to actualize their special relations to the clubs by means of a formal political relation. The concept of the customer has been central to the transformation of clubs into businesses, because this concept has legitimated the increase in admission prices. Simultaneously, by attempting to reduce the relationship between fan and club to a purely economic one, the notion of the customer serves the useful political purpose of making this socially exclusive process seem benign and commonsensical and of ruling any fans' protests about higher prices out of court *a priori*.

The conscious attempt of new directors to obviate the inconvenience of public, political debate is evinced by the experience of the chairman of Newcastle United's independent supporters' association, Kevin Miles. He related how in 1995, in a public debate on local radio with Freddie Fletcher, the chief executive at Newcastle United, the latter had dismissed Miles' suggestion that fans should have some representation on the board of the club. Fletcher asked Miles where he shopped, to which Miles replied that he shopped at Safeways. Fletcher then asked Miles whether he wished to be on the board of this supermarket, since he was a customer there, or whether such a demand would be considered legitimate by Safeways. In other words, Fletcher explicitly drew an analogy between the football club and its fans and the supermarket and its customers as the appropriate (economic) model to which the relation between fan and clubs should accord. Demonstrating the inadequacy of this purely economic model to the fans' consumption of football, Miles replied ironically that he did not spend his weekends and evenings visiting 'away' stores, nor did he possess a Safeway's away strip (Miles, personal interview, 10 September 1996). The special attachment and dedication which the fans demonstrate for their clubs demands the recognition of the social and political relationship of the fans and club in place of a flat, formal economic ideal.

The concept of the customer echoes the eighteenth- and nineteenth-century bourgeoisie's classical division of politics and economics, whereby they hoped to exempt themselves from the interferences of state legislation. Through the notion of the customer, the new directors have attempted to reduce their relationship with the football fans to a purely economic transaction. As Bates says, 'the customer gets what he pays for'. For the new directors, this is all they are willing to give to the customer; the only rights which they are willing to concede are economic ones of non-purchase. The concept of the customer conveniently rules out *a priori* any serious political intervention the fans might have in the administration of the football club.

Yet, despite the inadequacies of the concept of the customer with respect to the experience of fans and to the fans' relationship with the football club, the idea of the customer has become commonsensical in discussions about football in the 1990s. Since football is a major public ritual in contemporary Britain, the establishment of this concept at the core of 'metasocial commentary' about the ritual is important. In English football in the 1990s, fans are increasingly being asked to think of themselves as customers, echoing the much wider transformation of social relations in post-Fordist, Thatcherite Britain, where the idea that the primary form of social relationship is a purely economic or market one has become increasingly dominant. As a focus of public attention and imagination, the successful expression of the concept of the customer through football contributes to this hegemony, since it is through the game that we tell ourselves stories about ourselves. Increasingly, we tell tales about ourselves as customers whose social relations are mediated by the market, as the Thatcherite hegemony suggests. The employment of the concept of the customer in football is an important symbolic moment. Furthermore, the use which the new directors have made of the concept of the customer has also been important to the new consumption of football, since it has helped the clubs to increase ticket prices. Finally, the concept of the customer conceals the social significance of its implications through its apparent banality. It is in the very fact that the concept of the customer does not seem controversial, or even political at all, that its power lies.

The Success of the Second Wave

Although, as we shall see in the following chapters, the project of the new directors has been contested, it has at the same time been substantially implemented, so that football has undergone a radical transformation in the 1990s. The success of the second wave cannot merely be put down to the self-evident superiority of its project over the first wave's attempts at reform. For instance, Scholar attempted to implement a very similar strategy of reform in the game in the 1980s. Rather, the success of the second wave was facilitated by the wider social conditions in which the new directors operated in the 1990s.

The new directors' project of reform was closely linked to Thatcherite ideas of the free market. Consequently, the hegemonic establishment of Thatcherism as the dominant framework over British society by the 1990s legitimated the new directors' transformation of the game. In particular, the dominance of Thatcherism substantially assisted in confirming the new directors' belief that the game was now a business, although, as we shall see in the following chapters, the idea that fans have become customers has been partially resisted.

In addition, since Italia '90 and the Taylor report, football has attained a new cultural position and is increasingly attractive to the classes at the core of post-Fordist society. Thus, the new directors' attempts to reform the game were more likely to be successful in the 1990s, for, whereas Scholar attempted to widen the appeal of the game at a time when it seemed irredeemably wedded to the poor white male, the second wave's project coincided with a renewal of the game. This coincidence was not accidental, as many of the new directors (Sugar, Hall, Gibson), invested in the game in the 1990s after Italia '90 and the Taylor report. Unlike Scholar, they timed their project to coincide with an improvement in football's market position. Indeed, Sir John Hall has been explicit about the minimal attraction which the sport had for an entrepreneur before the 1990s: 'I never wanted to own a football club. Football is a bankrupt sport. A few years ago it was held together and still is, to a large degree, by the banks' (Naughton, 1996, p. 3). Hall, then, has recognised the historically specific financial and symbolic potential of football in the 1990s, although he is still realistic about the financial problems which face the sport. The huge BSkyB contracts have assisted in all this by providing funding for the necessary renovations of the stadia and broadcasting these transformations across the nation.

Finally, the organic transformation of football from the 1960s was crucial to the eventually successful implementation of the new directors' projects. In particular, the organic development of football necessitated the radical restructuring of the game by the mid-1980s. The development of the Premier League, which was the form that restructuring took, improved the market position and solvency of the top football clubs by increasing their television revenue and enabling them to maximize their own income by making each club more financial by independent. This new political economy contributed to the success of the new directors in the 1990s, because it funded their remarketing of the game. As Scholar demonstrated, the transformation of football into a thriving industry oriented to free-market values, before the creation of a new political economy for the game, was doomed to failure.

Conclusion

In line with the theoretical orientation of this study, I have emphasized that the new directors' transformation of football involves not simply an objective application of policy but rather the re-negotiation of the meaning of football. The new directors have, above all else, had to establish the legitimacy of profit-making as the clubs' central meaning and, following from this, the new directors have had to transform the relationship between fans and the club. Such a transformation can only be achieved through altering the way in which individuals understand themselves and, in particular, making fans see themselves as customers; a process which involves contestation and negotiation. Furthermore, the transformation of the meaningfulness of football (from public utility to profit-making business) is not only significant to the re-negotiation of the social relationship between fans and clubs but is central to the establishment of free-market principles as culturally hegemonic within post-Fordist society.

Notes

1 Many large European clubs had been bought up and integrated by multinational capitalist interests. For instance, Juventus and PSV Eindhoven are integrated with Fiat and Phillips respectively, while Olympique Marseilles and AC Milan have been integrated with the television companies of their respective owners, Bernard Tapie and Silvio Berlusconi (Duke, 1991, p. 634).

2 For instance, 'it is widely accepted that all Italian and Spanish Clubs run on huge deficits' (Inglis, 1992, p. 51).

3 David Dein, who joined the board of Arsenal in 1983, was a very successful commodity broker in the City, specializing in sugar.

4 Martin Edwards became chairman of Manchester United in 1980, after the death of his father, Louis. He sold his father's meat business in the early 1980s and invested all his money in the club; since his takeover he has sought to promote the financial strength of the club.

5 Ken Bates had previously been the chairman of Oldham Athletic (1965–1970) and Wigan Athletic (in the late 1970s) and rescued Chelsea from the financial ruin threatened by the construction of the East Stand undertaken

by the 'traditional' Mears family. Bates made money from quarrying gravel in Lancashire, but then reinvested this capital in sugar in Australia, land reclamation in the West Indies and a dairy farm in Buckinghamshire (*The Times*, 9 April 1994).

6   Scholar worked his way up from being a clerk in a north London estate agency to owning a multi-million pound property company by exploiting the crash in property prices in the 1970s.

7   In particular, the clubs outside the Premier League have continued to make losses, despite the notion that clubs should be profit-making. In 1994–1995 season, the Premier League had operating profits (pre-transfer fees) of £49 million, whereas the Football League had operating losses of £22.5 million (Deloitte and Touche, 1996, p. 4). After transfer fees are taken into account, the Premier League had profits of £6.2 million, while the Football League had losses of £20.4 million (and the First Division had losses of £12.5 million) (Deloitte and Touche, 1996, p. 7). Even so, there were clubs in the Premier League which recorded big losses after transfer fees: Everton £9.3 million, Newcastle United £8.1 million and Liverpool, £2.7 million, as well as Blackburn Rovers, Nottingham Forest and West Ham United, which all showed losses of £2 million or more (Deloitte and Touche, 1996, p. 20).

8   The same point was made by both Robert Chase, chairman of Norwich City, and by Peter Storrie, managing director of West Ham United. By this criterion, Jack Walker, the chairman of Blackburn Rovers, cannot be described as a new director, since he has invested enormous amounts of money in the club with no hope of a return and he does not seem to have any grand integrated project of accumulation, like Hall and Gibson.

9   Phillip Carter sold his shares in Everton in the 1990s but is considered here as a member of the new directors because he was concerned throughout the 1980s that professional football be profit-making and, above all, because he was a major figure in threatening the breakaways of the top clubs. In other words, he believed that football clubs should be profit-making and that those clubs which could not support themselves should fail. See for, instance, his demands for a breakaway in Chapter 6.

10   Sir John Smith died before the transformation of football in the 1990s was underway but, like Carter, he was a major figure in the breakaways and forthright in his condemnation of League rules and arrangements which hobbled the biggest clubs. See, for instance, his espousal of sponsorship in Chapter 5.

11   Scholar's flotation of Tottenham Hotspur was followed only by Manchester United and Millwall until the middle of the 1990s. New directors have now recognized the potential for public share issues. Newcastle United and Sunderland floated in 1997.

12   The opposition of the fans to the merger schemes is of interest, for it demonstrates that, although the new directors have risen to a position of dominance, its project must earn the consent of the fans. The new directors have to negotiate the transformation of football with the fans' own self-understandings. This complex negotiation is the subject of the final three chapters of the book.

13   Eventing involves increasing the price according to the opposition. This

strategy has caused discontent among the visiting fans of the more famous clubs.

14   Newcastle United, for instance, made £8.5 million from the sale of club merchandise, mainly through its sale of replica kits (Williams, 1996, p. 30).

15   This account of Steven Gibson's strategy at Middlesbrough is taken from a personal interview with Louise Taylor, north-eastern football correspondent for the *Sunday Times* (16 October 1996).

16   This speculation temporarily failed with the relegation of Middlesbrough FC at the end of the 1996–7 season.

17   Maxwell and Murdoch have adopted a similar strategy to that of Sir John Hall, although the profitability of the sign-value of football lies in the fact that it is a primary commodity by which newspapers (and satellite television) is sold, rather than a symbol by which a region is sold to global investors. In particular, football became a central symbolic value in Maxwell and Murdoch's battle over the circulation of papers. It is unnecessary to provide a full narrative account of Murdoch and Maxwell's more or less covert sparring over football clubs in the 1980s and 1990s, as this has been written up elsewhere (Horrie, 1992; Scholar, 1992). Maxwell and Murdoch came into competition over two principal clubs, Manchester United and Tottenham Hotspur. Maxwell had attempted to buy Martin Edwards' shares in 1983 and effectively challenged Murdoch over the club in 1989 when Murdoch secretly supported Michael Knighton's farcical attempt at purchasing the club (Crick and Smith, 1990, pp. 277–95; Horrie, 1992, pp. 193–6). A similarly covert struggle was waged over Tottenham Hotspur when Scholar got into financial difficulties (Horrie, 1992, pp. 198–9, 211). After Scholar's departure, Maxwell and Sugar, who was supported by Murdoch, struggled to gain control of the club (see Horrie, 1992, pp. 268–77).

18   Feminists would object strongly and rightly to the passive notion of women suggested by these arguments.

19   Sloane (1980) has recognized the peculiarity of sport as an economic form, although his arguments are very different from my own.

12

The Lads

Although the new directors have been very successful in transforming football in line with their entrepreneurial schemes, it is essential that the contestedness of the transformation of football in the 1990s is recognized. It would be a gross simplification to describe the development of the new consumption of football as if it were some smooth, technocratic procedure. Moreover, at the theoretical level, it must be emphasized that all conjunctural moments are inevitably contested and debated. At conjunctural moments, the metasocial commentary of which Geertz writes becomes particularly charged as participants recognize the social effects which transformation will entail. The next three chapters will interpret some of the main positions which fans have adopted towards the new consumption of football, not only to highlight the debates over this process, but also to demonstrate the way in which the fans have contributed to these changes in ways which they, themselves, may not recognize.

This chapter will analyse the interpretative practices of a particular kind of male fan at Manchester United in order to explore their responses to the new consumption of football and, in particular, their resistance and contribution to the creation of this new form of football. As I shall claim below, these male fans have developed a self-consciously masculine style of support which is related in complex ways to transformations which have taken place in working-class culture over the last thirty years, although I will emphasize their masculinity rather than their class position as the primary analytic here. In analysing the interpretative practices of these young men, 'the lads', I want to relate my discussion to the recent literature on fans and audiences.

Much of this recent literature on fans and audiences seeks to overcome the well-established theoretical approaches of the past. In particular, two main approaches which emphasize either resistance or hegemony have characterized the analysis of consumption. On the one hand, sociologists who have analysed popular pastimes have looked upon them with disdain (Jensen, 1992, p. 10), regarding their practitioners as cultural dupes whose mystified compliance ensures their continued exploitation (Vinnai, 1973; Hargreaves, 1982, pp. 33, 41; Clarke and Critcher, 1985, pp. 228–32,[1] Marcuse, 1968, pp. 2–17, 56–79;

Horkheimer and Adorno, 1973, pp. 120–67). On the other, there has been a tradition in cultural studies which has highlighted forms of resistance. The work of the Birmingham Centre for Contemporary Cultural Studies, notably *Resistance through Rituals* (Hall and Jefferson, 1976), constitutes the prime example of this position in British sociology. The articles in that collection examine the way in which various subcultures resist the hegemony of the dominant class through the adoption of particular styles of dress and behaviour. The theoretical framework, in which the selection is situated and which is laid out in a long introductory chapter (Clarke, *et al.*, 1976), rightly highlights the historical moment of the collapse of the post-war settlement in which these subcultures emerged but, despite this admirable historical consciousness, the collection tends to slip into an overly facile assumption that subcultures are somehow completely and successfully resistant. Consequently, Clarke and Jefferson argue, respectively, that skinheads and Teddy boys represented a fairly unproblematic attempt by working-class youth to reassert their traditional working-class identities in the face of the destruction of those traditions (Jefferson, 1976, pp. 81–3; Clarke, 1976, pp. 99–100).

Of the Birmingham School's work, *Learning to Labour* (Willis, 1977) unquestionably comes closest to the position which I want to adopt here. In that work, he shows how the sons of the rough working-class ensure the reproduction of their parents' subordinate class position by their resistance to school, which is regarded as the embodiment of middle-class and establishment values. In other words, their resistance at one moment leads to subordination and consent at another. Willis's approach is insightful but I want to go further and argue that the elements of resistance and compliance may not be temporally separate and causally related in the way Willis argues but that resistance and compliance may be simultaneous and paradoxically inseparable.

In line with the recent analysis of fans (Fiske, 1992, p. 35; Grossberg, 1992, pp. 59, 62; Portelli, 1993; Radway, 1987, p. 148), I want to suggest here that in analysing the interpretative practice of a particular type of male fan at football in the 1990s a more sophisticated approach is required than the examples of hegemony and resistance theory often suggest. The lads' fandom cannot be seen as fundamentally resistant to the transformation of football. Yet neither can this fandom be regarded as essentially compliant to hegemonic projects (and, therefore, mystified). Whereas hegemony theorists focus on compliance and mystification and resistance theorists on subversion and opposition, turning a blind eye to each other in their analytical process, I want to emphasize that, in fact, social relations consist of simultaneously compliant and resistant strands. Furthermore, theories of resistance and mystification both operate with an assumption of a contradiction of interests between the subordinate and dominant groups and then assume that either the subordinate group is aware of the reality of their position and resists it or is mystified into accepting it. This conception of social relations as self-evidently contra-dictory is naive. For instance, in the context of an international capitalist economy, the welfare and employment of the working-class is dependent upon the success of capitalist enterprises, and the working-class, therefore, shares some interests with the ruling capitalist class in the successful promotion of a capitalist enterprise. Yet capitalist and working-classes are, at the same time, in potential opposition over the distribution of wealth and goods within particular enterprises. The relationship between dominant and subordinate groups is textured by simultaneous opposing and shared interests which give rise to complex forms of compliance and resistance.

A similarly contradictory relationship of both mutual interest and opposition, of consent and resistance, is detectable within the field of consumption and in the lads' reactions to the transformation of football in the 1990s. Portelli has described this paradoxical fan culture of submission and resistance in an examination of Italian football fans, which he terms identification and resentment (Portelli, 1993). By identification and resentment, Portelli refers to the relationship between the fans of big Italian football clubs and the owners of those clubs. The fans support and, even adore, these owners who provide them with a successful team, but at the same time the fans resent the wealth and power of these owners, on whom the fans are so dependent. I want to follow Portelli's argument about the contradictory relationship between the rich and poor in Italian football culture and re-apply it to the experience of a particular type of male in England in the 1990s.

The Craic

The Love of the Team and the Lads' Pride

> I would say it's the modern equivalent of a religion, football. I would say that quite honestly. It's got all the same traits, like. You go to your place of worship, you have your icons, you follow your team. Even now out of season all you're thinking about is who they are going to sign, what's the new shirt going to be like, how you're going to do next season, who they're going to get in Europe. (Barry, 25 May 1994)

> It's passion. It runs a lot deeper than money. Money's no object. It's all about passion. That is the truth. 'Cause it's not support, it's an obsession. It's everything. As Bill Shankly said, it's not life and death, it's more important than that ... My family has been split up through it. I try to curb it but it's, it's just that little bit extra, you know what I mean. The boys. You're buzzing. You're on cloud cuckoo land. (Jeff, 1 July 1994)

These descriptions of fandom by two Manchester United 'lads' trace the contours of the analysis I want to offer of the lads' interpretative practice. Since the lads' self-understandings have determined their response to the transformation of the consumption of football, and that fandom has facilitated the new consumption of the game, it is necessary to go into some detail about the nature of the lads' identities and practices. The analysis of the lads' football fandom could usefully draw on Durkheim's classic work on aboriginal religions which was mentioned in Chapter 2.[2] As we can see from the above statement, the lads consciously conceive of their support as religious and they reach a heightened emotional state in it: 'The boys. You're buzzing.' In *The Elementary Forms of the Religious Life*, Durkheim (1964) argued that aboriginal clans, which had been involved in the profane and dispersed activity of hunter-gathering, periodically came together to worship their totem. In those ecstatic ritualistic celebrations, the aborigines experienced the social existence of their clan viscerally. The aborigines' emotions were focused on the totem of the clan and, since the totem represented the clan, the aborigines were, in fact, worshipping their own society in celebrating the totem.

The relevance of Durkheim's analysis of aboriginal religion and the lads' support for their team becomes apparent in the two quotations cited above. In their own accounts of their support for the team, the lads describe the ecstasy of support (see also Giulianotti *et al.*, 1994, p. 5; Finn, 1994, pp. 107–8; Bromberger, 1993). Such ecstasy is produced by the communal practice of singing and supporting the team. However, those communal practices are not only staged in the ground. The pub is also a crucial site for the creation of masculine solidarity. In the steamy and inebriated atmosphere of the pub before the game,[3] the lads first begin to re-create their sense of mutual solidarity, which (sometimes) reaches its height in the ground:

> At any club, the lads, inverted commas, who go and support the team and who go, who want the keg [alcohol] and want a bit of a craic, not necessarily fighting or anything or even to see an away fan but they just want to go to the boozer and have a good day and support the team.

> The craic is the great thing about football whether you support United or Lincoln City. Meeting up with the lads in the pub before the match, going to an away game with all your mates. That makes it more enjoyable definitely, I couldn't go to a game every week on me own. (Barry, 25 May 1994)

The craic, then, is only possible in so far as the lads mutually practise and demonstrate their support, by drinking and singing together, intensifying their emotions, raising them in some cases to a crescendo of excitement.

In line with Durkheim's argument, this ecstasy has a focus, which is expressed in the songs of the lads that resonate out of the doorways of a multitude of pubs and bars in towns and cities around England and Europe. That focus of solidarity is, of course, the team and the lads conceive of this relationship with the team, which acts as the medium for their masculine solidarity, in distinctive terms:

> It has been said that the nearest thing to unconditional love is that of a mother for her son. No matter what her son may do or say she will stick by him. No provisos, no conditions no bloody chance. The nearest thing to true unconditional love is that of a lad for his football team. (Steve Black, 'True Love', in *United We Stand*, Issue 35)

Or again:

> I reckon it's surrogate emotions, I really do. I think it's all these blokes that just can't say 'I love you'. I can't say 'oh, you're a really good mate, you are' but I can sing at the top of my voice, 'I love you City' or 'we love you City', or I can cry when we get promoted or I can cry when we get relegated. But if my mum dropped dead I probably wouldn't cry but I can cry if City won the Cup. (Mark Glynn, 14 July 1994)[4]

The lads conceive of their relationship with their team as a love affair. This conception links back to the creation of ecstatic solidarity in 'the craic' when the boys are 'buzzing'. On the one hand, the ecstasy of football fandom engages their emotions so deeply that they build up an affection for the club which is seen as love. However, the lads are only able to raise themselves to the level of excitement in their spectating because they invest the game with so much importance as a result of their love for the club. The ecstasy of the lads' support and the love they have for the club are symbiotic, therefore. Yet the lads' relationship of love is more significant than merely reinforcing the fans' ecstasy.

The love which the lads feel for their team is simultaneously also a love for the feeling of solidarity which they experience every time they see their team and participate in the communal practice of drinking and singing. Just as Durkheim suggested that aboriginal tribes worship their society through the totem, so do the lads reaffirm their identity as lads, with all the values and associations which go with that identity, and their relations with other lads through the love of the team. The love for the team is a transposed love of the lads' own social groups and the masculinity[5] which informs that group's relations with itself and others. The team, and the love invested in it, is a symbol of the values and friendships which exist between the lads. The love which the lads invest in the team affirms their notion of themselves as lads and their relations to each other at the deepest and most effective level.

One of the central elements of the lads' fandom is their 'pride'. By this, the lads refer to the status which their club earns through its success on the pitch. This status is reflected onto the lads, as supporters, but the lads also attain status or pride for themselves by the demonstration of loyal support; regular attendance, singing (even when losing) and fighting. This notion of pride is important in the lads' everyday lives, for it is football which substantially defines their masculinity. The pride they attain from the success of their club and their support of it brings them recognition in their everyday lives from other men who are supporters of the same club and those who are not. Since these masculine relations are substantially concerned with status and seeking recognition (Tolson, 1977, p. 43), the pride which a lad attains from football is important since it assists him in asserting himself in relations with other men in his community. Consequently, a fundamental part of the lads' support is emphasizing the rivalry of his club with another and the superiority of his club over others (see King, 1995b). This rivalry, which stems from the masculine competition for honour, is a central element in the lads' response to the new directors' project.

The Lads' Distinction

The masculinity which is celebrated by the lads by their drinking, singing and supporting is a distinctive practice. Not only does it divide the lads from the opposition, who are regarded as unmanly, but the lads also see themselves as a distinct body within the following of the club as a whole. This distinction has become particularly important at Manchester United since the transformation of the ground after the Taylor report, because the lads feel themselves under threat. Their style of support and the masculinity which it expresses is, as far as the lads can see, under a quite deliberate assault by the club's bureaucracy: 'People like us [the lads] ideally aren't wanted at United. We go to the matches, we don't spend any money in the souvenir shop, we don't buy the programmes' (Michael, 8 June 1994). As new support has been encouraged to attend games at Old Trafford as customers, the lads have been forced to recognize the distinctiveness of their support. The distinctiveness of this support is worth close examination, as it highlights the nature of the lads' fandom and also provides the categorical framework of the following chapters on the contemporary state of fandom in the light of the new consumption of football.

The lads are principally aware of two other fan groups (apart from those who watch from the executive boxes) and their difference from these other fans. Their ridiculing of these other fans constitutes a substantial part of their conversation and their understanding of themselves as fans. The two principal groups of fans which the lads view as distinct from themselves are the 'new consumer fans' and the producers and consumers of 'new football writing', as I shall call them in the following chapters. On the one hand, the new consumer fans are generally content with the new consumption of football and demonstrate this satisfaction by their willingness to purchase all manner of club merchandise. The new consumer fandom is more mixed, sexually, than the lads and often includes whole families. Since it is an expensive matter to attend matches, the new consumer fans' ability to bring the whole family points towards their being more affluent than the lads. The FA Carling Premiership's report carried out by the Sir Norman Chester Centre (1994) confirmed this, since it claimed that fans earning £30,000 a year or more were most likely to attend home matches with children and family (figures 18 and 19), although the wealth differential between new consumers and lads should not be overstated.[6] However, although the class position of the two groups overlaps with the more affluent sections of the lads holding equivalent positions to the new consumers, their styles of consumption are very different and, in particular, new consumers conform to the new directors' idea of the customer.

On the other hand, the new football writing fans comprise a very small body of any club's support. They are generally the college-educated sons and daughters of higher-grade white-collar workers or professionals and are often employed in the public sector, which, as noted in Chapter 3, was a middle-class fraction that had been increasingly squeezed during the 1980s and 1990s. I will discuss these particular styles of fandom and their significance in the following chapters, but for now I want to consider only the lads' perception of these other fan groups, highlighting the way in which the lads regard these groups as potential threats to their notion of fandom (and, therefore, to their masculine solidarity) and the attempts the lads make to maintain distinction from these groups so as to preserve the practices on which their masculinity relies.

At Manchester United, the new consumer fans are particularly distinguishable by their use of official club coaches (to away games), rather than travelling independently or with the fanzines' coaches, which are principally organised by and for the lads. The lads describe those individuals who travel with the club as 'trainspotters', and travelling with the club is called 'going with the trainspotters'. Thus, on a couple of occasions, Tim, a fan with whom I spent much time during the 1993–1994 season, described himself as going with the 'trainspotters' and joked that he had prepared his 'flask and butties'. The new consumer fans are mocked in this way by the lads because the official coaches are regarded as being overly protective and restrictive. In particular, the lads point to the fact that the coaches organise their journeys to arrive at away grounds so close to the kick-off time that there is little drinking time for the fans. This loss of drinking time is significant in the light of my earlier comments on the communal ritual of support. The lads are substantially only able to create the ecstatic solidarity, through which they express their masculinity, in so far as they are able to drink. Alcohol reduces inhibitions, while the mutual exchange through the buying of drinks and the shared practice of drinking are all fundamental to this visceral sense of togetherness. The lads do not only differentiate themselves from the new consumer fans because of the latter's dependence on the club for away trips; they also attach importance to styles of dress and deride the new consumer fans for their lack of 'style'. The lads wear much less official club merchandise than the new consumer fans. The origin of this rejection of official kit is linked to the development of the casual movement in the early 1980s (see Redhead, 1991a), which developed as a reaction against (hooligan) fan clothing of boots, denims and scarves of the 1970s, both as a means of avoiding police attention and as an expression of distinctiveness and superiority over other hooligan groups through the conspicuous expense of the designer clothes. This desire to dress well, thereby demonstrating financial and stylistic superiority, persists among the lads today, especially among those in their late teens and early twenties who are interested in violence.

Despite the fact that some lads still wear the club shirt, the lads are increasingly conscious of the distinctiveness of their style of dress, which is recognized by the lads as differentiating them from the 'trainspotters'. For the lads, to wear club merchandise is to be associated with fans who do not drink, who are dependent on the club for away-match travel, are uncritical of the changes to football, do not contribute to the atmosphere in the ground and will not stand up in a fight. The bitterness with which the lads now view the new consumer fans at Old Trafford stems from the fact that, with the reduction of capacities and increase in seat prices resulting from the development of all-seater stadia, the lads are threatened from exclusion from a ritual in which they reaffirm their masculinity and their relationship with other lads:

> It ruins it for me sometimes, the atmosphere, You know when you go out of the ground and all these people you just don't want there. It just ruins it for me. When I've been at some matches at Old Trafford this year and I've just been looking at the people around me. It just fucks me off so much to look at them all just sat there in shirts not singing. (Michael, July 1994)

The new consumer fans are distinguished by their dress and the passivity of their support; they are 'all sat there in shirts'.

The lads are quite conscious that their style of dress distinguishes them from new consumer fans:

> The reason people used to buy things [club merchandise] was for the identity and all that, but there isn't one there anymore, There's more

identity in a Ralph Lauren shirt as to be from Manchester than there is in a United or even a City top. Any football top like, you know, you walk round in a United top, they'd think you were from Manchester. You couldn't do that any more. (Nick, 8 June 1994)

Used to (buy the shirt) up to the age of seventeen. But there's no identity in a Manchester United shirt anymore. There's nothing. If I'd have worn one on holiday last week, it would have been you part-timer. Do you know what I mean? I couldn't take that. (Andy Mitten, 8 July 1994)

Both of these fans claim that there is no identity in a Manchester United shirt. Yet tens of thousands of individuals across Britain (and, indeed, the entire globe) disagree and happily purchase the various strips, doubtlessly regarding the shirt as meaningful when they pull it on; it symbolically represents their notion of themselves and their imagined relationship with Manchester United. Andy and Nick's argument that there is no identity anymore in a shirt cannot be sustained. Rather, they must mean that the identity that the shirt expresses is not consistent with their notion of themselves. For Andy and Nick, the Manchester United shirt, which for so many is the symbol of allegiance, ironically denotes inauthentic support; it is worn by part-timers and by individuals who do not come from Manchester.

The new consumer fans are uppermost in the lads' consciousness, and it is these fans whom they regard with most disdain because they threaten the masculine solidarity of the lads' fandom by taking the lads' places in the ground and failing to sing. Consequently, the lads try to distinguish themselves from such fans, thereby preserving the expression of their masculinity in their support. However, the lads are also aware of another new group of fans which has emerged since the mid-1980s: new football writing fans. To say that this group emerged in the mid-1980s does not suggest that individuals who eventually created this loose-knit fan group were not attending matches before that time, for individuals who are part of this group were involved in football in the late 1960s, but 'new football writing', as a discrete and recognizable form of fandom, emerged only after 1985.

As we shall see in the next chapter, new football writing fandom involves the production and consumption of the national fanzine *When Saturday Comes*, along with *Fever Pitch* and a wider and developing literature, and support for the FSA. The lads were disparaging about both. Of the 13 lads whom I interviewed, and one other, Tim, with whom I spent much time, only one read *When Saturday Comes* regularly and this individual, Harry, was only on the very edge of the lad category. Andy Mitten had read *When Saturday Comes* in the past but had stopped reading it some time ago because it 'had gone downhill' (8 July 1994). Of the 13 others, seven said they did not read it, four because they regarded it as 'too serious'. Five more did not mention it when fanzines were discussed in their interviews, so it is assumed that they did not read it. The apparent flippancy of the comment that *When Saturday Comes* was 'too serious' belies a significant distinction between the styles of support of the lads and that of new football writing fans: 'I always feel that they're trying to be too, too sensible, upright, level-headed supporters. 'Cause football supporters aren't like that' (Gordon, 26 May 1994). This notion of the level-headedness of *When Saturday Comes* refers to the fanzine's rejection of the rivalries between fans of different clubs. Gordon regards this as 'too sensible' because, as I have argued, one of the essential elements of the lads' support is rivalry with the male fans of other clubs; the success of a club reflects honour onto the male supporters and the whole point of masculine fandom is to try and establish superiority over other (masculine) rivals. The incompatibility of the new football writing's opposition to rivalry between fans sits uncomfortably with the very point of the lads' masculine support; the demonstration of and competition for male honour and status. This competition for honour is highlighted in another fan's criticisms of the FSA:

It seems like a good idea what I've seen of it but when all is said and done, like, I know we're all football fans but I just see some clubs ... [next clause unclear] ... who edit such fanzines are all right and all that but clubs that really dislike each other I can't see how they can work in unity. You could be from the same backgrounds and all that but even if you got individuals from each club who were prepared to work together, are you speaking for your fans? Cause if you could say you've got this plan to sort of have a go against ticket prices and you present it to the fans. You say me and such and such a person who is a Leeds fan and Liverpool fan and we're all agreed on this. It's hard to gain any respect apart from a few right-on people. (Stan, 28 May 1994)

Here Stan is presenting an interesting picture of the lads' mentality and of their distinctiveness from the producers and consumers of new football writing. Rivalry and competition is essential to the lads and, consistent with their masculinity, the struggle for recognition and supremacy is paramount. The producers and consumers of new football writing do not regard football primarily as an arena in which they achieve honour through the triumphs of their team. Rather they see the game as a communal celebration, through which they would like to express certain political sentiments.[7]

The difference in the styles of support between the new football writing fandom and the lads was demonstrated with particular clarity during my fieldwork. Two fans, Gary (5 February 1994, fieldnotes) and Phil, independently expressed similar sentiments about the comments of a member of the new football writing fandom on television. After the 1992 European Championship Finals, in which there had been some disturbances involving English fans, Channel 4 screened a programme, *Wake up England*, which examined the role of English fans in these disturbances. During this programme, Bill Brewster, who was on the editorial board of *When Saturday Comes* at the time, was interviewed after the initial violence in Malmo. He described how he was now fearful for his safety because every violently disposed fan would be out to get any English fan and he showed visible signs of anxiety on the screen. Both Phil (who had been in Sweden with England) and Gary mentioned this scene and ridiculed Brewster's fear. For them, it was inappropriate to show this fear – it was unmanly and negated their honour as men.

All-seater Stadia: Ticket Prices and Reduced Capacities

The development of all-seater stadia has had a serious impact on the ease of entry into the ground. Before the implementation of the Taylor report, almost all grounds had large standing areas,[8] entry to which was relatively simple, involving a payment of cash at the turnstile, and was almost always guaranteed. It was rare for any ground to be completely full. It is true that at the more popular clubs, such as Manchester United and Liverpool, entry to certain terraces would require substantial queuing. With the development of all-seater stadia, access to the ground has suddenly became problematic. Capacities have been reduced so that, on a purely arithmetic level, some of the fans who had been part of the crowd when Manchester United had a 60,000 capacity could not possibly gain entry. Furthermore, the reduction in capacity, the improvement in facilities, the cost of building and the fact that fans are now seen as customers has prompted a rise in prices which has been quite unprecedented in football history. Between 1988–1989 and 1992–1993, ticket prices rose by 222.9 per cent at Old Trafford (Williams, 1995) and, as Table 11.1 reveals, they have continued to rise since then at a lower rate.

This rapid increase in ticket prices has presented many of the lads with difficulties in gaining entry to the stadium, especially since, we have already noted, the lads are generally less affluent than the familial customers whom the club overtly seeks to attract. The lads who are still able to attend are generally employed in the jobs of the upwardly mobile sections of the new working-class. They are usually in reasonably well-paid manual or menial white-collar work, although some have risen to higher ranks in the white-collar bureaucracy,[9] but many have found it hard to pay for the 200 per cent increase in ticket prices. 'If they're going to keep putting like £30, £40, £50, you're going to have to jump off.

You're going to have to say 'I can't afford this anymore'. It's ridiculous' (Barry, 25 May 1994). Other fans expressed similar sentiments: 'Lately, they want more upper class people – they don't want the working-class there' (Phil, 1 June 1994). In addition to feeling threatened by eventual exclusion due to the inexorable rise in ticket prices, many of the lads already knew individuals who could no longer afford to go – and resented the fact. Craig described how friends he had always gone with could no longer go:

> there's a few who've been to the game and you're up in the pub later on and you know, and you can say, 'Oh, such and such a thing happened' and they're [lads who cannot afford to go] going 'Yeah, yeah, I heard that on the radio' but they didn't see it, didn't experience the atmosphere or anything. (Craig, 29 June 1994)

The lads who are excluded from the ground do not merely miss 90 minutes of football; they are also denied a fundamental resource which mediates their relationships with others.

At Old Trafford, the lads have faced the additional obstacle of a vast excess of demand for tickets. Between 1993 and 1995, after the reconstruction of the Stretford End but before the building of the new North Stand, Old Trafford had a stadium capacity of only 44,000. Since there were 120,000 members, of whom approximately 26,000[10] had season tickets (or the equivalent), the ground was vastly oversubscribed for the 1993–1994 and 1994–1995 seasons. During these seasons, it was theoretically possible for 94,000 members to apply for only 13,000 remaining seats at Old Trafford, although, of course, it was never the case that all members ever applied. In response to this demand for tickets, the club decided to extend the stadium and, during the summer of 1995 and throughout the following season, a new three-tier North Stand was erected which has raised capacity to 55,000. This has eased some (though not all) of the pressure for tickets but, even in the light of this new development, the lads in no way experience the ease of admission which had been typical before the 1990s.

Not only do tickets still have to be applied for in advance but there are certain strategies employed by the club which work against the lads (besides the increased cost of attendance). In the light of oversubscription for tickets, the club allocates tickets on the basis of a supposedly fair ballot system. There have been serious and widespread allegations that these ballots have been unfavourable to single males applying for tickets from the local area. Since the lads are least likely to spend money in the club shop on match day, due to their casual stylistic preferences, it has been suggested that the club has developed a deliberate ticket policy of awarding tickets to family groups who come from outside the Manchester area, knowing that these fans will be more likely to make purchases in the club shop. These accusations are at least partially confirmed in White's account of the 1993–1994 season (White, 1994), which includes an interview with Martin O'Neill, the branch secretary of the Cork United Supporters' Association. In discussing the organization of trips for Irish fans to Old Trafford, O'Neill poses the rhetorical question: 'Why do you think we Irish always do better than you lot [local fans] in the ticket draw?' He replies: 'Because they see our address, they know we'll make more of a trip of it. Spend more money' (White, 1994, p. 164). In particular, as O'Neill describes, the Irish fans will spend quite extraordinary amounts in the club shop purchasing souvenirs for themselves and their families. The success of the Irish fans in gaining tickets has little to do with the traditional luck of the Celts but demonstrates that the club does employ deliberate and slightly dubious strategies to exclude the lads. In addition to this, the club has implemented overt strategies which have disadvantaged the lads in comparison with new consumer fans. For instance, the 4000-seat family stand immediately excludes the lads, while the club class area of some 3000 seats in the middle of the Stretford End is marketed at a very different group from the lads (White, 1994, p. 230). In addition, as I have already argued, through merely raising prices, the club has excluded many local male fans who can no longer afford to attend matches (e.g. Jeff). It is likely that the club does formally discriminate against local masculine support but, even without doctoring the supposedly fair ticket ballot, the club has already instituted several methods of exclusion.

Yet the increased cost of attending games in an all-seater stadium and the new directors' explicit project of encouraging (more affluent) families to attend in order to create customers has not been the only transformation in the consumption of football to have interfered with the lads' masculine fandom. The creation of the all-seater stadium has also radically transformed the topography of the ground. The open terraces which had been central to the lads' creation of solidarity have disappeared, problematizing the lads' creation of solidarity, because this loss has restricted their ability to gather together in one area of the ground. The atomization and ordering of the crowd through seating restricts the formerly fundamental fan practices of jumping, swaying and communal celebration. The lads are quite conscious of these new obstacles that the apparently innocuous plastic bucket seat throws in the way of the expression of their identities:

> I think you tend, when you're stood up, you tend to drift into different crowds or into different people and really you end up with people who are most like yourself. That's the way I always thought of it. You can't choose who you're with now.

It should get back to the days when it was everyone together the same kind of people you're with. I'm not advocating mass rioting or anything like that. (Craig, 29 June 1994)

It might be added, though, that mass rioting was actually a potential feature of this ecstatic masculine solidarity.

By the 1980s, despite the reputation of the Stretford End, the key site of masculine congregation was actually in the United Road paddock.[11] This was the shallow area of terracing which ran adjacent to the Stretford End along the north side of Old Trafford, behind which runs United Road. The lads used to gather here and, in particular, in its most easterly corner next to the scoreboard paddock below the K-Stand, where the away supporters stood. The lads could consequently revel in their close proximity to their rivals, and thus their demonstrations of solidarity, pride and honour were most effective. The lads remember the United Road, whose bars sold two-pint mugs of beer (Tim, fieldnotes), with some fondness and it is still possible to hear songs at games which recall its atmosphere:[12] 'I used to stand in the United Road. I was obsessed with that corner' (Stan, 20 May 1994).

The terrace provided an open space in which it was easy to create an ecstatic solidarity. Furthermore, certain practices carried out in the communal anonymity of the terrace could become embarrassing from the isolation of a seat. The very anonymity of standing in a crowd protected the fan from humiliation if that fan started to sing alone or performed an action which no one followed. There is no such comfort in the panoptic isolation of the seat and, consequently, it has been doubly hard for the lads to regain the ecstatic masculine solidarity of the terrace. Thus, at the last home game of the 1993–1994 season, when the team paraded the trophy, the crowd celebrated in a restrained fashion, but Gordon incredulously described to me a scene in the bar area behind the K-Stand, where many of the lads have seats. The area was completely congested with male fans, who were singing and stamping in an extraordinary frenzy. Away from their atomizing seats, in the congested space of the bar area of the ground or the pubs outside the ground, the lads can re-create their ecstatic solidarity.

When it was all paddocks, it was all crushed in and everyone was swaying about and jumping about, and waving their fist at the opposition over the fence and all that. Now, it's not the same at all, it's almost like going to the cinema; it is at Old Trafford anyway. You pay at the start of the season to sit in the same seat. I mean it's all really nice – nice view, nice stadium and all that – but the atmosphere isn't the same and the whole thing is different almost like a different concept completely. (Paul, 13 June 1994)

The new consumption of football has threatened the lads' fandom because increased ticket prices, reduced capacities and the new topography of the ground are serious obstacles to the creation of the lads' identities.[13]

The Lads' Response to the Project of the New Directors

Resisting the New Consumption of Football

The interpretative practice of fans cannot be seen, on the one hand, as either straightforwardly resistant or, on the other, as simply mystified. The lads' masculine identity informs their response to the project of the new directors, mediating their opposition to the developments which obstruct the creation of ecstatic masculine solidarity, but, simultaneously, their notion of themselves as lads also ensures that they regard certain reforms favourably, as being in their interest. I want to trace this paradoxically resistant and compliant response of the lads to the new consumption of football, beginning with the way in which the lads' autonomous masculine culture is employed as a resource for resistance to the new consumption of football.

This opposition has at Manchester United been no more than a fusillade of small arms in the face of a full-scale bombardment but, nevertheless, it should not be ignored. In 1991, season tickets went up from £102 to £166 and, during the course of the 1991–1992 season, the club announced its intention to increase prices yet further to a minimum of £228 to pay for the reconstruction of the Stretford End. This leap in prices occasioned the first resistant volley from the lads against the transformation of the consumption of football at Old Trafford. Johnny Flacks, who has subsequently become a member of the FSA's national committee and the vice-chair of the Independent Manchester United Supporters' Association, organized a group of friends, who called themselves HOSTAGE (Holders of Season Tickets Against Gross Exploitation), to oppose this rise. Flacks organized a midweek meeting in February 1992 at Lancashire County Cricket Club, which some one thousand Manchester United fans attended at short notice to air their grievances. Nothing ever came of HOSTAGE in the end (much to the annoyance of many lads who attended the meeting and contributed money), but the attendance of so many at a meeting at such short notice demonstrated the potential for action.

That potential has been realized since April 1995 with the development of the Independent Manchester United Supporters' Association (IMUSA). This fan organization emerged ostensibly as the result of an announcement during a very important League match against Arsenal.

During that match, many masculine fans, who are concentrated in the K-Stand, stood up for long periods of time to demonstrate their support for the team. However, the club announced over the tannoy that the fans should remain seated, as they were obstructing the view for others and their actions were potentially hazardous. This demand demonstrated to the lads the extreme divide between their notion of themselves as fans and the club's idea of a desirable fandom, stimulating the creation of IMUSA, which was designed to provide an organized body which could lobby the club with the fans' views. Of course, the infamous announcement at the Arsenal game was very much the final conjunctural straw which was added to a much longer organic decline in the relationship between the lads and the club to which the accounts of the lads cited above are a testament. We will discuss the social composition of IMUSA in the next chapter.

Alongside the formal establishment of IMUSA and preceding its emergence, the lads have expressed their resistance to the new consumption of football through informal statements of opposition and complaint. In themselves, these complaints seem irrelevant but, as James Scott (1985) has argued, these everyday forms of seemingly futile resistance are effective political weapons, albeit 'weapons of the weak'. Scott argues that everyday forms of resistance themselves become incorporated into the negotiation of relations between dominant and subordinate groups and that such everyday resistances are essential to the development of more self-conscious forms of resistance. This is the case for the lads, because myriad informal debates with other lads about the direction of the club's transformation has facilitated the development of a self-consciously political body such as IMUSA. The lads regarded the announcement as the last straw because countless pub conversations had informed them of a common view among many of the fans that the club was nearing the point at which formal resistance was required.

One of the principal and regular appeals that the lads have made against the project of the Manchester United board and specifically against the idea that fans are no more than customers, with no political hold over the club beyond a market relationship, has been the appeal to tradition. The lads argue that the game was traditionally a working men's sport, of which they are the inheritors. 'We all believe it's a standing up sport. It's a working man's sport' (Jeff, 1 July 1994). Since, according to the lads, football is traditionally a working-class sport, the lads who still attend regard themselves as 'the bedrock of United's support' (Tim, fieldnotes, 27 October 1993); their support has sedimented over generations. Consequently, the lads argue that the present developments threaten the very foundations on which the success of Manchester United have been built:

United should be careful, they have effectively cut off the local young supporters who cannot get tickets for games now. I remember catching the 255 bus to Old Trafford as a kid and the bus was packed with lads the same age who knew they could pay in the match. That same bus is empty nowadays. (Andy Mitten, *United We Stand*, Issue 35)

This is a significant manoeuvre, as it questions the short-sighted pursuit of profit by the new directors. The club is easily able to fill the stadium now, with a championship-winning team, but, the argument runs, when the lean times return, the board will face a potential crisis. The affluent families will go elsewhere and the next generation of lads will not have built up a habit of going and, even if they wanted, would not be able to afford to attend in the future.

Potentially, it is an effective argument, although it is impossible to determine how seriously the club takes it. However, it is possible to apply a similar critical method to the lads' argument for their traditionalism as I used in the analysis of the new director's use of the term 'customer'. Such a critical approach goes against the easy populism which has characterized much recent writing on football discussed in Chapter 1 but is entirely necessary in the analysis of contemporary culture. Indeed, such critical analysis is incumbent upon the sociologists whose role is to provide some overarching insights into the social process. The following critical analysis of the lads' notion of tradition does not finally weaken their own demands for political recognition but, rather, it merely points up the parts of their arguments which are both potentially weak and actually exclusionary. The notion of tradition almost invariably refers to and legitimates a masculine and, indeed, male form of support which potentially excludes other – particularly female – forms of support. Thus, it is possible for the sociologist to favour the politics of one group over those of another while maintaining critical distance from these groups in the analysis of social change. Indeed, this critical analysis may, in the end, be of more use to the fans than the naive populism mentioned above.

The supposed traditionalism of the lads' support is an 'invented tradition' (Hobsbawm and Ranger, 1983). Although it is true that throughout this century football has been generally watched by working-class men, the lads' ecstatic style of support primarily developed in the 1960s when the terraces became the homes of potentially violent groups of young men from the newly affluent working-class. The caricatured figure of the Woodbine-smoking, flat-cap-wearing spectator (from whom the lads mythically draw a direct line to their own support) was no longer substantially present in the 1960s. In fact, throughout the twentieth century, although the football ground was predominantly a site of working-class leisure, the social composition of football crowds has fluctuated to include other classes (Dunning *et al.*, 1988 pp. 101, 119). It would be teleological and reductive to suggest that these fluctuations were merely superficial, belying the underlying reality of an essentially working-class game. On the contrary, the different constituencies of the crowds in different decades really gave the game different meanings at different times, which reflected the state of the wider social formation. To suggest that football remained fundamentally the same throughout the century is an exaggerated essentialism, and such claims of traditionalism must be treated with scepticism.

Furthermore, it is not simply the fact that the constituency of football crowds has changed over the course of the century which renders this appeal to tradition dubious, but the lads' own self-belief in their working-class status is itself problematic. Recent economic, social and cultural transformations suggest that any appeal to traditional class formations is necessarily imaginary, since every class has undergone quite radical change. It is certainly significant that the lads regard themselves as working-class, since this imaginary connection informs their under-standings and practices. For instance, their imagined working-class status carries with it a set of connotations about opposition to the owners of capital and an emphasis on physical toughness (which sits somewhat uneasily with the employment in the service industries which many of them now have) but they do not exist in a traditional working-class culture of which they sometimes imagine themselves to be part. Furthermore, the working-class tradition of which the lads consider themselves to be part is primarily a masculine one, and the complaint on which this invented tradition is predicated is not the exclusion of working-class fans in general but the exclusion of the working *man* in particular, of whom the lads regard themselves to be the descendants. Although this chapter certainly does not deny the connection between the lads' class position and their masculinity, the tradition which the lads invent is primarily masculine and is designed to legitimate and protect a very specific kind of masculine fandom which developed not in the traditional working-class but in the newly affluent working-class of the 1960s.

Furthermore, the fluctuation in the composition of football crowds across the century undermines not only the premise of the lads' appeal to tradition but finally its conclusion as well. If football crowds have not remained monolithic in social composition, culture or meaning, then it is also possible to conceive that the present sudden and fundamental shift in crowd composition, witnessed at its most extreme at Manchester United and at other top clubs in the Premier League, may not constitute a mere fluctuation but may indicate a 'real' transformation in crowd composi-tion.

The lads' imagined identity has informed their response to the transformations which face them in the 1990s. In the appeal to tradition, that response is actually flawed (although it may nevertheless succeed if enough people believe it). Yet the weakness of this particular response does not mean that it is politically pointless or that it reveals the illusions of fandom. Rather it demonstrates, in contradistinction to the dismissals of fandom as mere mystification, that fandom actually provides a resource by which the hegemonic projects can be combated. For instance, although the lads' claims of traditionalism cannot be sustained, their imagining of this traditionalism serves to reaffirm their notions of themselves and the distinctiveness of their style of support and acts as a resource for the development of other more formal strategies of resistance such as IMUSA.

Compliance to the New Consumption of Football

The love of the club

Although the lads have opposed the new consumption of football in an attempt to preserve the expression of their own masculine identities through football, they have, paradoxically, also finally assisted in the transformation of football, and this compliance to the new consumption of football has been informed, ironically, by the same notions of masculinity that have provided a resource and reason for resistance. This paradox of simultaneous resistance and compliance suggests the need to reconsider theories of resistance and hegemony which have often been employed in the analysis of consumption. Such a reconsideration of these theories in no way implies their total dismissal, for they have provided very useful insights into the social process, but these theories need to be nuanced with a realization of the complexity of the social process. Subcultures can be both resistant and compliant at the same time, and analysis which emphasizes only one aspect of the political relationship between subordinate and superordinate groups is inevitably facile. In particular, both hegemony theories and resistance theories operate with an unspoken premise that subordinate and superordinate groups are inevitably and inexorably opposed, with no shared interests between them.

In the analysis of the lads' fandom, I highlighted the love which the lads felt for their team. They conceived of this love as equivalent to, and as deep as, any love they might have for a woman. I went on to suggest that this love, though focused on the team, was actually an expression of their emotional attachment to their fellow (male) fans. Yet that attachment, which could be such a powerful resource of opposition, has facilitated the lads' acceptance of the transformation of football. Although the masculine fans experience a restricted kind of ecstasy in the stadium as a result of the demolition of the terraces, their love of the team compels them to continue attending. They may dislike the changes but at least they are capable of re-making the ecstatic solidarity in some way in the new grounds. As long as changes in football allow the lads to preserve some of the ecstatic solidarity of their fandom intact, they will accommodate major grievances and inconveniences – even the loss of the company of friends who can no longer attend the game with them.

The way in which the lads' love for the team has allowed them to accommodate the transformations of the 1990s emerged in several interviews. Lads would sublimate their opposition to Martin Edwards and his commercial policies simply by excluding them from their totemic image of the club that they loved. The lads have carried out an imaginary excision, which neatly slices the business side of the club from the team:

> I don't support the board. I support the team, Manchester United. That name. It doesn't matter who is running it. (Jeff, 1 June 1994)

> If some ruthless bastard can make a lot of money and make a company lot of money, he's going to get a big salary for it. That's the way society been pushed, that's the direction it's been pushed and that's the way it's gone and that's why they've floated the company to follow suit with the way businesses are run. There's two levels of the club. There's all that bullshit side of the club; there's the souvenir shop, there's the executive suite and the corporate lunches and all the rest – all that side of Manchester United. And there's the other side, which is like I said before, there's what really is the club which is the people who genuinely follow it. And for me, on that level, it's not altered at all and, no matter what they do, it never will because, I know without the likes of us that Martin Edwards wouldn't be earning a million pounds a year and they wouldn't be having all the rest of the bullshit. We are the most important factor. Maybe that should make us feel worse about it because they're profiting off our loyalty but, no, I don't feel that on the level that I'm involved in with the club. I don't feel up to that level, it has altered really. But then, maybe that's just the way I want to see ... No, I don't think they could alter it for me. (Gordon, 26 May 1994)

The separation which Gordon and Jeff attempt to effect in order to preserve their love is in 'bad faith', as Sartre would call it (Sartre, 1966, p. 89). The lads refuse to admit the fact, of which they are always aware, that the team is inseparable from the financial side of the club and that they have to submit to the board and its policies. By separating the team from the board, the lads hide this subordination from themselves in order to revel in the temporary expression of their imagined identities. They accommodate their subordination and comply to the transformation of football through this technique of self-deceit, which is most clearly shown in Gordon's statement, which openly wrestles with the contradiction between his knowledge of his position and the way he wants to conceive it. Yet the lads' compliance to the new consumption of football does not consist only or even most importantly of this negative method of bad faith, but rather the basis of the lads' acceptance of the changes to football and their subordination to the board's policies is active and self-conscious.

Rivalry

I have suggested that a central feature of the lads' fandom was masculine pride. Through their loyal support of the team and their team's success, the lads were able to gain recognition and status (Tolson, 1977, p. 43), as football support dispenses honour in the relationships of men from the working-class. The songs that the lads sing (and the conviction and frequency with which they sing them) in the ground demonstrate their status, and almost every song refers to their superiority and their opposition's inferiority.

The need for the masculine support to have a successful team, since their own status is informed by that success, drives the lads into alignment with the new directors, despite the fact that the project of the latter threatens the lads' fandom at another level. The masculine need for success draws the lads into accepting the interpretative framework which has informed the transformation of football. They accept the fundamental claim that football clubs are now profit-making businesses, and are willing to submit to that change so long as their club is successful:

> A football club is a capitalist institution. I mean, I'm not like going on about the revolution or anything but it is, that's what it is. Some of them are run well in that and some are run badly in that. (Barry, 25 May 1994)

Once the lads have accepted this major plank in the new commonsense that football is a business, it is logical that they should want the club to be successful as a 'capitalist institution' in the light of their masculine need for success. Consequently, the lads wholeheartedly approve of some of the commercial developments introduced by Edwards and the board which have improved the commercial standing of the club in the competitive economy of League football. In particular, the lads are pleased that the club shop has done well and that (other) fans buy the shirt:

> I reckon it's really good 'cause no one bashes me over the head when I walk past Old Trafford and say 'Buy this shirt or else'. I mean you only buy it if you want to, don't you? I can understand that like that it is bad with people who've got kids and the kids are under pressure 'cause all their mates have got shirts. I think that's a bit bad 'cause the parents have got to fork out loads of dosh for shirts but as far as everyone else goes and it's not the kids' shirts that bring in the most money, is it, it's all the rest of them. I've got no sympathy for these people who you see on the telly every time it's on Granada Report – United bring out a new shirt – and they're all there going, 'It's bloody terrible, they just don't care about the fans' and they're stood there

with the new shirt in their hands, aren't they? I mean if you want to buy, then you buy it. I'm well happy for the club to make as much money as it wants. It's not ripping people off. It's ripping people off by charging three hundred and fifty quid for a season ticket ... the more money the club has, the better as far as I'm concerned. (Paul, 13 June 1994)

They [the club] have spent quite a lot and I think they've spent wisely and doing the stadium up. I can't really see why people get stuck into him [Edwards] as they do. It's a lot different at City, where someone like Swales deserved the stick he was getting. I think Edwards has been a bit unfortunate really.

AK: The fact is he's brought success to the club.

That's the main thing. That's got to be the number one concern. (Craig, 29 June 1994)

As we have seen, the shirts, of which the lads approve, are very often worn by the type of people whose presence at Old Trafford rankles so deeply with the lads' notion of ecstatic masculine solidarity. The lads' masculinity welcomes certain commercial developments, which are simultaneously those which they revile.

A similar paradox is noticeable among the lads with regard to the stadium. On the one hand, the new all-seater Old Trafford is criticized because the old solidarities are no longer possible there. On the other hand, the lads have great pride in the ground, which they regard, not without reason, as the best in the English League. Indeed, the lads use the architectural impressiveness of the ground as ammunition in their competition for honour with other men. Manchester City is roundly abused because some of the stands are so shabby. In particular, the new Platt Lane (Umbro) stand at Maine Road is mocked because it is so obviously cheap. The financial power of Manchester United, symbolized in the architecture of the stadium, feeds into the lads' masculine pride. Yet the new architecture of the ground which fills the lads with pride also condemns them to a restricted expression of masculinity in their support.

Some commentators have argued that this rivalry between working-class men is itself mystified and that sport is a mirage thrown up by the capitalist class to hide the real contradictions within society. Echoing some of the work of the Frankfurt School, Vinnai, for instance, argues that football communicates ideas which are central to capitalism and to the domination of the capitalist class (Vinnai, 1973, p. 33–40) and thereby, in distracting the working-class, prevents the overthrow of the capitalist order (Vinnai, 1973, p. 95). Theories of mystification, like

Vinnai's, overemphasize the unity of the working-class and fail to recognize the essential benefits which the working-class derive from (admittedly problematic) alliances with capitalists. In the context of a competitive global market, it is not mystified for the working-class individuals to align themselves with a 'capitalist interest', because only through that alliance can those individuals earn a livelihood at all. In the light of this competitive economy, there are vertical divisions which run through the working-class and which link fragments of that class problematically to their capitalist employers. The working class is simply not as unified as these theories assume (and, indeed, it may be wrong to talk of the working class or any subordinate class in the singular), especially in the light of the post-Fordist fragmentation of this class.

In supporting a football club, working-class males symbolically re-create such an alignment with a capitalist interest. It is, however, a problematic and, indeed, paradoxical alignment because it must juggle the manifest inequality of the lads' position with the benefits which they reap as a result of their subordination. Hegemony theory, which operates with notions of mystification, exaggerates the unity of both the working-class interests and capital and consequently arrives at the false conclusion that any compliance must necessarily be a case of false consciousness. The lads certainly comply to dominant capitalist interests and, in complying, they are accepting a degree of subordination, but their compliance is complex. It is informed by the lads' partially autonomous masculinity, which demands their resistance to the new directors (as resistance theory has noted), but that masculine culture also explains their compliance because they share some genuine interests with the club, whose success increases their status as men.

The fanzines

Fanzines, fan magazines, have been an important medium through which the lads have expressed their paradoxical relationship with the club in the 1990s. However, there is a quite decisive division between club fanzines produced by and for the lads, articulating masculine understandings, and publications such as *When Saturday Comes*, which are produced and read (as we shall see in Chapter 13) principally by the educated members of the professional public sector middle class. The clearest demonstration of the division between these two forms of support and the fanzines which express that support was the banning of *Red Issue* from *When Saturday Comes*'s list of fanzines because *Red Issue* was regarded as divisive. Comments by a contributor to *Red Issue* concerning the banning of the fanzine demonstrate the distinction between new football writing fandom and the lads:

> There is, of course, a larger ideological split that underpins this sort of spat [the banning of *Red Issue* from the *When Saturday Comes* list]. All

too often, organisations and publications that seek to represent football fans as a whole tend to disparage so called 'sectarian' forces like *Red Ish*, accusing them of dividing fandom and thus reducing supporter power in general. (Kurt, 1994, p. 87)

Sure, there may be temporary alliances to halt the more brainless schemes of the senile FA or the cretins in Whitehall but there can be no permanent departure from the natural state of the true football fan that his support of the club is as much shaped by his hatred of others as by his love for his own team. (Kurt, 1994 pp. 87–8)

The producers and consumers of *When Saturday Comes* are 'ideologically split' from the lads because the former see the primary division of interests as not between fans but between fans and the directors. Yet for the lads the 'natural state' of support is to emphasize their rivalry with other fans, thereby achieving recognition and status for themselves. Kurt's statements neatly demonstrate both that the club fanzines at Manchester United are part of the lads' fandom and that these fanzines cannot be treated as if they were straightforwardly comparable with *When Saturday Comes*.

This is further reflected in the readership of the publications. *Red Issue* has always been one of the largest-selling club fanzines, with sales figures reputed to be over 10,000 per issue, though this is uncorroborated, while *United We Stand* began with a small readership which reached sales of about 5000 per issue by 1994 according to Andy Mitten (Andy Mitten, personal interview). Of course, these fanzines are read by both the new football writing and compliant fans, but their principal readership is the lads:

You get a real cross section. You get lads aged 16 'cause I know when I was sixteen I used to love buying fanzines, and you get 45 year old blokes coming up to you and saying, 'That was a great article last month'. I'd probably say 18 to 30 male is the vast majority of the readers. (Andy Mitten, editor, *United We Stand*, 27 June 1994)

We noted above that the lads have developed a style of dress by which they distinguish themselves. In recent editions, both club fanzines have drawn attention to styles of dress, and in this way they announce to the lads (who should be able to pick up on the references) which clothes are acceptable. In this way, the fanzines communicate the accepted form of masculine support to the lads. In an article describing the trip to Turkey for the game against Galatasaray in September 1994, a stylistic distinction was drawn heavily between the lads and the new consumer fans. Any lad reading that article could not fail to note the rules of membership which were being laid down:

> There seemed to be two distinct groups, those who regularly travel on
> the club's 'official' trips, invariably recognizable by their United tops,
> and the rest of us who wouldn't normally be seen dead travelling on
> the sanitised over-priced but nevertheless 'official' trips. If we wore a
> uniform it was definitely more Ralph Lauren than Umbro. (*Red Issue*,
> Vol. 7, Issue 35)

Another article, in *United We Stand*, draws on similar themes: 'Better
still, we've developed into a swaggering Lauren clad beast that couldn't
give a toss about any other club or any other supporters' (*United We
Stand*, Issue 41, p. 25). The discussion of the lads' stylistic distinction in
these club fanzines demonstrates that they are directed at the lads.

Like the lads' fandom more generally, the fanzines demonstrate a
complex combination of elements of resistance and compliance, in
contrast to Haynes' assertion that they are simply oppositional. Most
club fanzines emerged in 1989 or in response to the Hillsborough disaster
and the ensuing transformation of the game in the 1990s. *Red Issue* first
appeared in 1989, while *United We Stand* was first published in 1990. The
fanzines appeared exactly when the lads' fandom began to be seriously
threatened. As I have suggested above, the fanzines have expressed the
lads' specific understanding of themselves as 'true' fans and this has been
crucial. At a time of major changes which have threatened the lads'
fandom, the fanzines have sustained the lads' support by re-negotiating
the lads' identities to accommodate the new consumption of football. In
this sense, the fanzines have assisted in the compliance of the lads to the
project of the new directors. They have made it possible for lads to attend
the new ritual of football but to continue to imagine that their fandom is
'traditional', even though that fandom has actually had to be thoroughly
remade in the light of all-seater stadia.

Furthermore, the fanzines have contributed to the framework of
meanings which has made the new consumption of football possible. In
the last chapter, I argued that one of the principal changes which was
central to the new consumption of football was the establishment of the
clubs as primarily profit-making businesses. They were no longer to be
regarded as quasi-public institutions run for philanthropic reasons.
Ironically, although the fanzines oppose some of the developments which
have been introduced into football, the fanzines themselves have finally
contributed to the creation of the new free-market interpretative
framework which has increasingly informed football in the 1990s. The
fanzines legitimate entrepreneurialism as an economic practice.

The fanzines are commercial ventures; they are normally sold at £1 a
copy. Consequently, the editors of the fanzines, which, as I noted above,
sell between 5000 and 13,000 copies an issue, can earn quite substantial
amounts of income. Andy Mitten, the editor of *United We Stand*,
described himself as a motivated individual interested in developing new

projects (27 June 1994). He regards the fanzine as an appropriate expression of his entrepreneurial endeavours. The commercial and entrepreneurial element of the fanzines has not gone unnoticed by some of the lads. For instance, fans have noted that *Red Issue* makes a substantial revenue from its large sales (e.g. Stan, 20 May 1990). Andy Mitten is often the target of jokes about the revenue produced by his fanzine, and there is an element of seriousness to the comments. This is not to dismiss Andy's or other editors' serious commitment to producing a publication which the lads both enjoy and find useful as an interpretative resource. However, it is pointless idealizing the role of fanzines as fundamentally opposed to the commercial forces which are coursing through football, for, in very real ways, the fanzines are part of these same forces. They are themselves profit-making entrepreneurial endeavours. In Chapter 10, I argued that the political economy of Sky television itself was meaningful, expressing certain dominant values, and I want to make the same claim here. The very production and sale of the fanzines – the political economic origins of these texts – are themselves replete with meaning. When the lads purchase a fanzine, they are not simply buying an interpretative manual, detailing the correct method of masculine support; the fanzine also inevitably communicates the meaningfulness of its production – it announces its entrepreneurial origins. Thereby, fanzines both draw on and affirm the Thatcherite commonsense which emphasizes the free market and entrepreneurial activity and which has been central to the transformation of football in the 1990s.

Conclusion

The lads' interventions have constituted an important element in this conjunctural moment of transformation, and this chapter has examined the way in which masculine fandom has resisted but also, paradoxically, contributed to the new consumption of football in the 1990s. The discussion has situated itself within the contemporary sociological literature of fans and audiences, in that it has attempted to overcome some of the shortcomings of the theories of resistance and hegemony, which that literature seeks to develop. The lads' fandom has demonstrated that subcultural forms are paradoxically resistant and compliant because they are textured by cross-cutting ties of mutual and opposing interests with dominant groups. In this way, despite the lads' overt opposition to the new directors and their project, their masculine desire for status and honour (earned through football support) has led them into positions where they support the very developments which, at other moments, they resist. The lads' paradoxical compliance with the new directors' project has been crucial because, as the failure of the merger schemes in the 1980s demonstrated, the owners of football clubs are finally dependent on the fans. It is only in so far as fans attend games that the new directors have a valuable commodity. The lads' paradoxical compliance with the new consumption of football has ensured that in the end they have sustained the project of the new directors.

This chapter has drawn upon a period of fieldwork at one particular club. The concentration on a single club is not a particular problem *per se* as the lads of all clubs share much the same culture – a fact that is reflected by the lads' comprehension of the actions and songs of the opposition's lads. However, the fact that I have focused on Manchester United is significant and deliberate. That club has been in the vanguard of recent developments and inordinately successful in transforming itself in line with free-market values and principles. Consequently, the lads at Old Trafford have faced the project of the new directors at its strongest; other clubs in England will not be able to marginalize substantial parts of their masculine support with nearly such ease. Nevertheless, despite the extremity of the process in operation at Manchester United, it is not by any means unique to that club.[14] As the demonstrations and complaints in practically every fanzine attest, the reformulation of football consumption by the new directors to the detriment of the masculine support is a phenomenon which is sweeping through every club. Manchester United is an exceptional case but, in terms of the new consumption of football, it is an exceptional case which demonstrates the rule with special clarity.

Notes

1   Clarke and Critcher's work contains an interesting account of the historic construction of leisure in bourgeois society but, around the pages indicated, it is implied that subordinate classes must be mystified to have accepted leisure forms which are derived from a capitalist hegemony and which support that system both culturally and economically.

2   This use of Durkheim's theory of religion is not original and has been drawn upon before in the discussion of sport. See, for instance, Dunning, and Sheard (1979).

3   Tim provided an insight into the way in which the lads use the pub to create this ecstatic solidarity when he described his visit to Blackburn in October 1994. He proudly described how Manchester United fans had been packed into a pub and, when the time to leave came, they walked to the ground, singing euphorically, to the bewildered looks of the Blackburn Rovers fans, who were making their way quietly to the ground on the other side of the street. (Tim, fieldnotes, 29 October 1994).

4   Mark is not part of the lad category, being the head of the Manchester branch of the FSA, but this description seems valid, since he has spent many years attending games and therefore has a good insight into the fans' views and practices. He is also a Manchester City fan.

5   The centrality of masculinity for the male fans to their identities and

practices has been noted in much of the literature on fans, and especially hooliganism (see Dunning *et al.*, 1988, p. 16; Dunning, 1986, p. 87; Williams *et al.*, 1990, pp. xxv, 115, 132; Marsh *et al.*, 1978, p. 105; Holt, 1989, p. 330; Mason, 1988, p. 32; Buford, 1992; Ward, 1990; Allan, 1989).

6   The affluence of the lads who still attend football and constituted the majority of the network in which I established myself (which therefore implies a similar class position to the new consumer fans) is suggested by the very expensive designer clothes which many of these individuals wore.

7   One of the fans, whom I defined as part of the 'new football writing' group, suggested during his interview that in one sense he would like to see Manchester United get relegated to prove that football was not just about money and that the new directors had not succeeded (25 May 1995). In other words, just as the lads want the game to facilitate the expression of their identities, the new football writing fans would like to see their political beliefs expressed through the game.

8   Coventry City's stadium became all-seater in the mid-1980s but, due to fan protest, some of the seats had to be removed. Queens Park Rangers' stadium had very small standing areas before it finally went all-seater for the 1994–1995 season.

9   See Table A.1 for the lads' employment.

10   The figures take into account the 1000 – 1500 away allocation at Old Trafford.

11   Two interviews (Andy Walsh and Deborah) described the Stretford End as full of 'dickheads' (young lads trying to be hooligans) (Andy Walsh, 25 May 1994) and women and children (Deborah, 1 August 1994).

12   Manchester United fans sometimes sing a song to the tune of Culture Club's 'Karma Chameleon' with the words 'Karma United Road'!

13   Interestingly, the primarily masculine fans in the K-Stand (after discussions at IMUSA) have recently developed a strategy of countering the effect of seats by simply standing up *en masse* for long periods of the game. This action is announced with the song 'Stand up for the champions' and was particularly effective during a European Cup tie at Old Trafford against Juventus on 20 November 1996. However, the club stamped this practice out in the 1997–8 season.

14   At the inaugural meeting of IMUSA in June 1995, Kevin Miles, the chairman of the Independent Newcastle United Supporters' Association, revealed the level of disgruntlement among presumably masculine Newcastle United fans at the new developments which had occurred under Sir John Hall. Even though these fans, who have followed Newcastle United through 'thin and thin' in the past, now watched a team more successful than they had ever known, the level of dissatisfaction with the clubs' pricing system and ticketing policy was higher than ever.

13

New Football Writing[1]

Textual and Social Composition

New football writing began to emerge as a recognizable and self-conscious form of fandom after the disasters of 1985 in response to the crisis of football and in opposition to many of the arguments for reform which were being proposed in the press and in Parliament (see Chapters 7 to 9). As the name for this group suggests, the production and consumption of certain types of football literature is a central element of new football writing and, thus, the critical analysis of this form of fandom will concentrate on some of this fandom's major texts. In particular, I will focus on the national fanzine, *When Saturday Comes*, and Nick Hornby's *Fever Pitch*, although there is a much wider and developing literature which, it might be cogently argued, is part of new football writing (White, 1994; Watt, 1993; Hamilton, 1994). This chapter is not intended as a definitive analysis of the development of this kind of football literature and, therefore, although it acknowledges the publication of many books and football magazines in the 1990s which could certainly be described as new football writing, it will focus on *Fever Pitch* and *When Saturday Comes*, since these have achieved pre-eminence in the consciousness of the consumers and producers of new football writings. In addition, their existence has been very substantially responsible for creating the conditions in which subsequent publications have been possible.

The publication of *When Saturday Comes* in March 1986 was a critical moment for the development of new football writing. *When Saturday Comes* was an originally amateurish magazine created by a Chelsea fan, Mike Ticher, which sought to give the fans a place in which to air their discontents about the game in the mid-1980s. Originally, Ticher printed only a hundred copies of the first edition, using very rudimentary publishing techniques. However, within days of a review in the *Guardian*, Ticher received nearly a hundred requests for the next issue and, consequently, produced 1000 copies of the next edition (*When Saturday Comes*, 1992, introduction).

The Football Supporters Association (FSA) has also been a central part of new football writing as a style of fandom. The FSA was established in Liverpool in August 1985 in response principally to the Heysel disaster, expressing the outrage which was felt by many football supporters concerning that event, the media's representation of football fans, the treatment of fans and the government's proposals for reformation. The government's Football Spectators' Bill and its national identity card scheme became the FSA's main focus of attack. The prospect of the national membership scheme unified fans behind the FSA and, as a result of the FSA's campaign against the scheme, it was able to recruit some 20,000 members (*The Times*, 6 December 1988). The FSA has never been able to command such support since, and membership has dropped to below 2000. However, although membership had dwindled since 1990, the public profile of the FSA has remained disproportionately large in comparison with its formal size, and it is frequently required to express its opinions on the television and radio and in the newspapers. Despite the formal loss of support, then, the FSA is still able to articulate its views to an audience well beyond the declining constituency of its own members.

The final and crucial moment in the establishment of new football writing fandom was the publication of *Fever Pitch*, the ironic and best-selling autobiography of an Arsenal fan, in 1992: 30,000 hardback and 246,000 paperback copies were sold by March 1995 (Nick Hornby, personal communication, 1 March 1995). Although many of these copies were bought by fans who accorded more closely with the lads' style of fandom, the text itself expressed the sentiments of the emergent style of 'new football writing' fandom.[2] Drawing on the success of this first book, Hornby's edited volume, *My Favourite Year*, was published in 1993, by which time 'new football writing' fandom had become a self-conscious practice of consumption. The term 'new football writing', then, is intended to describe the new style of consumption which is based around *When Saturday Comes*, *Fever Pitch* and the FSA.

The common cultural links between the producers and consumers of new football writing are best established by an examination of the social backgrounds of the producers and consumers of new football writing, though the data on the producers and consumers of new football writing are certainly less solid than would ideally be the case. However, despite their shortcomings, we can gain some notion of the social location of this fandom. In particular, these data suggest a social and cultural reason behind the mutual aversion between the lads (and *Red Issue*, in particular) and *When Saturday Comes*.

In *Fever Pitch*, Nick Hornby reveals that he is a member of the London-based, professional, educated middle classes. Hornby was brought up by solidly professional parents in suburban Maidenhead, studied at Cambridge and taught for several years before becoming a writer. Hornby's social background is actually typical of the other writers who have been central to the production of new football writing. The authors who feature in his anthology, *My Favourite Year*, consist of similarly educated and professional individuals. Of the 13 contributors, including Hornby, five are professional writers, three write for or edit broadsheet newspapers (*Times Higher Education Supplement*, *Independent on Sunday*, *Sunday Times* and *Independent*), one teaches at a university, one is a pharmacist and one is the managing director of a market research company (Hornby, 1993, pp. 219–20).[3] A similar social background is reflected in David Bull's *We'll Support You Evermore* (Bull, 1992), which might also be termed 'new football writing', since it is a collection of short pieces by various fans, recalling memorable moments in their supporting careers. Of the 24 contributors, including John Major, 11 worked in higher education, a further three taught, two at comprehensive schools and one at a grammar school, four were professional writers or journalists, three more worked or have worked for local government, one was an MP and one worked in a private publishing company, which, incidentally printed fanzines, including the early editions of *When Saturday Comes* (Bull, 1992, pp. 9–12).[4]

When Saturday Comes' own marketing data[5] on their readership can be instructively examined to highlight the different social locations of the consumers of new football writing and the lads (as long as we are careful not to overemphasize this divide, as there is overlap between the groups). Although the readership was overwhelmingly (97 per cent) male, and aged between 18 and 34, and therefore had a similar sex and generational composition to that of the lads, the readers of *When Saturday Comes* were generally likely to have attended higher education and to be employed at the upper end of the labour market in professional jobs. Sixty-three per cent of the readership was classified as being from classes ABC1, i.e. from higher professional down to skilled manual workers. A further 15 per cent were students. This is potentially problematic for my classification of fans, since some of the individuals whom I have categorized as lads were also students. However, those individuals (Stan, Nick and Andy Mitten) were benefiting from the recent expansion in higher education by taking practical courses which would equip them for work in the service industries. I would suggest circumspectly that the students who read *When Saturday Comes* are not generally those studying at new universities on courses with practical intent, but are those who come from professional backgrounds who are reading formal academic subjects in the hope of gaining professional employment after college. This inference is at least partially sustained by the fact that the three students from my sample did not read *When Saturday Comes* (or, in Andy's case, had stopped reading it), implying that the kinds of student who consumed new football writing were different from those like Stan, Nick and Andy, who adopted masculine styles of support.

The (relatively) high-class composition of the *When Saturday Comes* readership is emphasized by the newspapers which its readers buy; 35 per cent bought the *Guardian*, 27 per cent the *Independent*, 20 per cent the *Daily Mirror*, 15 per cent the *Daily Telegraph*, 10 per cent the *Daily Mail* and 10 per cent the *Sun*. The popularity of the *Guardian* among the consumers of new football writing suggests a particular class position for these fans, since the *Guardian* is the preferred paper of the professional public sector service class. Furthermore, all of the three most popular papers are left wing or, at least in the case of the *Independent*, potentially acceptable to a left-wing audience. It would be wrong to suggest that the new football writing fan can be simplistically divided from the lad or the new consumer fan simply on the grounds of political alignment, but the popularity of the *Guardian* along with the other data on these fans does allow us to make some inferences about their class position.

The combination of the higher class position of the new football writing fans and their liberal or leftist political persuasion (as suggested by the favoured newspapers) gives new football writing a distinctive complexion, suggesting that its fandom is principally situated among the professional, public sector middle classes, where such views are common. Hornby confirmed this social composition of the new football writing when he said 'they [*When Saturday Comes* readers] are traditionalist and conservative as well as being Labour voting and liberal in their views' (Hornby, personal interview, 11 August 1994).

The social position of the producers and consumers of new football writing, is very specific. Both the producers (writers) and consumers (readers) are drawn principally from the well-educated professional classes. In this way, the social position of the producers and consumers of new football writing reflects Fowler's (1991) notion of a 'legitimate cultural group' in her analysis of women and romantic literature in the twentieth century, which draws on Bourdieu's notion of a 'left-bank' (intellectual and public sector) middle class (1984): 'Most strikingly, I have drawn attention to a new stratum which possesses such educational resources and which is found mainly in public sector administration and professional occupations' (Fowler, 1991, p. 170). In Chapter 2, I described the main social transformations which had occurred in Britain as a result of the restructuring of the economy in the light of global developments and, following Savage *et al.* (1992), I argued that a very significant social change has been the emergence of the private sector middle class and the concomitant (and relative) political and economic peripheralization of the public sector middle class. New football writing is principally produced and consumed within the latter social milieu.

The Principal Features of New Football Writing

In the Chapter 12, I argued that the lads' masculinity, which was the central feature of their fandom, informed their reactions to the new consumption of football, determining their paradoxical reactions to the new directors' projects. Similarly, the central understandings of new football writing fans have informed their responses to the changes in the game, establishing the lines of opposition and consent for these fans. In particular, the central meanings of new football writing are the notion of the 'golden age' of English football and the idea of authenticity, which constitute the core of new football writing's self-understandings.

'The Golden Age'

Although new football writing arose in response to the crisis of football in the mid-1980s, its roots lay in a period of English football which preceded that crisis by some two decades. New football writing germinated in the late 1960s and early 1970s in the boyhood experiences of those males who would go on to become central figures in the creation of new football writing.

The central role of memory and remembrance in new football writing is important and worth considering briefly before we go on to the shared memories of new football writers. Like history, memory can never return us directly to what is remembered in actuality. We can never recall or re-live the past according to Ranke's aphorism 'wie es eigentlich gewesen ist' (how it really was). Rather, the employment of memory in the present follows the process which Gadamer describes in his proposition of a hermeneutic historical method. Our understanding of the past proceeds via a 'fusion of horizons' (Gadamer, 1979, p. 273) whereby we interpret the past in terms of our present understandings which frame that past. However, these two horizons – our own culture and the historical culture we study – are never still but move in a constant upward spiral of ever-increasing understanding and interpretative depth. Similarly, our memories do not live in the mind as once and future thoughts but are permanently re-negotiated in the light of our changing circumstances and personal understandings. The sense and meaning of memories follow in the wake of contemporary experiences like geese which reform their echelon as new leaders take the lead in their flight south. A particular memory is, following Gadamer, constantly reinterpreted and given new meaning in the light of the developing circumstances of our existence. In other words, the changing meaning which we give to our existence as a whole transforms the meanings of particular memories which comprise that existence. Indeed, this reinterpretation of the past is, for Gadamer, constitutive of the continued history of humanity. Humanity makes its future by reinterpreting its past.

The necessarily mediated quality of memory leads to an important recognition about the nature of new football writing. The boyhood memories which are at the heart of new football writing's interpretative framework and which inform this fandom and its understandings of

180

contemporary changes cannot be considered to be really what these men thought about football when they were boys. Rather, they are imaginary constructions of what they now think they thought as children. The producers and consumers of new football writings – like the lads, and, indeed, like all social groups – must necessarily invent or imagine a tradition for themselves. They must actively re-create a boyhood which is gone and which can only be recovered through an imagination which is inevitably framed by their contemporary understandings.

The boyhood memories of the producers and consumers of new football writing have been particularly privileged in their fandom, acting as a primary resource for their understanding of the consumption of football. For them, the early experience of the game was of a 'golden age' of English football, when the League contained numerous good and entertaining teams, and England itself had won the World Cup in 1966. This 'golden age' constitutes a central resource for understanding the new consumption of football. In an interview with *When Saturday Comes*, both Eamonn Dunphy, the retired player and professional writer, and *When Saturday Comes* itself were explicit about the special nature of this period:

A lot of *When Saturday Comes*'s readers grew up watching football in the late Sixties, early Seventies and for them that is the 'Golden Era'. Do you think it's a simple case of childhood memories being romanticised or was the standard of play higher then?

I think standards were higher and there are solid reasons why. Before then, players were never properly paid, they were never as fit as they should have been, there was a lot of sloth and sort of stupid thinking, that's what Busby capitalised on really; that's why his team that died were so successful, it was a poor era in the game. Then the maximum wage was removed and players felt that they were getting rewarded properly for the first time. They became fitter and harder, but at the same time the individualism and the talent that had been around in the game before then was still present. So there was a period which I would claim, the golden age, when all the factors were evenly balanced. (*When Saturday Comes*, No. 58, p. 16)

Although the new football writers point to the quality of play as an essential factor in their sanctifying of this period of English football, it is noticeable how they refer to the fact that the players were rewarded 'properly'. The implications of this notion of a proper reward are significant, if we consider the discussion of the abolition of the maximum wage in Chapter 4. There I argued that, in fact, the abolition of the maximum wage was predicated on the acceptance of values which were at odds with the Keynesian post-war settlement; the abolition was based on a belief in the free market. However, in the construction of the late 1960s in the memories of the producers and consumers of new football writing, the rewards which players received were seen to be proper, in line with both their talents and with the social democratic affluence of that period. The late 1960s became a 'golden age' for new football writers not only because English football was of a high international standard but also because, in the invented memories of new football writers, it seemed to be informed by those very social democratic values which the producers and consumers of new football writing support. Such support is hardly surprising, since many of the producers and consumers of new football writing work in the public institutions which emerged or were substantially strengthened under the Keynesian post-war consensus.

For new football writing fans, the 1960s represented a mythological past in which their political understandings, which have been under increasing assault in the 1980s, were affirmed on the very pitches of the Football League; the period of the best English club and national team performances was conveniently coupled with an era of social democratic consensus. This connection of political preference and playing success was necessarily a subsequent act of imagination, because, at the time of the 'golden age', the future producers and consumers of new football writers were boys and could not have been aware of the political symbolism with which they would later invest this period. Furthermore, as I have already suggested, the abolition of the maximum wage was partly predicated on the adoption of free-market ideas which went against Keynesian and corporate principles and which the producers and consumers of new football writing would oppose.

The identification of new football writing as an imaginary construction which is founded upon certain political understandings is important, because this imaginary construction has informed new football writing's response to the transformation of football in the 1990s. New football writing's myth of origin has provided the interpretative framework by which this group of fans has understood and responded to recent developments in the game. Just as the lads regard the game as an arena of masculine solidarity and judge any transformation of the means of consuming the game by its effect on their masculine celebrations, so do the producers and consumers of new football writing view the new consumption of the game through an interpretative framework which emphasizes social democratic values and looks romantically back to a Keynesian past. In particular, operating within this social democratic framework, they oppose those developments which are informed by free-market thinking and which aim to subvert the corporatist basis of League football.

Authenticity

The producers and consumers of new football writing imagine not only that their earliest experiences of football were in the 'golden age' of English football but also that the terraces in those days were populated by a mythically authentic working class. By standing with these individuals, new football writing fans were experiencing the same traditional practices as these authentic individuals. New football writing has mistakenly taken the new styles of support which were developing in the 1960s (and hooliganism, in particular) for the authentic experience of a traditional working class.

Nick Hornby comically deprecates this mythological re-creation of himself from the suburban son of respectable professional parents into a member of the authentic working class in *Fever Pitch*. 'The white south of England middle-class Englishman and woman is the most rootless creature on earth; we would rather belong to any other community in the world' (Hornby, 1992, p. 47). Thus, the children of the suburban professional classes invent identities. Hornby denies that football should be seen as a working-class sport and that, therefore, individuals from other sections of society should feel neither ashamed of their background nor somehow worthy that they have lowered themselves to attending the game. For instance, Hornby argues: 'Football, famously, is the people's game, and as such is prey to all sorts of people who aren't as it were, the people' (Hornby, 1992, p. 96). However, at the same time as dismissing those individuals who attend the game because it is a working-class sport, Hornby confesses that he, in fact, does exactly that and that his attendance at Highbury was stimulated out of a need to create for himself an 'authentic', working-class identity:

> I have dropped as many aitches as I can; the only ones left in my diction have dug themselves too far into definite articles to be winkled out and I use plural verb forms with singular subjects whenever possible. This was a process that began shortly after my first visits to Highbury, continued throughout my suburban grammar school career, and escalated alarmingly when I arrived at university. (Hornby, 1992, p. 48)

When Saturday Comes has played upon similar notions of authenticity in which football is seen as a sport which represents the true working class and through which the leftist elements of the professional middle class can legitimate their own cultural and political position. Ed Horton is a principal figure here.[6] Horton's piece in *My Favourite Year* demonstrates the mythic populism of new football writing and, therefore, its putative attachment to the working class, despite his denial of the validity or importance of such a relationship. In that piece, Horton described the 1991–1992 season, when the Maxwells were forced to relinquish their ownership of Oxford United. Horton's populism peeps through at the end of the article when he declares that 'We took back what was ours, if only for a matter of months' (Horton, 1993, p. 73). The question which this sentence raises is who is the 'we' and what was the 'ours' to which Horton refers. Obviously, Horton means the fans at Oxford who were united by their opposition to the Maxwells and the club itself. Horton then speaks for this group. Yet as these chapters on the fans are designed to show, any club's fans are a very problematic and differentiated body and to call them 'we' so easily denies that differentiation; a differentiation which, at other moments, Horton recognizes when he distinguishes himself (like Hornby) from the 'people'. Yet Horton easily slips into an unsustained populist claim that all the fans felt like him. Horton, therefore, falls into the very trap which Hornby (and Horton himself) consciously mark out; that of seeing football as a populist, working-class sport and enjoying it because it offers the opportunity of a mythical solidarity with that class. Despite the denials, new football writing imagines itself as speaking for a mythical traditional working-class fan, thereby legitimating itself, since it appears to represent the understandings of a wider fandom than it actually does. The producers and consumers of new football writing imaginarily align themselves with the working class in their consumption of the game, thereby demonstrating their support for this class.

The origin of new football writing within the leftist sections of the professional middle class in the late 1960s and a mythic affiliation with the traditional working class among this fandom have determined new football writing's position in the debates about football in the 1990s. Although new football writing has a curious dependence on the lads' (working-class) fandom, the meanings which new football writing fans would like to see expressed through the game are very different. The producers and consumers of new football writing want football to express their (leftist) political views, just as the lads wanted the retention of the terraces because these concrete spaces facilitated their demonstrations of masculinity. Since the terraces are associated with authentic working-class support, new football writing fans have generally opposed not only the demolition of the terraces but also any other developments introduced by the new directors which threaten the 'authenticity' of football as a ritual.

This political project has been explicitly recognized by the producers and consumers of new football writing: 'The way they're [the new directors] taking the game is the very opposite of what the *When Saturday Comes* people and all that would want out of the game' (Hornby, personal interview, 11 August 1994). Other fans express similar sentiments, demonstrating that they want to consume a football which accords with their political project:

When I get really bitter and twisted about [Manchester] United, I half wish that they got relegated so that it clears out all the shit, including the shit that are running the club and so that there's some sort of purging really. Let's see where we are, let's see who's still going to watch them then. And that's why at the end of this season, I was, I've not got any particular allegiance to Oldham, Ipswich or Sheffield United but I'd much rather see a big club go down than a smaller club. (Andy Walsh, personal interview, 25 May 1994)

Officials in the FSA were equally explicit in their aims. Mark Glynn, the secretary of the Manchester branch of the FSA, hoped that by campaigning, the FSA could sneak social democracy in through the back door (Mark Glynn, personal interview, 14 June 1994). Johnny Flacks, the FSA's representative to the FA, revealed the basis for his affiliation to the association: 'The FSA suits me perfectly because it gives me an opportunity to combine two things, if you like; the love of football and the love of social justice' (Johnny Flacks, personal interview, 8 June 1994). For new football writers, football should embody an egalitarian and social democratic message. The construction of the golden age in the late 1960s is significant because it symbolically coincides with a period when the principle (if not the reality) of inclusive and egalitarian provision was still dominant. New football writing, therefore, imagines a past which informs this style of fandom and which is then drawn upon to legitimate its arguments against developments which threaten that fandom. The producers of new football writing have opposed those aspects of the new consumption of football which go against their social democratic sensibilities and which seem to exclude an 'authentic' working class, of which these fans imagine themselves to be part.

The Historic Role of the Professional Middle Classes: Before *Fever Pitch*

If the social location of new football writing is to be found principally in the intellectual and public sector professional middle class – Bourdieu's 'left bank' – then the origins of this form of fandom can certainly be traced back beyond the mid-1980s. I have already noted that the producers and consumers of new football writing in this conjunctural moment first experienced football as boys in the late 1960s and early 1970s, but it seems likely that older members of the professional public sector middle class have themselves been interested in football since at least this period and that, similarly, they produced literature which informed their consumption of the game. In this way, England's World Cup triumph in 1966 had a somewhat similar effect on this class fragment as Italia '90 did for their counterparts later, legitimating and emphasizing their interest in the game. Significantly, in 1972, Ian Taylor wrote 'It's also the middle brow button-down-collar intellectuals of the Sunday press and academics from various disciplines who can now write about their football hang-ups without loss of respectability' (cited in Haynes, 1995, p. 4).

Just as the boys who would produce new football writing in the 1980s and 1990s became interested in the game in the late 1960s and early 1970s, so did the adult members of this class fragment demonstrate a similar form of fandom some twenty-five years before new football writing. In particular, this class fragment began, in the late 1960s, to produce literature whose themes would be explored more fully in the l990s. Signally, in 1968 Arthur Hopcraft published *The Football Man*. Although this work did not involve the self-conscious and self-deprecating style of later new football writing, and *Fever Pitch* in particular, it discussed the transformation of football in the 1960s and included interviews with major players in the post-war period, giving a detailed picture of the state of the game in the 1960s. In this way, though less explicitly than *Fever Pitch*, which is interested more or less exclusively with the fans' consumption of the game, *The Football Man* constituted a handbook for the consumption of the game. It laid out the wider meaningfulness of the consumption of football. Thus, Hopcraft claimed that 'football was not so much an opiate of the people as a flag run up against the gaffer bolting his gates and the landlord armed with his bailiffs' (Hopcraft, 1990, p. 23). As we have seen, this construction of the sport as an authentic ritual of working-class solidarity and opposition is important to new football writing.

In the late 1960s and early 1970s, this class was content to demonstrate its affiliation to the game publicly, as Taylor's comment reveals. That public affiliation became problematic later in the 1970s and 1980s and, although this class fragment was certainly still involved in consuming the game, its public discussion of its consumption of football was muted. However, this was not the case for the entire class fragment. In Chapter 1, I argued that the sociology of football has to become self-conscious in order to improve itself and set itself upon properly critical and academic foundations. The recognition of the social origin of new football writing in the public sector and intellectual professional middle class and its historical existence back at least to the late 1960s allows us to self-consciously and critically situate the sociology of football. In effect, the sociology of football in Britain over the last twenty-five years, which emerged principally in response to the appearance of hooliganism in the 1960s, is a form of new football writing. It is the discussion of a segment of the professional middle classes about the consumption of the game and, like new football writing more generally, is heavily concerned with the working-class consumption of the game.

Taylor's (1971) well-known piece on football hooliganism might be read not only as an early example of the sociological analysis of football violence but also as an early piece of new football writing. Interestingly, Taylor effectively anticipates some of the themes which would feature in the new football writing of the 1980s and 1990s. He focuses on the consumption of the game – the violent fandom of a 'subcultural rump' of the working class. Furthermore, and more importantly, in his attribution of hooliganism to the growing alienation of a subcultural rump of the working class due to the internationalization and commercialization of the game, Taylor ultimately evokes a past in which the working class actively participated in the club and in which the club was effectively a form of social democratic institution. This working-class subcultural rump protested against its alienation from the formerly democratic club through violent confrontation. In effect, Taylor anticipates the invention of tradition of new football writing in the 1990s. The past is constructed mythically as the site of a social democratic emancipation, but whereas Taylor locates that past some time between the 1930s and 1950s, new football writers construct the 1960s as a period in which the game was healthy because it was situated in a similarly imagined Keynesian consensus.[7]

New Football Writing's Contribution to the New Consumption of Football

In Chapter 10, I argued that the representation of Italia '90 on English television played a significant role in facilitating the transformation of the game, and throughout the present chapter I have argued that Nick Hornby's work, *Fever Pitch*, has been central to new football writing. Significantly, the two were connected. It was very unlikely that Nick Hornby's book would even have been published (or written at all) in the mid-1980s. The transformation in the public perception of the game, which was substantially achieved through the media's representation of the World Cup, encouraged the publishers, Victor Gollancz, to commission *Fever Pitch* on the evidence of the first chapters (Hornby, personal interview 11 August 1994). It can be inferred that this publishing house recognized the potential market for this book in the light of the new cultural position of football. A crucial moment in new football writing's establishment was, therefore, substantially determined by the marketing needs of a specific media conglomerate, the very kind of commercial enterprise to which new football writing is often opposed.

The publication of *Fever Pitch* was the result of entrepreneurial forces, whose implementation in football Hornby himself opposed (in complex ways), while the outstanding success of the book contributed to the establishment of football's new cultural position, thereby assisting the new directors' project. After the publication of the book (and its wide acclaim), new television programmes and other (new football writing) books[8] began to appear which confirmed the transformation of football. Nick Hornby cited an example of this dialectical influence which *Fever Pitch* had on the cultural position of football:

> It's hard to talk about [the influence of *Fever Pitch*] without being poncey about it. All I can say is after a few months, a lot more started to be written about football after the book. Certain things on TV probably wouldn't have happened without it. (Hornby, personal interview, 11 August 1994)

Specifically, Hornby revealed that a programme called *There's Only One Brian Moore* was commissioned after one unnamed individual had read *Fever Pitch*. Since 1995, the production of football-related cultural products has continued apace. Nick Hornby himself has appeared regularly on a comic programme called *Fantasy Football League*, and *Fever Pitch* has been turned into a stage play and a film. By making the game meaningful (and attractive) to the wider public, new football writing, and *Fever Pitch* in particular, has contributed into the remarketing of football which has been the primary objective of the new directors and other entrepreneurs more widely involved in the use of football in the media.

New football writing's central understandings of the 'golden age' and 'authenticity' have been important to this remarketing of football, since this 'invented' past emphasizes the traditional authenticity of the game just at a time when the English game has been transformed more radically than ever before in the twentieth century. The connection with the past facilitates the new consumption of football because it enables fans to imagine that, despite the novelty of football in the 1990s, it is actually founded in the traditions of the past. In this way, new football writing enables those individuals who have become interested in football in the 1990s to consume the game.

Independent Supporters' Associations: the Alliance of the Lads and New Football Writing Fans

Although new football writing has contributed to the new consumption of football, it has also provided an important resource for the resistance to the new directors' project. In Chapter 12, I noted the emergence of an independent supporters' association at Manchester United (IMUSA) which I located initially among the lads. In fact, the social location of IMUSA is more complex and much more interesting. After the announcement at the home match against Arsenal, prominent figures among Manchester United fans decided that some formal opposition to the club was required. Significantly, the individuals who came to the fore in this conjuncture were both lads and new football writing fans, who had not previously been aligned with each other. Three central figures emerged at the forefront of the development of IMUSA, two of whom I knew before the development of this group – Andy Walsh and Johnny Flacks[9] – and who were situated within new football writing fandom, and a third, Chris Robinson, who was the editor of *Red Issue* and therefore, up to that point, had been representative of the extreme masculine support from whom the new football writing fans were differentiated. For instance, both Andy Walsh and Johnny Flacks independently expressed some mild but nevertheless significant reservations about the more controversial aspects of *Red Issue* in their personal interviews.

The development of IMUSA reveals an interesting and important social development in the new consumption of football. The project of the new directors, at its most extreme at Old Trafford, has driven two groups, many of whose orientations and values were different, into an alliance. In particular, the imagined past of new football writing has been central to this important alliance; the rapprochement between the two groups has been possible because the new football writing fans share a very similar notion with the lads about what constitutes the appropriate consumption of football at the ground. The kind of fandom which the new football writers take as appropriate is their remembered interpretation of the atmosphere of the grounds in the late 1960s, which was also the formative experience for the lads. That common experience – taken by both to be traditional and authentic working-class culture – has allowed this unification of the lads and the new football writers.

In particular, IMUSA has developed two strategies for opposing the policies of the board. First, in 1995, IMUSA published 'A Redprint for Change' which was, in effect, a manifesto of IMUSA's intentions and main areas of concern. The 'Redprint' was especially concerned with the atmosphere in the ground and the exclusion of young, local fans from the stadium. In effect, the 'Redprint' and IMUSA, although consciously anti-sexist in their demands, emphasized the need to preserve masculine styles of consumption within football. The concern about the exclusion of young, local fans was related to the invented tradition discussed in Chapter 12, although it was also rooted in genuinely egalitarian concerns about universal access to the stadium.

The second strategy which IMUSA has implemented and which is now in operation is the buying up of shares so that IMUSA can at least attend shareholders' meetings and thereby earn the right to question the board's economic policies directly. This share strategy is very interesting in the light of the new directors' use of the concept of the customer. One of the principal effects of the notion of the customer was to obviate political debate by reducing discussion to a matter of pure economic procedure. Fans could not dispute their exclusion or the increase in prices because these were purely economic matters, which the company must have the freedom to deal with within the constraints of the market. Through their purchase of shares, IMUSA has effectively politicized the economic and undermined the new directors' attempts to obviate political discussion with the fans. IMUSA has in actual social practice effected an extremely radical political project which turns a fundamental commonsense of capitalist culture on its head. It has demonstrated that the economy is always and inevitably political. Thus, although new football writing has assisted in the remarketing of football and thereby contributed to the new directors' project at one level by improving the cultural position of football, new football writing has been equally and simultaneously important in the creation of an autonomous subculture which is in the process of developing strategies of resistance against the new consumption of football. Clearly, it would be wrong to idealize the extent which IMUSA will be allowed to politicize shareholders' meetings, and the board has already developed policies which aim at limiting debate in these meetings by insisting that questions can only be raised in direct relation to the (purely economic) agenda.

Conclusion

Like those of the lads, the understandings of the producers and consumers of new football writing inform their response to the new consumption of football so that their reactions to the development of football in the 1990s form a complex and textured pattern of resistance and consent. Although new football writing opposes the new consumption of football on one level (informed by notions of the authenticity of the game), their very appeals to authenticity through texts has facilitated the remarketing of football to a wider audience. Consequently, new football writing has made some contribution to the very project which it overtly opposes. Yet, at the same time, even that paradox must itself be countered by a further one, where the imagined construction of the new football writing fandom has provided the central resource for them in the formalizing their opposition to the new directors and has facilitated an important alliance between the lads and the new football writing fans. In particular, this alliance in the form of independent supporters' organizations has, above all, opposed the idea that fans are simply customers. The producers and consumers of new football writing may be open to criticism on the grounds that their tradition is 'invented' and that at certain points they are in bad faith, since they fail to recognize the points at which they have assisted the new directors whom they openly oppose, but their notion of authenticity counters the reduction of the football fan to a customer. The notion of authenticity, with all its richly meaningful connotations and memories, undermines the flat one-dimensionality of the notion of the customer. New football writing demonstrates that there is more to fandom than the new directors wish to concede when they use free-market ideas of the customer.

Notes

1   The term 'new football writing' to describe this fandom is derived from the subtitle of a volume of collected essays which was edited by Nick Hornby, called *My Favourite Year: a Collection of New Football Writing*. In fact, as I intend to show, 'new football writing' may not in fact be so 'new', and the use of this title is employed to emphasize the connection of this style of fandom to the conjunctural moment of the 1990s.

2   The difference between the lads and new football writing as a style of fandom was illustrated by the lads' reaction to *Fever Pitch*. Although the book was generally well received by the lads with whom I carried out fieldwork, some of them were surprised that Hornby changed teams, and spent some seasons following Cambridge United (e.g. Barry). This change of allegiance is more or less impossible for the lads, since their relationships with other men (and their honour) is dependent on their affiliation to one club and the friendships which are forged through the support of that one club. To change clubs would have involved a loss of face and would imply a rejection of the relations which were founded on the mutual celebration of a team.

3   The social location of new football writing fandom among the professional (public sector or intellectual) middle class was highlighted in an article in the London *Evening Standard* (7 April 1994), 'Putting the BA into football'. The article was written by David Baddiel, the 'comedian' and 'Cambridge arts graduate with a double first' (*Evening Standard*, 7 April 1994) and, citing Melvyn Bragg's, Martin Amis's, Nigel Kennedy's and Salman Rushdie's open support for the game, discusses the recent attraction of the game to intellectuals:

> These are intellectuals who are coming out of the closet, not going into it to see if an Umbro top goes with an Armani jacket. They're coming out of it, singing, crying and clutching copies of *Fever Pitch* because, they feel safe, at last admitting it.

It is notable that Baddiel deploys *Fever Pitch* as a central symbolic expression of this new practice of consumption.

4   Other books which might be considered to be new football writing include Hamilton (1994), Kuper (1994), White (1994) and Watt (1993), although new publications are appearing all the time. There has also been a rapid increase in the number of magazine titles available; notable more recently launched periodicals include *Four-Four-Two*, *Total Football* and *Perfect Pitch*.

5   *When Saturday Comes'* readership profile was conducted by *Further Thought* in April 1992.

6   Horton's argument against middle-class individuals using the game as a means of experiencing the working class is quoted by Hornby (1992, p. 97).

7   The close connection between recent academic writing (in particular) and new football writing is revealed by the connection between younger football academics and the FSA. Tim Crabbe, the chairman of the FSA between 1994 and 1996, is presently employed at Goldsmiths College as a research fellow on a project concerned with racism in football. Adam Brown, the secretary of the FSA, gained a PhD from the Manchester Institute for Popular Culture, published an article in a collected volume (1993) and is now employed as a research fellow on a project about popular music at the Manchester Metropolitan University and Liverpool University. In the late 1990s, Adam Brown became a very important figure in IMUSA, employing his professional training to great effect in aiding the development of this organization for which he was widely recognized and applauded. He played an important role in the protest against the takeover by Murdoch's BSkyB and, with Andy Walsh, has written an excellent book on the subject called *Not for Sale* (1999).

8   Television programmes which have been inspired by the recent transformation in the perception of football include: *Standing Room Only* (BBC2) (which was originally going to be called *When Saturday Comes*), *Fantasy Football League* and *The Rock and Goal Years*.

9   Since the research for this book was carried out, there has been a dispute between Johnny Flacks and IMUSA which resulted in Johnny Flacks leaving the organization.

14

The New Consumer Fans

In Chapter 11, I argued that a central strategy which the new directors had tried to implement in the 1990s was to attract 'customers', by which they meant disciplined and affluent families, to football. Chapters 12 and 13 examined two types of fandom which were closely associated with the game before the new consumption of football and which have strongly opposed many aspects of the transformations which occurred in the 1990s. In this chapter, I want to examine new forms of fandom which have developed in line with the new directors' strategies. It should be noted that the prominence of new consumer fans is certainly at its highest at Manchester United, which has since the late 1950s been able to attract the largest nationwide support of any club. The peculiarity of Manchester United must make us wary of exaggerating the presence of new consumer fans at football grounds across England. For instance, the 1994 Carling Premiership survey carried out by the Sir Norman Chester Centre revealed that 12.8 per cent of its sample were women and this was taken as a sign of an increase in female attendances. However, Waddington *et al.* (1996), pointing up the methodological shortcomings of this Premiership survey, have questioned whether this figure really constitutes an increase at all and whether women have not always attended football as a minority, which was ignored over the last thirty years as a result of the focus on hooliganism. For instance, Waddington *et al.* note that many surveys carried out in the last decade or so, several by the Sir Norman Chester Centre, have consistently shown the proportion of females fans to be somewhere between 10 and 13 per cent (Waddington *et al.*, 1996).

Although the differences between clubs have to be recognized, it might be tentatively suggested (on purely intuitive grounds) that, at the biggest clubs in the Premier League, more families and women are attending than in previous decades, but that at clubs outside this elite there has been little change. Nevertheless, even if this 12.8 per cent constitutes an increase in the attendance of women, they are in the minority at football grounds, which are still dominated by the presence of males. In the light of the persistence of male support, it is possible that the emphasis on the attendance of women by the new directors is more a rhetorical device intended to prove that the transformation of football has been achieved than a real sign of a fundamental shift in the support of football. By insisting on the increased attendance of women, the new directors may hope that this claim becomes a self-fulfilling prophecy, attracting more women to the game.

However, although the announcement of the development of new audiences for football across England may be premature, it is clear that the policies implemented by the board at Manchester United have been successful in attracting the new types of fans which had been proposed in the arguments for reform. The relative growth in the attendance of these new consumer fans, who approve the marketization of football, has been important in the political debates about the transformation of Manchester United. The presence of new consumer fans in the ground has increasingly threatened the lads' ability to attend and very significantly reduced their bargaining position with the new directors. Knowing that they are replaceable as supporters, the lads are effectively compelled into compliance themselves; as they can be replaced by other fans.

Despite the lads' denigration of the new consumer fans, they are not, in fact, inauthentic or peripheral to football in the 1990s. On the contrary, the new consumer fans are as 'real' as lads who have been attending for years. Fandom of any variety cannot be regarded as unreal or inauthentic, because fandom is always finally only a matter of imagination (Anderson, 1990).[1] Fans become fans simply by considering themselves to be so; it is impossible to suggest that fans who consider themselves fans are not so. New consumer fans believe themselves to be Manchester United fans and, therefore, they are real Manchester United fans. Yet they are fans in a different way from the lads (and from the producers and consumers of new football writing).

Adequate research into fans and their practices of fandom is a necessarily demanding and time-consuming procedure, since it is vital that close contacts are established with individuals in order that a 'deep' interpretation of their fandom can be gained. The research into fans in this book concentrated first on the lads, because they have been the most prominent fan group for the last thirty years, and second on new football writing fans, since they have proposed explicitly political agendas against the new consumption of football. The research into new consumer fans, a group whose importance only emerged during the course of research, was consequently brief and, ultimately, inadequate. The discussion of this group here is proposed not as a definitive statement of their composition or self-understandings but rather as an indication of the importance of this group, suggesting that future researchers could usefully attempt the detailed analysis of this group which was not possible here. In particular, serious critical research into this type of fandom could offset the poverty which has characterized recent work on football.

The Composition of New Consumer Fandom

New consumer fans are recognizable by their attitudes to the recent transformation of the game, as will be shown below, and by their style of dress, which does not involve the conscious display of certain designer labels, such as Henri Lloyd or Ralph Lauren, which the lads favour. Most often, new consumers wear several items of official club merchandise, typically the shirt, the manager's jacket, a hat and scarf. Through this style, new consumer fans physically demonstrate their allegiance to the club and their agreement with the project of the new directors.

Within new consumer fandom, there are three subgroups which can be recognized and defined. First, there are those fans in the 1990s of both sexes who have been attending games for a long time but who approve of the changes which have been effected by the new directors. At Manchester United, a significant number of middle-aged and quite elderly single women make up part of this group, and it was suggested that this unusual element of Manchester United's support was a result of popular reactions to the Munich disaster in 1958, when many individuals became fans of the club out of sympathy for the loss of its potentially great team (Deborah, personal interview, 1 August 1994). These fans cannot really be described as 'new', therefore, but since they have willingly adopted the styles of fandom which the genuinely new fans demonstrate and because they share the latter's support for the new consumption of football, I include these (old) consumer fans within this category.

Second, there are the new family groups which have been consciously encouraged to attend by the creation of a 4000-seat family stand in the new Stretford End (now called the West Stand). Many family groups have not bought season tickets in the family stand but come only a few times a season to Old Trafford, in which case they might be situated in any part of the stadium: thus there are many more than 4000 new consumer families in the ground at any game. As already mentioned in Chapter 11, it is likely that Manchester United has cultivated this style of support by favouring supporters who come from outside Manchester in family groups in the postal ballot for League tickets, because these individuals are more likely to spend money in the club shop (White, 1994, p. 164).

Third, there are the groups of teenage girls whose presence at games has been more prominent since the 1990s and has been especially noticeable at Manchester United, where the sexual attractiveness of their star players, such as Ryan Giggs and David Beckham (until the latter's transfer to Leeds in the summer of 1996), has been drawn upon by the new directors as a quite explicit marketing strategy. In addition to these three main subgroups of new consumer fans, I want to suggest tentatively from some evidence which I cite below that some lads show a potential to move towards this form of fandom. In particular, lads with young families are likely to find the facilities offered by the club to be convenient. If the new directors are capable of winning the compliance of the lads through the provision of facilities for their children, then the free-market argument will have been substantially implemented. The family will have been successfully instituted in post-Fordist football as a disciplined apparatus of consumption which is efficiently economic, since it offers greater market potential at the same time as a means of social control. This will have been an important symbolic achievement in Britain's post-Fordist transformation.

Since my analysis of new consumer fans is avowedly cursory, the social location of these fans is more difficult to establish. However, since the new consumer fans approve of the better facilities, are willing to pay more for these facilities and do not make many complaints about the higher prices, it is possible to conclude that new consumer fans are generally more affluent than the lads. This is implied (though not proved) by the fact that some of the lads, who could move towards the new consumer style of fandom by taking their families or at least their children with them to the ground, are prevented from doing so by the expense (e.g. Jeff). Similarly, the ability of new consumer fans to attend as whole families suggests considerable affluence. I would suggest, then, that new consumer fans are generally employed in the well-paid and secure positions at the core of post-Fordist society; they work in the white-collar positions of the private service industries. Clearly, the class difference between the lads and new consumer fans should not be overstated, because many of the lads who are still able to attend football are, despite their complaints regarding increased prices, employed in similar jobs. However, although the more affluent sections of the lads' support is in a comparable social location to that of the new consumer fans, the lower end of the lads' fandom, which includes elements from the 'underclass', is significantly less affluent than the new consumer fans.

This occupational position is implied by four of the fans whom I classified as new consumer fans; Malcolm was a former laboratory assistant at Ferodo, examining brake pads, who used his redundancy pay to invest in shares, which have shown returns; Lillian[2] worked for British Gas in a white-collar service job; Deborah[3] worked in an engineering company in Middlewich; and Chris[4] worked in an administrative role in a textile company in Leeds. Again, it must be emphasized that no definitive conclusions can be drawn from such a small sample.

New Consumer Fans and the Transformation of Football

Despite the lads' contention that new consumer fans (who do not sing) are not real supporters, my interviews with the individuals named above demonstrated that they experienced just as visceral an attachment to the club as any of the lads. It should be noted, however, that all four of these individuals were in the first subgroup mentioned above. They had been attending games at Old Trafford for years and, in Chris's case, decades. The lads' accusation that new consumer fans are not as dedicated to the club is probably more accurate for new consumer fans from the second and third groups; those fans who attend only one or two games a season (often as a family) or only watch games to see Ryan Giggs. However, even in this case, the lads are wrong to describe these individuals as not 'real' fans. It is simply that their understanding of themselves and their relationship to the club is different to that of the lads.

The new consumer fans whom I interviewed demonstrated a remarkable dedication to the club and, indeed, their lives were dominated by their support for Manchester United. Malcolm started attending home games in 1978, and within five years began to attend away matches. In the last six or seven years he has attended every game played in England and goes to reserve matches as well (Malcolm, 31 May 1994). Lillian demonstrated a similar dedication, revealing that she did not miss games any more and even attends reserve, A and B games.[5]

Although the club features as centrally in the identities of these fans as it does with the lads, the new consumer fans are distinguishable from the lads and new football writing fans by the type of literature in which they are interested. They take little interest in the club (the lads') fanzines:

> I bought my first fanzine last year. And I'd seen them for years, well not years and years. I'd seen people selling them. I thought they were University Rag mags – full of stupid jokes and adverts. So I never bought one. (Chris, 21 June 1994)

> I used to get *United We Stand*, which was quite good, but I didn't think it worth me buying – I didn't get enough out of it. I did get *Red Issue* when it first used to be about but it used to annoy me so much. (Deborah, 1 August 1994)

Their lack of interest in the masculine fandom which is expressed in these publications is reflected in their attitudes towards the recent changes in football. For instance, new consumer fans are not especially disadvantaged by the introduction of all-seater stadia:

> I enjoyed standing up but seating doesn't bother me. Sometimes seats are beneficial because if you want to have a drink you can get to your seat five minutes before the game and your seat will be there. Standing up you used to be there an hour and you had to be there early to get a good view. So it didn't really matter to me having seats really. In the end now, I enjoy having a seat. (Malcolm, 31 May 1994)

Since Malcolm's fandom was not primarily based on an ecstatic celebration of masculinity, seating did not threaten him. However, he was aware that others may have lost something through the development of all-seater grounds. He referred to those fans who used to like 'giving it some' (i.e. shouting, singing, using threatening behaviour, etc.). For Malcolm, seats are merely a more convenient way to consume football; it is easier to watch the game from them.

Chris demonstrated similar sentiments, for, although he always enjoyed listening to the singing, he himself always sat, as he was primarily interested in spectating, which was best undertaken in the stands rather than on the terrace. So, although he was somewhat ambivalent about the way in which grounds have improved, he was convinced that this improvement was necessary, as grounds had become places which had, during the 1970s and 1980s, become severely dilapidated:

> It's [the state of the grounds] got better. In the Second Division, I can't think of which ground it was but there used to be glass bottles broken, set in concrete on top of walls to stop people getting over. You couldn't get a good view so you had to virtually stand on this glass and you'd feel it coming through your pumps. And then there'd be all these barriers, and you'd be squashed against barriers and you'd be herded around. And there were no toilet facilities and so you did it outside and you could see it all streaming down into the hot-dog stall. It was just filth. (Chris, 21 June 1994)

Since the development of all-seater stadia has been very substantially undertaken to encourage the attendance of families, it is not surprising that new consumer fans, who approve of all seating, also applaud the influx of families into the game:

> I think it's good, really, 'cause it gets the family out as well. Instead of husbands going to football or vice versa, the families go and then, on the way home, whatever happens, then can have a talk, instead of husbands just going, explaining something to their wives when they get home. (Malcolm, 31 May 1994)

The introduction of families into football through the improvement of the grounds has been a strategically important manoeuvre for the new directors, because there is some suggestion that the lads' masculinity might itself be accommodated through this growth of familial consumption.

> Jeff: Families are not being encouraged to go to the game.
> Phil: All the fucking Stretford End upper tier should be a fucking family stand.
> Jeff: To take the wife, me, two kids, you're talking £100. What average family can afford that?
> Phil: None in fucking Manchester, in the Greater Manchester area.
> Jeff: Not where we come from. The average wage down there is £140 a week. (Jeff and Phil, 1 June 1994)

This dialogue demonstrates that some of the lads are potentially willing new consumer fans; they approve of the fact that the new stadia are suitable for families to attend. Indeed, both argue that families should be encouraged to attend. However, the sorts of family which the club has in mind and the sorts of family from which lads, such as Phil and Jeff, come and to which they refer in their statements are very different and are separated by a wide differential in wages. For these lads, the ground is not open to their families because it is impossible for them to afford the admission charges. Phil and Jeff reveal both that some lads could drift towards new consumerism once they have children and that new consumer fans are generally more affluent than the lads.

Paralleling the new consumer fans' approval of the transformation of the grounds and therefore the means of consuming football, there is support for the new directors themselves among the new consumer fans. For instance, although we noted that many of the lads no longer held Martin Edwards in the contempt which he provoked in the 1980s before the club started winning trophies regularly, he still finds much more sympathy among the new consumer fans than among the lads, or indeed, among new football writing fans. When asked his opinion of Edwards' policies, Chris merely replied 'Business is business' (Chris, 21 June 1994). Chris' brief statement is important because it demonstrates that new consumer fans have accepted one of the major planks in the new commonsense of British post-Fordist society. Since business operates according to the 'laws' of the free market and is primarily concerned with profit, Chris both affirms that interpretative framework and legitimates individuals like Martin Edwards, who have risen to dominance within its context.

Lillian echoed Chris' comments:

> Obviously, he [Martin Edwards] does make money but which chairman of a company doesn't make money. And at least he is a United fan at heart and, to me, he made the ultimate sacrifice. That club had

been in his family for donkey's years ... [libellous comment about Louis Edwards omitted] but it must have hurt him because the only way he could raise the cash to build the stadium and finance that was by doing a share issue and actually losing overall control. That is the ultimate sacrifice; he gave up ownership of the club he loved. (Lillian, 8 August 1994)

Lillian's statement operates in a similar fashion to Chris', affirming the centrality of business to contemporary culture, but she goes further and assents to the legitimacy of the new directors to whom this new hegemony has given rise. Edwards' profit from the club is justified on the grounds that he himself has contributed towards its success. Indeed, in Lillian's eyes, he has relinquished a style of autocracy which, we noted, was typical in pre-1980s football, and reinvented his relationship to the club on purely market lines in the best interests of the club. The consent to the recent transformations at Manchester United presumes an acceptance of free-market understandings more widely.

As argued in Chapter 11, one of the principal strategies of the new directors, of which Edwards is one, has been to expand the commercial operations of the club by producing and selling more merchandise. We have noted the lads' somewhat paradoxical disdain for this strategy. The new consumer fans, unsurprisingly, support the club's commercial strategy more or less unreservedly and are both willing to buy merchandise themselves and approve of others purchasing it:

> I think it's [club merchandise] all right, good, yeah. Like any sport, like America, the baseball, they have all the merchandise, don't they? Whatever sport they have, you'll always have this, won't you. I think it's good, yeah. For kids, for anyone really, it's great but for kids it's great; shirt, socks and shorts – the whole stuff. (Malcolm, 31 May 1994)

Lillian was equally approving of the replica kits: 'I didn't get the last red one. So I decided to get the new one but I'm really pleased with it. I think it's brilliant – the imprint of the stadium in the shirt' (Lillian, 8 August 1994). Although Lillian finds that the shirt gives her the opportunity to express her affiliation to the club, she also approves of the money which the shirts make for the club:

> On Wednesday morning [when the new shirt went on sale], they had crush barriers out at Old Trafford for the queues. There were people queuing from five in the morning. You can't expect the club to turn down that kind of money. (Lillian, 8 August 1994)

The compatibility between the club's strategy and the new consumer fans' understandings of themselves is further revealed by the way in which new consumer fans travel to away games. In Chapter 12, it was noticed that one of the lads' principal jibes at new consumer fans was their use of the club's official transport to away games. The consent to the club's policies which the use of the official transport suggests was demonstrated explicitly by Lillian when, in the light of the disorder which had occurred the previous year, she considered the prospect of unofficial groups travelling to Turkey for the match against Galatasaray in September 1994:

> You can't be a United fan if you're contemplating going [to Turkey unofficially]. I've not missed a game for four years. It will kill me not to go. I'm desperate, but when it comes down to it, if the club aren't going to run a trip then I'm not going to go on it. (Lillian, 8 August 1994)

Lillian would not go to a game which the club had not sanctioned, because to go would threaten the club's reputation and its position in the competition. If fans attended the match in Turkey despite the ban and there was trouble, the club could be ejected from European competition. Lillian's commitment to official club policy highlights the decisive divide between new consumer and masculine fandom. Whereas the lads reject any club directives which threaten their practice of masculine fandom, new consumer fans have fully subsumed their identities within the interests of the club. They abide by the club's strategies because the club regards these strategies as likely to bring the most success, and that success is the focus of the new consumer fans' concerns. They comply with the new directors because to do so accords with their interests, determined by their self-understandings, whereas the lads resist some of the club's strategies because these strategies threaten their different interests, given by their different cultural orientation.

Although new consumer fans, like all fans, are subordinate to the board and its projects, the new consumer fans are not mystified. They submit to the authority of the board because they believe that they will thereby achieve the most desirable ends for themselves. If anything, the lads and the producers and consumers of new football writing operate with more contradictory and illusory notions of themselves as fans because, on the one hand, they submit to the authority of the board, and invest time and money in the club, but on the other, the very project of the board is knowingly at odds with their own self-understandings.

Conclusions

The purpose of the last three chapters has been to analyse some of the complex ways in which these three main forms of fandom have negotiated, resisted and complied with the new consumption of football. I have tried to look over the shoulders of the new directors and the fan groups in order to read the texts which they have produced for themselves, though I have tried to read critically through situating the particular texts in a wider historical whole. However, this analysis does not claim to be complete or final, and nor could it ever be. In his *Negative Dialectics*, Adorno (1990) argued that concepts are never adequate to their objects and that human knowledge proceeds by the eternal dialectical realization of the shortcomings of each concept. If we take Adorno's philosophy seriously, then it is important to avoid reifying the concepts by which I have analysed football fandom in the 1990s. Although I would, of course, argue that the three concepts of fandom which I have employed here accurately reflect the contemporary state of the consumption of football, it must be realized that they are historically specific to the early 1990s to mid-1990s. This analysis, which focuses for the most part on the state of these fandoms in one conjunctural moment, must be limited.

In addition to the necessarily historical specificity of this research, the fandoms of which I have written are not the essential properties of individuals and are, therefore, inherently changeable. Since fandom is actively imagined by individuals, it is fundamentally fluid, changing as individuals' self-understandings change. Fandom is open to the eternal and dialectical workings of the self-consciousness. Consequently, in the course of their lives, fans can alter their style of fandom so that, as we have seen, it is possible for lads, for example, to drift towards new consumer fandom. Furthermore, every fan mediates a particular form of fandom to his or her own particular identity and, consequently it is possible for fans to exist in the interstices of the three categories which I have employed. Fans can exist on the periphery of the lads and new consumer categories, demonstrating features of either style at different moments. Indeed, as I have noted, three of the four new consumer fans whom I have quoted here demonstrate this interstitial fandom, while the fourth new consumer, Chris, moved towards the lads in my year of fieldwork. The mutability of fandom, because it is founded in inevitably changeable self-understandings, is demonstrated by the alliance of the lads and new football writing fans at Manchester United in IMUSA in the face of the development of what were, for them, unacceptable policies by the board.

Throughout a recent collection of essays about fandom (Lewis, 1992), a common theme on which the various writers drew was the disdainful dismissal of fandom by orthodox sociology; fandom was regarded as either trivial or mystified, in either of which cases it was peripheral to the concerns of sociology. These three chapters on the contemporary condition of football fandom should undermine that arrogance. Football fans express self-understandings which are informed by values and ideas from the wider social formation, but through the ritualistic arena of football these values gain a more public hearing than might normally be the case. In particular, the new consumption of football has very substantially involved the contested application of free-market principles to football and, with regard to the fans, one of the main areas of debate has been the contested accommodation of the notion that fans are now customers. This debate reflects wider post-Fordist and post-Keynesian transformations of Britain, which have involved the process of transforming citizens into consumers, as multinationals have become increasingly dominant over the nation state. Since football is a public ritual, the game has assisted in the establishment of this free-market hegemony in which the concept of the customer is embedded.

Consequently, football fandom as part of this ritual is not peripheral to cultural reproduction but a fundamental practice in which important social groups in English society constitute and reformulate themselves. Football fandom has become particularly significant as a symbolic practice in which social relations are expressed and negotiated. Furthermore, since football has become a prime site in the post-Fordist economy, performing an important symbolic role whereby commodities are identified and branded, fandom is a crucial element of this economic practice and, therefore, is fundamental to the economic development of post-Fordist Britain. The significance of the analysis of football fandoms in the 1990s goes well beyond the temporal and spatial confines of the game itself. Football fandom constitutes a central mechanism of the emerging class compromise developing under the interpretative framework of a Thatcherite hegemony which informs Britain's post-Fordist transformation.

Notes

1   Anderson argues that imagining is not mystified but inevitable and necessary, and sociologists should not dismiss the use of imagination in the creation of communities as 'false' in a search for a true social form but rather examine the different ways in which communities imagine themselves into being. 'In fact, all communities larger than primordial villages of face to face contact (and perhaps even these) are imagined. Communities are to be distinguished, not by their falsity/genuineness, but by the style in which they are imagined' (Anderson, 1990, p. 15).

2   Lillian was not straightforwardly a new consumer fan, as she reads *When Saturday Comes*.

3   Deborah's fandom was nearer new football writing; she was a member of the FSA and reads *When Saturday Comes*. However, she does use official club travel to away games and likes to wear the official club merchandise.

4   Chris moved towards the lads' style of fandom during the year of my fieldwork.

5   The reserve team is drawn from the first team squad. The A and B teams consist of junior teams which have signed with the club but are too young to be part of the squad.

15

English Football in the New Europe

In this book, I have analysed the transformation of football in the 1990s by situating that specific development within a wider historical context. In turn, however, the examination of the specific by means of a general framework 'dialectically' throws light on that general framework itself, and it is hoped that the book will contribute to an understanding not just of the changes in football but also more generally of Britain's move towards a post-Fordist settlement. The form of English football which is emerging as we approach the year 2000 is in line with Britain's peculiar form of post-Fordism and it both reflects and contributes to the development of that social and economic formation. Increasingly, the professional game is economically concentrated around the biggest financial actors, while the active participation of the social core of post-Fordist society in the game is growing with the concomitant marginalization of the periphery. Furthermore, this new consumption of football is informed by notions of the free market and the concept of the customer in particular. In this, football in the 1990s is increasingly expressing wider social understandings but, as a ritualistic arena, these meanings have greater resonance in the ecstatic celebrations of the game and thereby gain a special hold over the social formation.

In order to explain the specific development of the Premier League and the new consumption of football, I have followed the emphasis which has been placed in sociology since the 1960s on the interpretations of active agents in the social process. Through the myriad of individual acts of exchange which are informed by a dominant framework of meaning, the social formation is itself slowly and organically transformed until it reaches a point when it is patently in contradiction with this framework of meaning. At such a conjunctural moment, various dominant groups come to the fore, demanding reform of the framework of meaning in line with their own interests and understandings. The group which most adequately represents the line of the organic development and is most favoured by that development is able to establish its framework of understanding over the emergent social formation, since that understanding is already informally and organically accepted by large parts of society. As arenas for the public expression of meaning, rituals are bound up with this process of transformation, because as societies develop organically, various groups demand that the ritual be transformed in line with those wider social changes. However, rituals themselves are spheres of exchange which have an organic trajectory of their own. Since rituals are informed by the same framework as the wider society, the organic development of the ritual substantially parallels the historical trajectory of the society, so the ritual will eventually face similar conjunctural difficulties which society at large faces.

Employing this theoretical framework, I have sought to interpret the transformation of football in the 1990s but, to do that, in line with its historical method, the book has traced the origins of the present changes to the late 1950s. In the light of growing European competition, the maximum wage became increasingly unsustainable by the late 1950s and was abolished in 1961. Significantly, organic developments rendered the restriction of the market for players untenable and the corporatist basis of the maximum wage was overruled in favour of a free market for players' wages. From 1961, English professional football was effectively framed by two incompatible principles. On the one hand, there was a set of rules and arrangements which were corporatist in intent and which sought to maintain the League as a whole, while, on the other, the abolition of the maximum wage represented the emergence of free-market principles into the game. Over the *longue durée*, the free-market principles which determined labour relations in the game increasingly brought the political economic constitution of the Football League into contradiction with its (corporatist) framework, especially in the light of the declining attendance of football. This brought the League to a conjunctural crisis in the mid-1980s which was eventually resolved by the creation of the Premier League which was founded on notions of the free market and the rightful independence of the clubs.

The Bradford fire initiated the conjunctural moment in which football was recognized to be in crisis. The values that the game expressed were regarded as being intolerably at odds with wider social developments. In effect, then, there was something of a dual conjunctural moment for football from the mid-1980s because, on the one hand, its own administration was inadequate with respect to its political economic realities (and was undergoing internal reform), and, on the other hand, the media, government and judiciary were increasingly demanding that football be brought into line with the direction of social and economic change, over which they had a privileged say. The internal political economic transformation of football and the external demands for reform were related because the external demands for the reform of the game highlighted the inadequacies of football's political economy. In a society which was increasingly highlighting economic transformations as the fundamental remedy to the collapse of the post-war settlement and free-market reforms in particular, the political economic anachronism of the League became especially galling. However, although there were demands for the political economic reform of the League in the 1980s and some of these were effected, the free-market demands for the new consumption of football became dominant only after Hillsborough, when they were established as the central means of sustaining football, both economically and in terms of reducing crowd disorder.

In the 1990s, the Premier League provided the top clubs with the financial resources to transform the consumption of the game in line with the free-market understandings which were, by the 1990s, hegemonic in British society. However, this application of free-market principles has not been straightforward. Since the application of the free market to football has involved the transformation of understandings and meanings, it has necessarily involved extensive social debate and resistance. The previous three chapters were intended to demonstrate some of the major lines of debate and resistance, to show the complexity of the new consumption of football, although at the same time recognizing that the transformations which were envisaged in the 1980s have for the most part been implemented. The interpretation of the conjunctural moment of the 1980s and the 1990s has involved more than merely 'looking over the shoulders' of the social actors in the manner which Geertz advocated but it has above all been a critical interpretation.

Although the hermeneutic method which is drawn upon throughout this text suggests that sociologists must look backwards – the owl of Minerva flies only at dusk – the tracing of the organic development of the political economy of football allows at least some tentative and short-term predictions about the potential direction of future developments in the Football League. Within England, it is highly probable that the two lower divisions will be entirely separated from the League by the end of this century and that there will be only two fully professional football divisions. If this is the case, then it is likely that both divisions will come under the auspices of the FA, and the Football League will effectively disappear, absorbed into the FA. However, the most interesting and important developments would seem to lie, not within the provincial horizons of English football, but rather at the grander level of European football, and the potential lines of development here seem to be both sociologically interesting and politically extremely important.

Recent commentary about the social and economic transformations which have resulted from the rapid flow of international capital in the post-Fordist global economy has emphasized the (partial) breakdown of the nation state as an effective manager of the national economy and a concomitant transformation of social identities. Although Amin and Malmberg (1994, p. 228) have disputed the notion of a 'Europe of regions', arguing that such a notion exaggerates the extent of post-

Fordist transformations (Amin and Malmberg, 1994, p. 233) and ignores the crucial role of multinationals in the emergent economy, they maintain that a central feature of contemporary social and economic change is the emergence of particular cities which have come to the forefront since the mid-1970s (Amin and Malmberg, 1994, p. 232). Amin and Malmberg argue that London, Milan, Frankfurt and Paris have been at the centre of this reconsolidation of large metropolitan areas through their command of finances, management, business services and infrastructure. Alongside these major metropolises, smaller but still very large provincial cities have also begun to emerge through new combinations of industry, office relocation and their intermediary roles in the financial and service sector. Birmingham, Turin and Manchester are examples of these burgeoning provincial cities (Amin and Malmberg, 1994, p. 232).

Harvey (1988) has also emphasized the importance of the city in the global post-Fordist economy, arguing that they have become 'lures for capital'. The city constitutes an increasingly important site in the new Europe as the nodal point of the global markets and local economic and social needs, which have been ever more important to multinationals. Multinationals have looked for appropriate cities in which to invest, while the cities themselves have made themselves as attractive as possible for such investment. Thus, in the early 1970s Seattle attempted to eradicate its mass unemployment problem by encouraging the intervention of business leaders and planners who would be capable of promoting investment to expand the city's arts infrastructure. Seattle went on to describe itself as a 'quality of life capital' (Harvey, 1994, p. 401). Similarly, in the 1980s the city of Glasgow declared that 'Glasgow's miles better', and in 1990 Glasgow became the European City of Culture, carrying out radical and successful urban regeneration projects in the city's centre, while, in true post-Fordist fashion, leaving the economically and socially deprived areas of the city as peripheral as ever.

In the context of the emergence of multinational corporations, the predominance of flows of global capital and the concomitant decline of the nation state as an effective economic manager, the city has become a key site of economic development and social and political integration in the new Europe. It is here that the future of football clubs is most interesting, because in this new European context, as the repressed ('medieval') city-state returns, the football club increasingly promises to be a public symbol of any city's status in the new social order. Football clubs will not only be important economic actors in their own right but will increasingly denote which cities are politically and economically important because they can afford to support a good team and, therefore, are worthy of investment by international capital. It might be noted that the reversal of fortunes between Liverpool Football Club and Manchester United in the 1990s may say more about the respective cities than merely the contingent success of 11 men on the field of play. From the mid-1970s until 1989 and, especially in the 1980s, Liverpool dominated domestic and European competitions, winning 11 Championships and four European Cups. Although by no means marginalized in the 1990s, Liverpool has been displaced by Manchester United as the dominant force. This football reversal correlates symbolically with the economic development of the cities, where, despite persistent social problems in parts of the city, Manchester has been increasingly able to consolidate and advance its position over the last two decades – but in the 1990s, in particular – as the dominant city in the north-west of England. It is highly likely that the fame of Manchester United has contributed to this re-resurgence of the city in the post-Fordist world economy. As we have seen in Chapter 11, both Sir John Hall and Steven Gibson have employed their respective football clubs at Newcastle and Middlesbrough to put those once-decaying industrial and Fordist cities back onto the global map.

The development of sponsorship has contributed to this symbolic role of the football club in the new Europe, particularly at the biggest clubs. The development of shirt sponsorship has expressed this post-Fordist emergence of the relationship between multinational corporations and cities as the sites of local markets. On the one hand, the formal expression of a relationship with a football club (and, therefore, a city) through sponsorship has provided the corporation with publicity. Moreover, and equally importantly in the context of fragmented post-Fordist markets, the football club effectively brands the sponsoring corporation's products. This is particularly noticeable at a club like Newcastle United, which is sponsored by the international (but locally based) Newcastle Breweries. Through sponsorship of Newcastle United, the brewery identifies itself with the city and symbolically marks its product.

More interestingly, the sponsorship of major football clubs by large corporations has contributed to the transformation of the identities which the fans express through the football club and the community which they imagine therein. The introduction of sponsorship into football effectively re-negotiates the kind of institution which the football club is and therefore the kind of identity which football fans can express in their support. When fans support a sponsored club, they are no longer simply supporting that club (as a representative of a local town or city) but also the capitalist business which has allied itself to that club. The development of this sponsorship re-negotiates the position of the club symbolically and implies a new kind of fan attachment to this institution. Especially at the biggest English clubs which attract nationwide support, the localism which was once expressed through the club is being re-negotiated in the light of the club's attachment to a multinational sponsor. Through the support of their club, the fans are affectively connected with the wider global economy through their mediated identification with a multinational actor in that economy. The development of sponsorship in football can be interpreted as part of this process whereby large capitalist interests are gaining increasing political, economic and affective hold over individuals who are becoming not primarily citizens of a nation state but consumers of a corporation. In that way, sponsorship symbolically represents the growing dominance of private multinationals over the public nation state, and the deep attachment of the football fan for the club is an important site for this connection of consumers to increasingly dominant multinationals. The old symbolism of the football club as a sign of local solidarities is developed by sponsorship into a metropolitan symbolism that assists in orienting individuals to the new global economy and in recognizing their new dependence on multinationals.[1]

The big city clubs in England and across Europe as a whole are increasingly the sites of a very interesting transformation. Through a club's connection with large capitalist enterprises and its growing integration into European competition, it has become a central site of social identification in the new Europe. Individuals, as fans (and consumers), are related to the developing political and economic realities of Europe through their football team. The football club, then, symbolically represents the re-emergence of the city (linked to international capital) as a central focus of identification in the new Europe, potentially replacing the nation and the state as the key sites of allegiance (Delanty, 1995, p. 160).[2]

The development of the biggest football clubs as the symbolic representatives of emergent regional identities which are focused on major cities has important implications for contemporary politics. In his recent critique of the Thatcherite state of Britain, Hutton (1996) demands the creation of a new and active citizenship which addresses post-Fordist transformations. Similarly, in a book which examines the historical origins and political consequences of the idea of Europe, Delanty (1995) argues for the need for an active 'post-national' citizenship which will combat the potential dangers of newly emergent nationalisms. Although these demands for active citizenship are proper, they are (especially in Delanty's case) abstract in that they make their demands for citizenship with little consideration of actual areas and specific ways in which such a citizenship might be developed. The point is that in the end, as history has shown, no amount of academic pontification (separated from social reality) has the least effect on the historical trajectory of a society if academics fail to make themselves aware of what individuals outside universities generally think.

In so far as the new Europe is concerned, the central cultural role which football clubs have attained in representing cities and in expressing the nascent social identities should not be ignored. As a ritualistic arena which provides a focus for public debate, the football club is a potential site for the new citizenship of which Delanty and Hutton talk. In particular, the football club is a possible site for this citizenship because the fans' identities are invested deeply in the club and they care sufficiently about the fortunes of the club to be galvanized into political activity over its activities. In a sense, the deep affective relationship that the fans have with their club and their concern for its welfare replicate the patriotism which political theorists, such as Rousseau, have regarded as essential to the political health of any community. The problem with the kinds of citizenship which Hutton and Delanty envisage is that, outside intellectual circles, there is very little sense of commitment to the issues or institutions concerning which Hutton and Delanty propose active political participation. Many football fans, however, are politically committed, albeit in a manner which Hutton and Delanty and, indeed, many other academics might not recognize. In the light of the emergence of the new Europe, the development of fan organizations such as IMUSA becomes particularly interesting. Clearly, it is important not to exaggerate the political position of a small, economically weak fan organization within the vast context of the European Union and the global economic network which flows through it, but the birth of these groups at more and more clubs throughout England suggests the development of grass-roots political activism. Combined with the development of new social movements, such as environmental groups, these independent supporters' organization have sought to expand political debate into areas which were once regarded as beyond this type of debate. Independent supporters' organizations insist that the economic sphere is not an apolitical one, nor are companies only answerable to large shareholders whose only concern is profit. In particular, they have countered the one-dimensional free-market rhetoric that we are all only customers now.

The sociological examination of these new European identities which are being expressed through the football club and the rise of political activism among the fans in this wide European context is a crucial area of study which would prove worthwhile both in itself and to sociology more widely. Detailed research projects (across the whole of Europe) into these issues of the expression of post-national, metropolitan or regional identities at football clubs would provide a rich insight into contemporary social practices which would be 'deep' in the Geertzian sense. They would genuinely concern themselves with the way in which individuals actually think and manage their social relations. Such research would be beneficial to the sociology of football in Britain, since illuminating research into these areas would rectify this subdiscipline's marginal position in the academic world. Furthermore, and far more importantly, such work would turn the tables on conventional academic research, which has often focused on the issues which its own researchers regard as important rather than those which fill the public's imagination. Then, the analysis of football would no longer be sociology's poor cousin but would be a central element in setting sociology on its feet by ensuring the discipline's close contact with the individuals whom it putatively seeks to understand. Sociology would then no longer be guilty of mere ivory-tower abstractions but would be capable of the 'deep' understanding of contemporary social processes which it professes to seek. From that 'deep' understanding, the social and political attention to which sociologists rightly aspire would follow. Sociologists would no longer be marginalized as the new Europe emerges around us, called upon only infrequently for childish soundbites on television, but would provide essential insights into these epochal social processes for the public – insights which were always sociology's purpose.

Notes

1   For a discussion of the emergence of regionalism and its relationship to the development of multinationals in the post-Fordist global economy, see Sabel (1994) and Amin and Malmberg (1994).
2   For an argument about the re-emergence of the city as the locus of economic development, see Amin and Malmberg (1994 p. 232), Harvey (1988, 1994) and Featherstone (1994).

Appendix

Methodology

I employed three principal methods: participant observation, interviews and documentary research.

Participant Observation

In order to analyse the transformation of the consumption of football, it was necessary to gain an understanding of the new means of consumption and the perception of the fans, who were most affected by these changes in the means of consumption. To that end, I carried out participant observation at Manchester United during the 1993–1994 season, although I did attend games in the previous year and also maintained the contacts I had made in that season by continuing to attend home games up to the present time. I am still in contact with the core of original informants. Manchester United was chosen as a site of research because, as a single researcher, it was only possible to attain the level of detailed knowledge which I required by concentrating on one club. Since Manchester United was in the forefront of the move to a Premier League and to the new consumption of football, and the stadium was one of the first to be converted to being all-seated after the Taylor report, it was logical to focus on that club.

Participant observation was chosen as a method in advance of a large-scale survey, because the research was concerned with an interpretative (hermeneutic) analysis of the changes. This interpretative method was only possible through thorough immersion into the understandings of the fans themselves. I gained close contact with over 20 fans at Manchester United, and made acquaintances with 20 more. Finally, this method suited my focus on 'the lads', since young males have been consistently difficult to attract to surveys and focus groups. 'Becoming a fan' alongside the lads and thereby gaining their trust and building up a rapport with them not only made it possible to gain accurate knowledge of their fandom, but was also the only effective way to gain any reliable understanding of them. The advantages of participant observation are highlighted by the recent shortcoming of the survey as a method which was demonstrated by the 1994 report by Sir Norman Chester Centre for Football Research for the Premier League (see Waddington, *et al.* (1996).

My fieldwork began at the start of the 1993–1994 season. I simply began attending all the games, home and away. I started to travel to away games on coaches organized by the two principal fanzines at Manchester United, *Red Issue* and *United We Stand*. I knew from the previous year attending some home games and two away games that these fanzines were principally written and read by the lads (see Chapter 12) and that the coaches would be principally populated by the lads. In addition, in order to gain more direct contact with the lads, I wrote to both fanzine editors to ask if they required any assistance. Andy Mitten, the editor of *United We Stand*, replied and I assisted him with a couple of issues. He was able to get me a ticket for the first game of the 1993–1994 season, at Norwich, to which I travelled on the fanzine coaches, making contact with some fans. Manchester United was playing its first game in the European Cup in September 1993 against Honved in Budapest, and Andy Mitten suggested I go with UF Tours, who were run by a well-known Manchester United fan and with whom many other 'lads' were travelling. The trip involved a four-day return coach journey and I was able to make several very good contacts. Out of these initial contacts, I was able to establish myself in the informal network of lads which operates around the football club. This informal network constituted the principal site of my fieldwork.

Although the main site of my fieldwork was the lads, I did make contact with other types of fan. In particular, by way of attending the meetings of the FSA throughout the 1992–3 and 1993–4 seasons, including the AGM in 1993, I was able to make contact with a different network of fans from the lads (though there was a problem with these meetings as a research resource; see Note 8, Chapter 13).

Finally, I was much less successful in contacting the third group of fans, whom I have termed 'new consumer fans' (see Chapter 14). This was due principally to limitations in time and finance. My sample of new consumer fans is, consequently, far from satisfactory but I include these fans for discussion since they are an important feature of the Premier League and may be usefully targeted as a future topic of research.

Interviews

Fans

After my fieldwork with the lads, I interviewed a selection of my contacts (principally those with whom I had attained the best rapport). This meant that the selection of lads tended to be those who were more respectable, rather than those Manchester United fans who are known to be involved in more illicit activities. The interviews were informal, although they were focused on several central questions, and lasted for between half an hour and over an hour. Out of respect for the rapport I had built up, I had to be flexible about how and where I interviewed the lads. Some were interviewed at my flat, while it was necessary to go to others' houses. Others had to be interviewed in the pub (once in a group of two and once in a group of three). The same procedure was adopted for the 'new football writing' fandom and the new consumer fans. The purpose of the interviews was to provide fans with an opportunity to express their views on the changes which have occurred in football in the 1990s.

I interviewed 26 fans (although several others agreed to be interviewed but were subsequently too busy). Table A.1 shows the categories of the fans whom I interviewed or cited from my fieldnotes. Although I did not interview Tim, I spent most of the 1993–1994 season with him and so have included his comments in Chapter 12 and counted him as the fourteenth member of 'the Lads' in that chapter. Gary was also not interviewed but he is cited from my fieldnotes. Kevin Miles, the chairman of the Newcastle United Independent Supporters' Association, was interviewed over the telephone after my initial period of fieldwork.

The ages given are those at the time of the interview or fieldwork.

Table A.1 The fans

Name	Sex/Age	Occupation	Fan Category
Andy Mitten	Male, 19	Student	Lads
Michael	Male, 21	Unemployed	Lads
Nick	Male, 19	Student	Lads
Tim	Male, 33	Clerk	Lads
Jeff	Male, 27	Unemployed (ex-army)	Lads
Phil	Male, 28	Nightshift	Lads
Gordon	Male, 31	Crane driver	Lads
Barry	Male, 32	Taxi driver	Lads
Paul	Male, 24	Technician with Plessey	Lads
Craig	Male, 24	Clerk, DHSS	Lads
Bob	Male, 45	Plumber	Lads
Jack	Male, 24	Trainee accountant	Lads
Harry	Male, 36	Administrator, FE	Lads[a]
Gary	Male, 17	Builder	Lads
Kevin Miles	Male, early 30s	–	Lads
Stan	Male, 24	Student	Lads
Andy Walsh	Male, 32	Student, ex-bank clerk	NFW
Mark Glynn	Male, 27	Official, Salford council	NFW

Sally	Female, 28	Teacher	NFW
Philip Cornwall	Male, late 20s	Editor, *When Saturday Comes*	NFW
Nick Hornby	Male, late 30s	Writer	NFW
Barry	Male, 50	Rep. for security firm at Manchester airport	NFW
Dan	Male, 59	Skilled engineer	NFW[a]
Johnny Flacks	Male, early 40s	Owns textile business	NFW
Malcolm	Male, 37	Ex-laboratory assistant, Ferodo	New consumer
Lillian	Female, 29	Clerk, British Gas	New consumer[a]
Deborah	Female, 28	Skilled worker, engineering company	New consumer[a]
Chris	Male, 36	Administrator, textile company	New consumer[a]

[a] Denotes problematic characterization: individual shows some defining features of other fan groups.
NFW = New Football Writing.

Elites: Chairman, FA officials, Television Executives

Tables A.2, A.3 and A.4 show which individuals I contacted, their positions and whether they were willing to be interviewed.

Table A.2 The chairmen

Name	Club	Response	Date/Length of interview
D. Ellis	Aston Villa	No reply	
D. Dein	Arsenal	No reply	
J. Walker	Blackburn Rovers	Refused	
K. Bates	Chelsea	Accept	10/10/94, 30 mins
R. Noades	Crystal Palace	No reply	
P. Johnson	Everton	No reply	
L. Silver	Leeds United	No reply	
D. Moores	Liverpool	Refused	
P. Swales	Manchester City	No reply	
M. Edwards	Manchester United	Refused	
J. Hall	Newcastle United	No reply	
J. Dunnett[a]	Notts County	No reply	
F. Reacher	Nottingham Forest	No reply	
R. Chase	Norwich	Accepted	6/8/94, 60 mins
I. Stott	Oldham Athletic	Accepted	21/6/94, 45 mins
R. Thompson	Queens Park Rangers	No reply	

215

D. Dooley	Sheffield United	Accepted	17/8/94, 45 mins
D. Richards	Sheffield Wednesday	No reply	
G. Askham	Southampton	Accepted but too busy in the end	
A. Sugar	Tottenham Hotspur	No reply	
T. Brown	West Ham United	Accepted – interviewed Peter Storrie, managing director	25/7/94, 45 mins
S. Hammam	Wimbledon	Refused	

[a] Jack Dunnett, the chairman of Notts County, was president of the League from 1981 to 1986.

Table A.3 Miscellaneous football elites

Name	Position	Response	Date/Length of interview
J. Hill	Chairman PFA, 1956–1961	Accepted	13/3/94, 45 mins[a]
G. Kelly	Secretary, FA	Refused	
D. Macgregor	Commercial manager, MUFC	Accepted	19/8/94, 25 mins
K. Merrett	Secretary, MUFC	Refused	
B. Moorhouse	Membership secretary, MUFC	Accepted	27/7/94, 30 mins
R. Parry	Chief executive, the Premier League	Refused	
T. Phillips	Commercial manager, the Premier League	Refused	

[a] Interviewed over telephone.[1]   MUFC = Manchester United Football Club.

Table A.4 Media and television elites

Name	Position	Response	Date/Length of interview
J. Bromley	Former head of ITV Sport	Accepted	23/6/94, 25 mins
G. Dyke	Head of LWT	No reply	
A. Fynn	Advertising consultant, Saatchi and Saatchi[a]	Accepted	11/8/94, 30 mins[b]
J. Martin	Head of Sport, BBC	No reply	
V. Wakeling	Head of Sport, BSkyB	Accepted	24/5/94, 30 mins

| L. Taylor | North-east football correspondent, *Sunday Times* | Accepted | 16/10/96, 25 mins |
| H. Winter | Football correspondent, *Daily Telegraph* | Accepted | 16/8/94, 40 mins |

[a] Fynn is also the author of four books about the game, and especially its poor management and marketing
[b] Interviewed over telephone.[1]

Documentary Research

I used three types of documentary resources: the newspapers, books and fanzines.

Newspapers

I used *The Times*, *Sunday Times*, *Daily Telegraph*, *Sunday Telegraph*, *Financial Times* and the *Guardian* as my chief sources of information, though I did examine tabloid reactions to major issues such as Bradford and Hillsborough. The newspapers were crucial in providing information on concrete events and they were also very useful in providing quotations from the chairmen. In the light of the difficulty of interviewing the chairmen, these quotations constituted more discursive material which could be analysed alongside my recordings of interviews.

Books

Like any academic work, this book situates itself within a wider theoretical and empirical literature. However, the particular focus of interest, football, has required an examination of football literature, going back to the 1960s. This examination has been selective, concentrating on those books which have, in particular, been concerned with the economics of football and the restructuring of the game. In addition, the recent growth of fan literature has been surveyed and, as I have shown in Chapter 13, is highly significant.

Fanzines

Fanzines are fan magazines which are produced cheaply on an amateurish basis[2] and include the views of the editor as well as articles and letters submitted by fans. They are generally concerned with one club, although there are some national fanzines, notably *When Saturday Comes*. Although there were examples of fanzines in the 1970s (e.g. *Foul*), the fanzine movement, as a conscious attempt by the fans of nearly every club to express their dissatisfaction with the game (to other fans), emerged after the disasters of 1985, so that by 1989 almost every club had its own major fanzine, potentially selling thousands of copies each issue. As a new phenomenon and as a central element of fandom in the late 1980s and early 1990s, I have studied *When Saturday Comes* and the two main fanzines at Manchester United, *Red Issue* and *United We Stand*, in some depth.

Notes

1 I was able to use a recording machine to tape my telephone conversation with Fynn, but not for my conversation with Jimmy Hill.
2 The production and printing of fanzines is becoming more and more professional and complex all the time, and certain fanzines are extraordinarily well published, notably Tottenham Hotspur's fanzine *The Spur*. I discuss the significance of the developing glossiness of fanzines in Chapter 11.

References

Abercrombie, N. (1990) *Dominant Ideologies*, London: Unwin and Hyman.

Abercrombie, N. and Urry, J. (1983) *Capital, Labour and the Middle Classes*. London: George Allen and Unwin.

Abercrombie, N. and Warde, A. (1988) *Contemporary British Society*. Cambridge: Polity.

Abercrombie, N., Hill, S. and Turner, B.S. (1980) *The Dominant Ideology Thesis*. London: George Allen and Unwin.

Abrams, M. (1960) *Must Labour Lose?* Harmondsworth: Penguin.

Addison, P. (1982) *The Road to 1945: British Politics and the Second World War*. London: Quartet Books.

Adorno, T. (1990) *Negative Dialectics*. London: Routledge.

Aglietta, M. (1979) *A Theory of Capitalist Regulation*. London: New Left Books.

Allan, J. (1989) *Bloody Casuals*. Scotland: Famedram.

All England Law Reports (1963) 'George Eastham *v*. Newcastle United Football Club, Ltd, and others', pp. 139–60. London: Butterworth.

Althusser, L. (1971a) *Lenin and Philosophy*. London: New Left Books.

Althusser, L. (1971b) *For Marx*. London: Allen Lane.

Althusser, L. and Balibar, E. (1975) *Reading Capital*. London: New Left Books.

Amin, A. (1994) Postfordism: models, fantasies and phantoms of transition. In Amin, A. (ed.), *Postfordism: A Reader*. Oxford: Blackwell.

Amin, A. and Malmberg, A. (1994) 'Competing structural and institutional influences on the geography of production in Europe'. In Amin, A (ed.), *PostFordism: A Reader*. Oxford: Blackwell.

Anderson, B. (1990) *Imagined Communities*. London: Verso.

Anderson, P. and Blackburn, R. (eds) (1966) *Towards Socialism*. London: Collins.

Archetti, E. (1994) Masculinity and football: the formation of national identity in Argentina. In Giulianotti, R. and Williams, J. (eds), *Game Without Frontiers*. Aldershot: Arena.

Armstrong, G. (1994) False Leeds: the construction of hooligan confrontations. In Giulianotti, R. and Williams, J. (eds), *Game Without Frontiers*. Aldershot: Arena.

References

Armstrong, G. and Harris, R. (1991) Football hooligans: theory and evidence. *Sociological Review*, **39** (3), 427–58.

Arnold, A. and Beneviste, I. (1987a) Producer cartels in English league football. *Economic Affairs*, October/November, 18–23.

Arnold, A. and Beneviste, I. (1987b) Wealth and poverty in the English football league. *Accounting and Business Research*, **17** (67), 195–203.

Baistow, T. (1985) *Fourth Rate Estate*. London: Comedia Publishing Group.

Bale, J. (1989) *Sports Geography*. London: E. and F.N. Spon.

Bale, J. (1995) *The Stadium and the City*. Keele: University of Keele.

Barnett, S. and Corry, A. (1994) *The Battle for the BBC*. London: Aurum.

Barthes, R. (1972) *Mythologies*. London: Paladin.

Baudrillard, J. (1981) *For the Political Economy of the Sign*. St Louis: Telos.

Baudrillard, J. (ed. Poster, M.) (1988) *Selected Writings*. Cambridge: Polity.

Baudrillard, J. (1994) *Simulacra and Simulation*. Ann Arbor: University of Michigan.

Bedarida, F. (1990) *A Social History of England*. London: Routledge.

Belfield, R., Hird, C. and Kelly, S. (1991) *Murdoch: The Decline of an Empire*. London: Macdonald.

Beneviste, I. (1985) Soccer clubs need a new line-up to score financially. *Accountancy*, January, 77–9.

Bernstein, R (ed.) (1985) *Habermas and Modernity*. Cambridge: Polity.

Bird, P. (1982) The demand for league football. *Applied Economics*, **14**, 637–49.

Bleaney, M. (1983) Conservative economic strategy. In Hall, S. and Jacques, M. (eds), *The Politics of Thatcherism*. London: Lawrence and Wishart.

Bocock, R. (1992) *Consumption*. London: Routledge.

Boggs, C. (1976) *Gramsci's Marxism*. London: Pluto.

Boon, G., Thorpe, D. and Shah, A. (1994) *Survey of Football Club Accounts*. Manchester: Touche Ross.

Bottomore, T. and Brym, R. (1989) *The Capitalist Class*. London: Harvester Wheatsheaf.

Boudon, R. (1986) *Theories of Social Change*. Cambridge: Polity.

Bourdieu, P. (1984) *Distinction*. London: Routledge and Kegan Paul.

Briggs, A. (1979) *Sound and Vision: the History of Broadcasting in the United Kingdom*, Vol. IV. Oxford: OUP.

Bromberger, C. (1993) Fire-works and the ass. In Redhead, S. (ed), *The Passion and the Fashion*. Aldershot: Avebury.

Brook, S. (1992) *Labour's War*. Oxford: Clarendon.

Brown, A. and Walsh, A. (1999) *Not for Sale: Manchester United, Murdoch and the Defeat of BskyB* (Edinburgh: Mainstream).

Brunsdon, C. (1991) Satellite dishes and the landscape of taste. *New Formations*, no. 15, 23–43.

220

Buford, B. (1992) *Among the Thugs*. London: Mandarin.

Bull, D. (ed.) (1992) *We'll Support You Evermore*. London: Duckworth.

Burrows, R (1991) *Deciphering Enterprise Culture*. London: Routledge.

Burrows, R. and Marsh, C. (eds) (1992) *Consumption and Class*. New York: St Martins.

Campbell, B. (1993) *Goliath*. London: Methuen.

Canter, D., Comber, M. and Uzzell, D. (1989) *Football in Its Place*. London: Routledge.

Carchedi, G. (1977) *On the Economic Identification of Social Classes*. London: Routledge and Kegan Paul.

Chester, N. (1983) *Report of the Committee of Enquiry into Structure and Finance*. Blackpool: Football League.

Chippendale, P. and Franks, S. (1992) *Dished! The Rise and Fall of British Satellite Broadcasting*. London: Simon and Schuster.

Chippendale, P. and Horrie, C. (1985) *Stick It up You Punter! The Rise and Fall of the* Sun. London: Simon and Schuster.

Christian, H. (ed.) (1980) *The Sociology of Journalism and the Press*. Keele: University of Keele Press.

Clarke, A., Taylor, I. and Wren Lewis, J. (1982) Inequality of access to political television: the case of the general election 1979. In Robbins, D. (ed.), *Rethinking Inequalities*. Aldershot: Gower.

Clarke, J. (1976) The skinheads and the magical recovery of the community. In Hall, S. and Jefferson, T. (eds), *Resistance Through Rituals*. London: Hutchinson.

Clarke, J. and Critcher, C. (1985) *The Devil Makes Work: Leisure in Capitalist Britain*. London: Macmillan.

Clarke, J., Hall, S., Jefferson, T. and Roberts, B. (1976) Subcultures, cultures and class. In Hall, S. and Jefferson, T. (eds), *Resistance Through Rituals*. London: Hutchinson.

Cockerell, M. (1988) *Live from Number 10*. London: Faber and Faber.

Cohen, S. (1971) *Images of Deviance*. Harmondsworth: Penguin.

Cohen, S. and Young, J. (eds) (1981) *The Manufacture of News*. London: Constable.

Colemen, S. Jemphrey, A., Scruton, P. and Skidmore, P. (1990) *Hillsborough and After: The Liverpool Experience*. Ormskirk: Centre for Studies in Crime and Social Justice, Edgehill College.

Collins, J. (1989) *Uncommon Cultures*. London: Routledge.

Commission on Industrial Relations (1974) *Professional Football*, No. 87. London: HMSO.

Congdon, T. *et al.* (1992) *Paying for Broadcasting*. London: Routledge.

Cornwall, A. and Lindisfarne, N. (1994) *Dislocating Masculinity*. London: Routledge.

Corry, D., Williamson, P. and Moore, S. (1993) *A Game Without a Vision*. London: IPPR.

Crick, M. and Smith, D. (1990) *Manchester United: The Betrayal of a Legend*. London: Pan Books.

Critcher, C. (1991) Putting on the style: aspects of recent English football. In Williams, J. and Wagg, S. (eds), *British Football and Social Change*. Leicester: Leicester University Press.

Crompton, R. and Jones, G. (1989) Clerical 'proletarianization': myth or reality. In McDowell, L., Sarre, P. and Hammett, C. (eds), *Divided Nation*. London: Hodder and Stoughton.

Curran, J. and Seaton, J. (1988) *Power Without Responsibility*. London: Routledge.

Curran, J. and Gurevitch, M. (eds) (1977) *Mass Communication and Society*. London: Edward Arnold.

Curran, J., Ecclestone, J., Oakley, G. and Richardson, A. (eds) (1986) *Bending Reality*. London: Pluto.

Davies, P. (1990) *All Played Out*. London: Heinemann.

Delanty, G. (1995) *Inventing Europe*. London: Macmillan.

Deloitte and Touche (1996) *Annual Review of Football Finance*. Manchester: Deloitte and Touche.

Dennis, N., Henriques, F. and Slaughter, C. (1956) *Coal Is Our Life*. London: Eyre and Spottiswoode.

Department of Education and Science (1968) *Report of the Committee on Football* (The first Chester report). London: HMSO.

Derrida, J. (1976) *Of Grammatology*. London: Johns Hopkins University Press.

Dosi, G., Freeman, C., Nelson, R., Silverberg, G. and Soete, L. (eds) (1988) *Technical Change and Economic Theory*. London: Frances Pinter.

Dougan, D. (1981) *How Not to Run Football*. Wolverhampton: All Seasons.

Dougan, D. and Young, P. (1974) *On the Spot: Football as a Profession*. London: Stanley Paul.

Douglas, M. and Isherwood, J. (1980) *The World of Goods*. Harmondsworth: Penguin.

Douglas, P. (1973) *The Football Industry*. London: George Allen and Unwin.

Duke, V. (1991) The sociology of football: a research agenda for the 1990s. *Sociological Review*, **39**(3), 627–45.

Duke, V. (1994) The drive to modernization and the supermarket imperative: who needs a new football stadium? In Giulianotti, R. and Williams, J. (eds), *Game Without Frontiers*. Aldershot: Arena.

Dunning, E. (1986) Sport as a male preserve: notes on the social sources of male identity and its transformations. *Theory, Culture and Society*, **3**(1), 79–90.

Dunning, E. (1988) Football and British society. In Sir Norman Chester Centre for Football Research (ed.), *Football into the 1990s*. Leicester: University of Leicester.

Dunning, E. (1994) The social roots of football hooliganism. In Giulianotti, R., Bonney, N. and Hepworth, M. (eds), *Football, Violence and Social Identity*. London: Routledge.

Dunning, E. (1996) On problems of the emotions in sport and leisure: critical and counter-critical comments on the conventional and figurational sociologies of sport and leisure. *Leisure Studies*, **15**, 185–207.

Dunning, E. (1998) *Sports Matters*. London: Routledge.

Dunning, E. and Sheard, K. (1979) *Barbarians, Gentleman and Players: A Sociological Study of the Development of Rugby Football*. Oxford: Martin Robertson.

Dunning, E., Murphy, P. and Williams, J. (1988) *The Roots of Football Hooliganism*. London: Routledge.

Dunning, E., Murphy, P. and Waddington, I. (1991) Anthropological versus sociological approaches to the study of soccer hooligans: some critical notes. *Sociological Review*, **39**(3), 459–78.

Dunphy, E. (1994) *A Strange Kind of Glory: Matt Busby and Manchester United*. London: Mandarin.

Durkheim, E. (1964) *The Elementary Forms of the Religious Life*. London: Allen and Unwin.

Dyson, K. and Humphreys, P., with Negrine, R. and Simon, J.-P. (1990) *Broadcasting and New Media Policies in Western Europe*. London: Routledge.

Eagleton, T. (1976) *Marxism and Literary Criticism*. London: Methuen.

Eastham, G. (1964) *Determined to Win*. London: Stanley Paul and Co.

Economist (1986) Association Football: a battered sport and a tired business. 31 May, pp. 45–54.

Economist (1989) Britain: football's nemesis. 22 April, pp. 27–38.

Edgell, S. and Duke, V. (1991) *A Measure of Thatcherism*. London: Harper Collins.

Ekstein, J. and Feist, A. (eds) (1992) *Cultural Trends*, Issue 13. London: Policy Study Institute.

Elias, N. (1978) *What Is Sociology?* London: Hutchinson.

Elias, N. and Dunning, E. (1986) *Quest for Excitement*. Oxford: Blackwell.

Evans, H. (1983) *Good Times, Bad Times*. London: Weidenfeld and Nicolson.

Ewing, A. (1974) *A Short Commentary on Kant's Critique of Pure Reason*. Chicago: University of Chicago Press.

Featherstone, M. (1990) *Consumer Culture and Postmodernism*. London: Sage.

Featherstone, M. (1994) City cultures and post-modern lifestyles. In Amin, A. (ed.), *Postfordism: A Reader*. Oxford: Blackwell.

Ferguson, M. (1991) *Public Communication*. London: Sage.

Fine, B. and Leopold, E. (1993) *The World of Consumption*. London: Routledge.

Finn, G. (1994) Football violence: a societal psychological perspective. In Guilianotti, R., Bonney, N. and Hepworth, M. (eds), *Football, Violence and Social Identity*. London: Routledge.

Fishwick, N. (1989) *English Football and Society, 1910–1950*. Manchester: MUP.

Fiske, J. (1992) The cultural economy of fandom. In Lewis, L. (ed.), *The Adoring Audience*. London: Routledge.

Football Association (1991) *The Blueprint for the Future of Football*. London: Football Association.

Football League (1959) *The Football League Handbook: 1959–60*. Preston: Football League.

Football League (1964) *The Football League Handbook: 1964–5*. Preston: Football League.

Football League (1981) *Management Committee Report*. Lytham St Anne's: Football League.

Football League (1990) *One Game, One Team, One Voice*. Lytham St Anne's: Football League.

Football Trust (1991) *Digest of Football Statistics: 1990–1*. London: Football Trust.

Football Trust (1996) *Digest of Football Statistics: 1994–5*. London: Football Trust.

Foucault, M. (1979) *Discipline and Punish*. Harmondsworth: Penguin.

Fowler, B. (1991) *The Alienated Reader*. London: Harvester Wheatsheaf.

Frankenburg, R. (1970) *Communities in Britain*. Harmondsworth: Penguin.

Freeman, C. and Perez, C. (1988) Structural crisis of adjustment, business cycles and investment behaviour. In Dosi, G., Freeman, C., Nelson, R., Silverberg, G. and Soete, L. (eds), *Technical Change and Economic Theory*. London: Frances Pinter.

Freeman, C., Clarke, J. and Soete, L. (1982) *Unemployment and Technical Innovation*. London: Frances Pinter.

Fynn, A. and Guest, L. (1994) *Out of Time*. London: Simon and Schuster.

Gadamer, H.-G. (1979) *Truth and Method*. London: Sheed and Ward.

Gamble, A. (1983) Thatcherism and Conservative politics. In Hall, S. and Jacques, M. (eds), *The Politics of Thatcherism*. London: Lawrence and Wishart.

Gamble, A. (1985) *Britain in Decline*. London: Macmillan.

Gamble, A. (1988) *The Free Market and the Strong State*. London: Macmillan.

Gamble, A. and Walton, P. (1976) *Capitalism in Decline*. London: Macmillan.

Gardner, C. and Sheppard, J. (1989) *Consuming Passions*. London: Unwin and Hyman.

Geertz, C. (1973) Deep play: notes on the Balinese cockfight. In *The Interpretation of Cultures*. New York: Basic Books.

Gerth, H. and Wright Mills, C. (1991) *From Max Weber*. London: Routledge.

Giddens, A. (1977) *The Class Structure of Advanced Societies*. London: Hutchinson.

Giddens, A. (1984) *The Constitution of Society*. Cambridge: Polity.

Giddens, A. (1985) Reason without revolution: Habermas's *Theorie des kommunikativen Handelns*. In Bernstein, R. (ed.), *Habermas and Modernity*. Cambridge: Polity.

Giddens, A. and Mackenzie, G. (1982) *Social Class and the Division of Labour*. Cambridge: Cambridge University Press.

Gilmore, D. (1990) *Manhood in the Making*. New Haven: Yale University Press.

Giulianotti, R. (1993) Soccer casuals as cultural intermediaries. In Redhead, S. (ed.), *The Passion and the Fashion*. Aldershot: Avebury.

Guilianotti, R. (1994a) Social identity and public order: political and academic discourses on football violence. In Giulianotti, R., Bonney, N. and Hepworth, M. (eds), *Football, Violence and Social Identity*. London: Routledge.

Giulianotti, R. (1994b) 'Keep it in the family': an outline of Hib's football hooligans' social ontology. In Giulianotti, R. and Williams, J. (eds), *Game Without Frontiers*. Aldershot: Arena.

Giulianotti, R. and Williams, J. (eds) (1994a) *Game Without Frontiers*. Aldershot: Arena.

Giulianotti, R. and Williams, J. (1994b) Introduction: Stillborn in the USA? In Giulianotti, R. and Williams, J. (eds), *Game Without Frontiers*. Aldershot: Arena.

Giulianotti, R., Bonney, N. and Hepworth, M. (eds) (1994) *Football, Violence and Social Identity*. London: Routledge.

Glaser, B. and Strauss, A. (1968) *The Discovery of Grounded Theory*. London: Unwin and Hyman.

Glasgow University Media Group (1976) *Bad News*. London: Routledge and Kegan Paul.

Golding, P. and Elliot, P. (1979) *Making the News*. London: Longman.

Goldthorpe, J. (1980) *Social Mobility in Modern Britain*. Oxford: Clarendon.

Goldthorpe, J., Lockwood, D., Bechofer, F. and Platt, J. (1968a) *The Affluent Worker: Industrial Attitudes and Behaviour*. Cambridge: Cambridge University Press.

Goldthorpe, J., Lockwood, D., Bechofer, F. and Platt, J. (1968b) *The Affluent Worker: Political Attitudes and Behaviour*. Cambridge: Cambridge University Press.

Goldthorpe, J., Lockwood, D., Bechofer, F. and Platt, J. (1969) *The Affluent Worker in the Class Structure*. Cambridge: Cambridge University Press.

Gramsci, A., Hoare, Q. and Nowell-Smith, G. (eds) (1971) *Selections from The Prison Notebooks*. London: Lawrence and Wishart.

Green, D. (1990) *A Better BBC*. London: Centre for Policy Studies.

Green, G. (1953) *The History of the Football Association*. London: Naldrett Press.

Grossberg, L. (1992) Is there a fan in the house? The affective sensibility of fandom. In Lewis, L. (ed.), *The Adoring Audience*. London: Routledge.

Gruneau, R. and Cantelon, H. (eds) (1982) *Sport, Culture and the State*. Toronto: University of Toronto Press.

Habermas, J. (1971) *Knowledge and Human Interests*. London: Heinemann.

Habermas, J. (1979) What is universal pragmatics? In *Communication and the Evolution of Society*. London: Heinemann.

Haferkamp, H. and Smelser, N. (eds) (1992) *Social Change and Modernity*. Oxford: University of California Press.

Haines, J. (1988) *Maxwell*. London: Futura.

Hall, S. (ed.) (1980a) *Culture, Media and Language*. London: Hutchinson.

Hall, S. (1980b) Encoding/decoding. In Hall, S. (ed.), *Culture, Media and Language*. London: Hutchinson.

Hall, S. (1983) The great moving right show. In Hall, S. and Jacques, M. (eds), *The Politics of Thatcherism*. London: Lawrence and Wishart.

Hall, S. (1986) Media power and class power. In Curran, J., Ecclestone, J., Oakley, G. and Richardson, A. (eds), *Bending Reality*. London: Pluto.

Hall, S. (1990) The meaning of new times. In Hall, S. and Jacques, M. (eds), *New Times*. London: Lawrence and Wishart.

Hall, S. and Jacques, M. (eds) (1983) *The Politics of Thatcherism*. London: Lawrence and Wishart.

Hall, S. and Jacques, M. (eds) (1990) *New Times*. London: Lawrence and Wishart.

Hall, S. and Jefferson, T. (eds) (1976) *Resistance Through Rituals*. London: Hutchinson.

Hall, S., Critcher, C., Jefferson, T., Clarke, J. and Roberts, B. (1978) *Policing the Crisis: Mugging, the State and Law and Order*. London: Macmillan.

Halloran, J., Elliot, P. and Murdock, G. (1970) *Demonstrations and Communications*. Harmondsworth: Penguin.

Halsey, A. (1989) Social trends since World War II. In McDowell, L., Sarre, P. and Hammett, C. (eds) (1989), *Divided Nation*. London: Hodder and Stoughton.

Hamilton, I. (1994) *Gazza Italia*. Harmondsworth: Penguin.

Hannah, L. (1983) *The Rise of the Corporate Economy*. London: Methuen.

Hardaker, A. (1963) *Pattern for Football*. Lytham St Anne's: Football League.

Hardaker, A. (1977) *Hardaker of the League*. London: Pelham.

Harding, J. (1991) *For the Good of the Game*. London: Robson.

Hargreaves, J. (ed.) (1982) *Sport, Culture and Ideology*. London: Routledge and Kegan Paul.

Harvey, D. (1988) Video cities. *New Statesman and Society*, 30 September.

Harvey, D. (1994) Flexible accumulation through urbanization: reflections on 'post-modernism' in the American city. In Amin, A. (ed.), *Postfordism: A Reader*. Oxford: Blackwell.

Haynes, R. (1995) *The Football Imagination: The Rise of Football Fanzine Culture*. Aldershot: Arena.

Heath, A. and McDonald, S.K. (1989) Social change and the future of the left. In McDowell, L. *et al.* (eds), *Divided Nation*. London: Hodder and Stoughton.

Hegel, G. (1967a) *Philosophy of Right*. New York: Oxford University Press.

Hegel, G. (1967b) *The Phenomenology of Mind*. New York: Harper Torch.

Hill, J. (1961) *Striking for Soccer*. London: Peter Davies.

Hobsbawm, E. and Ranger, T. (eds) (1983) *The Invention of Tradition* . London: Macmillan.

Hoggart, R. (1957) *The Uses of Literacy*. London: Chatto and Windus.

Holmes, M. and Horsewood, N. (1988) The post-war consensus. *Contemporary Record*, Summer, pp. 24–7.

Holt, R. (1989) *Sport and the British*. Oxford: Clarendon.

Home Affairs Committee, 3rd Report (1988) *The Future of Broadcasting*. London: HMSO.

Home Office (1982) *Report of the Inquiry into Cable Expansion and Broadcasting Policy* (The Hunt Report). London: HMSO.

Home Office (1986) *Report of the Committee on Financing the BBC* (The Peacock Report). London: HMSO.

Home Office (1988) *Broadcasting in the 90's: Competition, Choice and Quality*. London: HMSO.

Hopcraft, A. (1990) *The Football Man*. London: Sportspages.

Horkheimer, M. and Adorno, T. (1973) *Dialectic of Enlightenment*. London: Allen Lane.

Hornby, N. (1992) *Fever Pitch*. London: Victor Gollancz.

Hornby, N. (ed.) (1993) *My Favourite Year*. London: Witherby.

Horrie, C. (1992) *Sick as a Parrot*. London: Virgin.

Horton, E. (1993) Going down? In Hornby, N. (ed.), *My Favourite Year*. London: Witherby.

House of Commons Official Reports (1989) *Hansard: Parliamentary Debates*. London: HMSO.

How, A. (1995) *The Habermas–Gadamer Debate and the Nature of the Social*. Aldershot: Avebury.

Hutton, W. (1996) *The State We're In*. London: Vintage.

Ingham, R. (ed.) (1978) *Football Hooliganism: The Wider Context*. London: Interaction.

Inglis, S. (1988) *League Football and the Men Who Made It*. London: Collins.

Inglis, S. (1991) *The Football Grounds of Great Britain*. London: Collins.

Inglis, S. (1992) Football's business league. *International Management*, March, pp. 50–4.

Jackson, B. (1968) *Working Class Community*. London: Routledge and Kegan Paul.

Jameson, F. (1991) *Postmodernism or the Cultural Logic of Late Capitalism*. London: Pluto.

Jefferson, T. (1976) The cultural responses of Teds. In Hall, S. and Jefferson, T. (eds), *Resistance Through Rituals*. London: Hutchinson.

Jenkins, H. (1992) *Textual Poachers*. London: Routledge.

Jensen, J. (1992) Fandom as pathology: the consequences of characterization. In Lewis, L. (ed.), *The Adoring Audience*. London: Routledge.

Jessop, B., Bonnett, K., Bromley, S. and Ling, T. (1988) *Thatcherism*. Cambridge: Polity.

Joll, J. (1977) *Gramsci*. Glasgow: Fontana.

Kant, I. (1996) *Critique of Pure Reason*. London: Macmillan.

Kavanagh, D. (1990) *Thatcherism and British Politics*. Oxford: Oxford University Press.

Kavanagh, D. and Morris, P. (1989) *Consensus Politics from Attlee to Thatcher*. Oxford: Blackwell.

Keaton, G. (1972) *The Football Revolution*. Newton Abbott: David and Charles.

Keen, S. (1992) *Fire in the Belly*. London: Piatkas.

King, A. (1995a) The problem of identity and the cult of Cantona. *Salford Papers in Sociology*.

King, A. (1995b) Outline of a practical theory of football violence. *Sociology*, **29**(4), 635–51.

King, A. (1995c) *The Premier League and the New Consumption of Football*. PhD Thesis, Institute for Social Research, University of Salford.

King, A. (1996) The fining of Vinnie Jones. *International Review for the Sociology of Sport*, **31**(2), 119–37.

King, A. (1997a) The lads: masculinity and the new consumption of football. *Sociology*, **31**(2), 329–46.

King, A. (1997b) New directors, customers and fans: the transformation of English football in the 1990s. *Sociology of Sport Journal*, **14**(3), 224–40.

King, A. (1997c) The postmodernity of football hooliganism. *British Journal of Sociology*, **48**(4), 576–93.

King, A. (1998a) Thatcherism and the emergence of Sky television. *Media, Culture and Society*, **20**(2), 277–93.

King, A. (1998b) A critique of Baudrillard's hyperreality: towards a sociology of postmodernism. *Philosophy and Social Criticism*, **24**(6): 47–66.

Klein, J. (1970) *Samples from English Cultures*. London: Routledge and Kegan Paul.

Körner, S. (1955) *Kant*. New Haven: Yale University Press.

Kuper, S. (1994) *Football Against the Enemy*. London: Orion.

Kurt, R. (1994) *United We Stood*. Wilmslow: Sigma Leisure.

Landes, D. (1989) *The Prometheus Unbound*. Cambridge: Cambridge University Press.

Lash, S. and Urry, J. (1987) *The End of Organised Capitalism*. Cambridge: Polity.

Lash, S. and Urry, J. (1994) *Economies of Signs and Space*. London: Sage.

Leadbeater, C. (1989) In the land of the dispossessed. In McDowell, L., Sarre, P. and Hammett, C. (eds) (1989), *Divided Nation*. London: Hodder and Stoughton.

Lee, M. (1993) *Consumer Culture Reborn*. London: Routledge.

Lever, J. (1983) *Soccer Madness*. Chicago: University of Chicago Press.

Levitas, R. (ed.) (1986) *The Ideology of the New Right*. Cambridge: Polity.

Lewis, L. (ed.) (1992) *The Adoring Audience*. London: Routledge.

Lister, R. (ed.) (1996) *Charles Murray and the Underclass*. London: IEA.

Liverpool Football Club and Athletics Grounds Plc (1993) *Annual Report*. Prescot: Stephenson Print.

Lovell, T. (1987) *Consuming Fiction*. London: Verso.

Lury, C. (1993) *Cultural Rights*. London: Routledge.

Mannheim, K. (1952) *Essays on the Sociology of Knowledge*. London: Routledge and Kegan Paul.

Mannheim, K. (1976) *Ideology and Utopia*. London: Routledge and Kegan Paul.

Marcuse, H. (1968) *One-Dimensional Man*. London: Routledge and Kegan Paul.

Marquand, D. (1988) *The Unprincipled Society*. London: Jonathan Cape.

Marris, R. (1996) *How to Save the Underclass*. London: Macmillan.

Marsh, P., Rosser, E. and Harré, R. (1978) *The Rules of Disorder*. London: Routledge and Kegan Paul.

Martin, B. (1985) *A Sociology of Contemporary Cultural Change*. Oxford: Blackwell.

Marx, K. (1971) *A Contribution to the Critique of Political Economy*. London: Lawrence and Wishart.

Marx, K. (1977) *The German Ideology*. London: Lawrence and Wishart.

Mason, T. (1980) *Association Football and English Society*. London: Harvester.

Mason, T. (1988) *Sport in Britain*. London: Faber and Faber.

McCarthy, T. (1978) *The Critical Theory of Jurgen Habermas*. London: Hutchinson.

McDowell, L., Sarre, P. and Hammett, C. (eds) (1989) *Divided Nation*. London: Hodder and Stoughton.

McLuhan, M. (1968) *Understanding Media*. London: Routledge and Kegan Paul.

McNair, B. (1994) *News and Journalism in the UK*. London: Rout-ledge.

Merton, R. (1968) *Social Theory and Social Structure*. London: Free Press.

Miedzian, M. (1992) *Boys Will Be Boys*. London: Virago.

Miliband, R. and Savile, J. (eds) (1973) *The Socialist Register*. London: Merlin.

Miller, D. (1987) *Material Culture and Mass Consumption*. Oxford: Blackwell.

Molotch, H. and Lester, M. (1974) News as purposive behaviour: on the strategic use of routing events, accidents and scandals. *American Sociological Review*, **39**, 101–12.

Molotch, H. and Lester, M. (1975) Accidental news: the great oil spill as local occurrence and national event. *American Journal of Sociology*, **81**(2), 235–58.

Moorhouse, H.F. (1991a) On the periphery: Scotland, Scottish football and the new Europe. In Williams, J. and Wagg, S. (eds), *British Football and Social Change*. Leicester: Leicester University Press.

Moorhouse, H.F. (1991b) Football hooligans: old bottles, new whines? *Sociological Review*, **3**(39), 489–502.

Morgan, D. (1992) *Rediscovering Men*. London: Routledge.

Morgan, K. (1990) *The People's Peace: British History 1945–89*. Oxford: Oxford University Press.

Mosse, G. (1985) *Nationalism and Sexuality*. Wisconsin: University of Wisconsin.

Mouffe, C. (1979) *Gramsci and Marxist Theory*. London: Routledge and Kegan Paul.

Murdock, G. (1980) Class, power and the press: problems of conceptualisation and evidence. In Christian, H. (ed.), *The Sociology of Journalism and the Press*. Keele: University of Keele Press.

Murdock, G. (1981) Political deviance: the press presentation of a militant demonstration. In Cohen, S. and Young, J. (eds), *The Manufacture of News*. London: Constable.

Murdock, G. and Golding, P. (1973) For a political economy of mass communications. In Miliband, R. and Saville, J. (eds), *The Socialist Register*. London: Merlin.

Murdock, G. and Golding, P. (1977) Capitalism, communications and class relations. In Curran, J. and Gurevitch, M. (eds), *Mass Communication and Society*. London: Edward Arnold.

Murphy, P., Williams, J. and Dunning, E. (1990) *Football on Trial*. London: Routledge.

Murray, C. (1990) *The Emerging British Underclass*. London: IEA.

Murray, R. (1990) Fordism and post Fordism. In Hall, S. and Jacques, M. (eds), *New Times*. London: Lawrence and Wishart.

Nairn, T. (1981) *The Break-up of Britain*. London: New Left Books and Verso.

Naughton, J. (1996) Children of the Revolution. *Total Sport*, February.

Overbeek, H. (1990) *Global Capitalism and National Decline*. London: Unwin and Hyman.

Pimlott, B. (1988) The myth of consensus. In Smith, L. (ed.), *The Making of Britain: Echoes of Greatness*. London: Macmillan.

Piore, M. and Sabel, C. (1984) *The Second Industrial Divide*. New York: Basic Books.

Political and Economic Planning (1966) English professional football. *Planning*, **32**(496), 77–161.

Portelli, A. (1993) The rich and poor in the culture of football. In Redhead, S. (ed.), *The Passion and the Fashion*. Aldershot: Avebury.

Popplewell, Mr Justice O. (1985) *Committee of Inquiry into Crowd Safety and Control at Sports Grounds*. London: HMSO.

Popplewell, Mr Justice O. (1986) *Committee of Inquiry into Crowd Safety and Control at Sports Grounds: Final Report*. London: HMSO.

Poulantzas, N. (1979) *Classes in Contemporary Society*. London: New Left Books.

Radway, J. (1987) *Reading the Romance*. London: Verso.

Redhead, S. (1991a) An era of the end, or the end of an era: football and youth subculture in Britain. In Williams, J. and Wagg, S. (eds), *British Football and Social Change*. Leicester: Leicester University Press.

Redhead, S. (1991b) *Football with Attitude*. Manchester: Wordsmith.

Redhead, S. (ed.) (1993) *The Passion and the Fashion*. Aldershot: Avebury.

Ricoeur, P. (1982) *Hermeneutics and the Human Sciences*. Cambridge: Cambridge University Press.

Rippon, A. (1982) *Soccer: The Road to Crisis*. Ashbourne: Moorland Publishing Co.

Robbins, D. (ed.) (1982) *Rethinking Inequalities*. Aldershot: Gower.

Roberts, R. (1983) *The Classic Slum*. Harmondsworth: Penguin.

Robins, D. (1984) *We Hate Humans*. Harmondsworth: Penguin.

Sabel, C. (1994) Flexible specialisation and the re-emergence of regional economies. In Amin, A. (ed.), *Postfordism: A Reader*. Oxford: Blackwell.

Sampson, A. (1965) *Anatomy of Britain Today*. London: Hodder and Stoughton.

Sartre, J.-P. (1966) *Being and Nothingness*. New York: Washington Square Press.

Savage, M., Barlow, J., Dickens, P. and Fielding, T. (1992) *Property, Bureaucracy and Culture*. London: Routledge.

Sawers, D. (1989) Financing the BBC. In Veljanovksi, C. (ed.), *Freedom in Broadcasting*. London: Institute for Economic Affairs.

Scholar, I. (1992) *Behind Closed Doors*. London: Andre Deutsch.

Scott, James (1985) *The Weapons of the Weak*. New Haven: Yale University Press.

Scott, John (1985) *Corporations, Classes and Capitalism*. London: Hutchinson.

Scott, J. (1986) *Capitalist Property and Financial Power*. Brighton: Wheatsheaf.

Scott, J. (1991) *Who Rules Britain?* Cambridge: Polity.

Scruton, R. (1980) *The Meaning of Conservatism*. Harmondsworth: Penguin.

Seidler, V. (1989) *Rediscovering Masculinity*. London: Routledge.

Shields, R. (1992) *Lifestyle Shopping*. London; Routledge.

Sir Norman Chester Centre for Football Research (1988) *Football into the 1990s*. Leicester: University of Leicester.

Sir Norman Chester Centre for Football Research (1994) *FA Carling Premiership: Fans' Surveys 1993–4: General Sample Report*. Leicester: University of Leicester.

Sked, A. and Cook, C. (1979) *Post-War Britain: A Political History*. Harmondsworth: Penguin.

Sloane, P. (1969) The labour market in professional football. *British Journal of Industrial Relations*, **7**, 181–99.

Sloane, P. (1971) The economics of professional football: The football clubs as utility maximiser. *Scottish Journal of Political Economy*, **18**, 121–45.

Sloane, P. (1980) *Sport in the Market*. London: IEA.

Smith, L. (ed.) (1988) *The Making of Britain: Echoes of Greatness*. London: Macmillan.

Sutherland, R. and Haworth, M. (1980) The economics of the industry. *Managerial Finance*, **12**(1), 1–5.

Sztompka, P. (1992) *The Sociology of Social Change*. Oxford: Blackwell.

Szymanski, S. (1991) Measuring the success of football clubs. *Working Paper Series*, London Business School.

Szymanski, S. and Smith, R. (1993) The English football industry: profit, performance and industrial structure. *Working Paper Series*, London Business School.

Szymanski, S. and Wilkins, S. (1993) Concentration, persistence and the English football league. *Working Paper Series*, London Business School.

Taylor, I. (1971) Soccer and soccer consciousness. In Cohen, S. (ed.), *Images of Deviance*. Harmondsworth: Penguin.

Taylor, I. (1982) Class, violence and sport: the case of soccer hooliganism in Britain. In Gruneau, R. and Cantelon, H. (eds), *Sport, Culture and the State*. Toronto: University of Toronto Press.

Taylor, I. (1984) Professional sport and the recession: the case of British soccer. *International Review for the Sociology of Sport*, **19**(1), 7–29.

Taylor, I. (1986) Spectator violence around football. *Research Papers in Physical Education*, **4**.

Taylor, I. (1987) Putting the boot into a working class sport: British soccer after Bradford and Brussels. *Sociology of Sport Journal*, no. 4, 171–91.

Taylor, I. (1989) Hillsborough, 15 April 1989: some personal contemplation. *New Left Review*, no. 177, 89–110.

Taylor, I. (1995) 'It's a Whole New Ball Game': sports television, the cultural industries and the condition of football in England. *Salford Papers in Sociology*.

Taylor, Lord Justice P. (1989) *The Hillsborough Stadium Disaster 15th April 1989: Interim Report*. London: HMSO.

Taylor, Lord Justice P. (1990) *The Hillsborough Stadium Disaster 15th April 1989: Final Report*. London: HMSO.

Taylor, R. (1992) *Football and Its Fans*. Leicester: Leicester University Press.

Thatcher, M. (1993) *The Downing Street Years*. London: HarperCollins.

Therborn, G. (1990) Two thirds, one third society. In Hall, S. and Jacques, M. (eds), *New Times*. London: Lawrence and Wishart.

Theweleit, K. (1987) *Male Fantasies*, Vol. I. Cambridge: Polity.

Thomas, D. (1990) *The Amstrad Story*. London: Century.

Tischler, S. (1981) *Footballers and Businessmen*. London: Holmes and Meier Publishers.

Tolson, A. (1977) *The Limits of Masculinity*. London: Tavistock.

Tomlinson, A. (ed.) (1990) *Consumption, Identity and Style*. London: Routledge.

Tomlinson, A. and Whannel, G. (eds) (1986) *Off the Ball*. London: Pluto.

Tuchman, G. (1971) Objectivity as strategic ritual: an examination of newsmen's notions of objectivity. *American Journal of Sociology*, 77(4), 660–80.

Tuchman, G. (1978) *Making News: A Study in the Construction of Reality*. London: Free Press.

Tunstall, J. (1983) *The Media in Britain*. London: Constable.

Tunstall, J. and Palmer, M. (1991) *Media Moguls*. London: Routledge.

Urry, J. and Wakeford, J. (eds) (1973) *Power in Britain*. London: Heinemann.

Veblen, T. (1970) *The Theory of the Leisure Classes*. London: Unwin.

Veljanovski, C. (1989) *Freedom in Broadcasting*. London: Institute for Economic Affairs.

Veljanovski, C. (1990) *The Media in Britain Today*. London: News International.

Vinnai, G. (1973) *Football Mania*. London: Ocean Books.

Waddington, I., Dunning, E. and Murphy, P. (1996) Research note: surveying the social composition of football crowds. *Leisure Studies*, 15, 215–19.

Wagg, S. (1984) *The Football World*. Brighton: Harvester.

Walvin, J. (1986) *Football and the Decline of Britain*. London: Macmillan.

Ward, C. (1990) *Steaming In*. London: Sportspages.

Watt, T. (1993) *The End*. Edinburgh: Mainstream.

Weiner, M. (1985) *English Culture and the Decline of the Industrial Spirit 1850–1980*. Harmondsworth: Penguin.

Whannel, G. (1983) *Blowing the Whistle*. London: Pluto.

White, J. (1994) *Are You Watching Liverpool?* London: Heinemann.

When Saturday Comes (1992) *The 1st Eleven*. Harpenden: Queen Anne.

Williams, J. (1994) Rangers is a black club: 'race', identity and local football in England. In Giulianotti, R. and Williams, J. (eds), *Game Without Frontiers*. Aldershot: Arena.

Williams, J. (1995) English football stadia after Hillsborough. In Bale, J. (ed.), *The Stadium and the City*. Keele: University of Keele.

Williams, J. (1996) The 'New Football' in England and Sir John Hall's New Geordie Nation. Paper presented for the conference on Football and Regionalism, Essen.

Williams, J. and Wagg, S. (eds) (1991) *British Football and Social Change*. Leicester: Leicester University Press.

Williams, J., Dunning, E. and Murphy, P. (1990) *Hooligans Abroad*. London: Routledge.

Williams, R. (1961) *The Long Revolution*. New York: Columbia University Press.

Williams, R. (1977) *Marxism and Literature*. Oxford: Oxford University Press.

Williams, R. (1985) *Towards 2000*. Harmondsworth: Penguin.

Williams, R. (1990) *Television: Technology and Cultural Form*. London: Routledge.

Willis, P. (1977) *Learning to Labour*. Farnborough: Saxon House.

Wittgenstein, L. (1974) *Philosophical Investigations*. Oxford: Blackwell.

Wright, E. (1985) *Classes*. London: Verso.

Wright Mills, C. (1959) *The Sociological Imagination*. Oxford: Oxford University Press.

Young, M. and Wilmott, P. (1986) *Family and Kinship in East London*. Harmondsworth: Penguin.

Zweig, F. (1962) *The British Worker in an Affluent Society*. London: Heinemann.

Fanzines:

Red Issue, PO Box 16, Urmston, Manchester M31 1LX.

United We Stand, PO Box 45, Manchester M31 1GQ.

When Saturday Comes, 4th Floor, 2 Pear Tree Court, London EC1 ODS.

Index